How to Find
Health Information
on the
INTERNET

How to Find
Health Information
on the
INTERNET

BRUCE MAXWELL
bmaxwell@mindspring.com

Congressional Quarterly Inc.
Washington, D.C.

For Barbara—she believed

Cover and book design: Debra Naylor

Library of Congress Cataloging-in-Publication Data

Maxwell, Bruce, 1959-
    How to find health information on the internet / Bruce Maxwell.
        p.   cm.
    Includes index.
    ISBN: 1-56802-271-9 (alk. paper)
    1. Medical care--Computer network resources--Directories.
2. Medicine--Computer network resources--Directories. 3.
Health--Computer network resources--Directories. 4. Internet
addresses--Directories. 5. Telecommunication in medicine. 6.
Medical informatics. I. Title.
RA773.6 M39 1998   98-20101
025.06'61--dc21

SUMMARY CONTENTS

CONTENTS

CONTENTS

PREFACE

People are taking more responsibility for their health today than ever before. They're eager for information about how to cope with medical problems that strike them or their loved ones, how to reduce their risk for various diseases, and how to get the best health care possible.

Just as this thirst for health information has developed, so has a remarkable source for satisfying it: the Internet. It's currently estimated that more than 10,000 Internet sites offer a huge array of health information, and more are going online every day.

These health sites provide medical journal articles, patient publications from the National Institutes of Health and patient support groups, annotated lists of books about specific illnesses, lists of medical experts in various illnesses, answers to all of your basic questions about virtually every health topic imaginable, and lots, lots more.

Equally important are the hundreds of Internet mailing lists and Usenet news-groups where users provide support and information to each other regarding an enormous number of medical topics. No matter where you live or what time of day or night it is, with the Internet you're never alone with your health problem.

How to Find Health Information on the Internet is a guide to more than 600 of the best health-related Web sites, mailing lists, and Usenet newsgroups. The book is not a directory of every health-related resource on the Internet. Instead, it attempts to provide useful starting points in your Internet search for health information.

I have personally examined every site listed in this book. To be included, a site has to offer a large quantity of useful information, provide information that appears reliable, not charge for access, be stable, and be reasonably easy to access. Since I'm not a doctor, I cannot personally vouch for the accuracy of every document at every site listed in this book. Always, always, always check with your doctor to confirm the accuracy and usefulness of anything you find on the Internet.

Some may question why a book like this is necessary. With all the search engines now available, why not just type in a keyword and go from there?

To see the answer for yourself, try typing the word "cancer" into your favorite search engine. When I did this recently with the AltaVista search engine, I got 197,716 "hits." If I spent just ten seconds checking each link, it would take nearly twenty-three days to visit them all. That's obviously not practical.

Even with a more limited search term, the number of hits produced by search engines is often overwhelming. Using the narrower term "breast cancer" still provides more than 93,000 hits with AltaVista, and "prostate cancer" produces more than 31,000 hits. Even if you leave the cancer field and try a less obvious term such as "sleep disorders," you still get more than 12,000 hits.

By contrast, if you use this book you can instantly find some of the best sites about your topic. Along with the address, I provide a description of each site that tells you exactly what you'll find there. The table of contents contains a complete listing of all sites in the book; the index is a great aid in finding sites related to your topic that might be listed in other categories.

I plan to update this book regularly. If you have suggestions for sites that should be included in new editions, please send me an e-mail message at bmaxwell@mind-spring.com

If you'd like to be informed about new editions of this book, please visit my Web site at http://bmaxwell.home.mindspring.com

I've been most fortunate to work with lots of great people in producing this book. I'm grateful to Debra Naylor for creating the cover and doing the preliminary interior design, Paul Pressau for refining the interior design and shepherding the book's electronic composition, Joan Stout for creating the index, and Kristen Beach and Meredith Masse for their publicity work. I'd especially like to thank Jon Preimesberger for his careful editing, wise counsel, and unflagging graciousness throughout this project.

My greatest thanks are reserved for the two people to whom this book is dedicated. They are rare individuals, and this book would not have been possible without them. Dave Tarr, executive editor at Congressional Quarterly Books, is the kind of editor most authors spend their entire careers searching for without success. It is both an honor and a pleasure to work with him. And my wife, Barbara, continues to amaze me each and every day with her support, her caring, and her love. How I got lucky enough to find her I'll never know.

Bruce Maxwell

INTRODUCTION

INTRODUCTION

Health information on the Internet can help save your life. I'm living proof. A few years ago, over a period of months my doctor treated me for a variety of medical symptoms. It seemed like as soon as one was under control, another developed. Finally, based on my symptoms, my medical history, and recent tests, my doctor suggested a diagnosis that might explain everything. I had an ignorant, lay-person's view of the illness he mentioned, and rejected his diagnosis.

I continued getting more and more sick—and more and more scared. In desperation, I turned to the Internet. Within minutes, I found a National Institutes of Health site that offered several documents about the illness my doctor had mentioned. I only had to read the first two pages to realize that my doctor's diagnosis was correct. I immediately returned to him and started treatment—a treatment that I'm fully convinced saved my life. Today, with ongoing treatment I'm largely able to control my illness and can lead a normal life.

My case is an extreme example of the benefits available from Internet health information. Yet millions of people have similar—if less dramatic—stories to tell about how health information they found on the Internet has helped improve their lives.

People have found background information about an illness that struck them, news about new drugs or research developments that could help a loved one, or simply information about how to pursue a fit and healthy lifestyle. And just as important as the hard-core medical information, they've found support, comfort, and insights through the hundreds of Usenet newsgroups and mailing lists where people with specific illnesses can exchange messages. Some doctors are even starting to use the Internet to communicate with their patients.

Yet for all the promise that health information on the Internet offers, there also are perils. There's a lot of bad information floating around—everything from information that's just plain wrong to fraudulent claims by quacks, hucksters, and con artists. And separating the junk from the good stuff isn't always easy.

HOW TO JUDGE THE QUALITY OF
INTERNET HEALTH INFORMATION

So how do you, as a consumer with no formal medical training, judge the quality of health information you find on the Internet? Most importantly, you have to use your common sense. If a claim that you read sounds too good to be true, it probably is. If a "cure" for a particular illness falls outside commonly accepted medical knowledge, steer clear. And if someone promises a "miracle cure," stay away. Much as you might want to believe in miracle cures—especially when you or someone you love is desperately ill—they don't exist.

When seeking health information on the Internet, you're particularly vulnerable because in many cases you're doing so in response to a medical crisis involving yourself or someone you love. You're stressed, you're frightened, and you may not have had a lot of sleep lately. You may jump on the Internet, desperately looking for information and—most importantly—looking for a cure that will make the medical crisis disappear. Under these circumstances you may be tempted to suspend your normal good judgment and latch onto anything that promises hope, no matter how outlandish it seems. You must resist that temptation, as hard as it is, and carefully assess any information that you find.

Sometimes it's easy to determine whether a piece of health information is reliable. For example, if someone sends you an unsolicited e-mail message trying to sell you some health product, throw it away. Unscrupulous folks send millions of these unsolicited messages, known in Internet circles as spam. It costs virtually nothing to send the messages, which makes them real popular with scam artists, hucksters, and their ilk. No reputable company sends spam.

But what about when you're out on the Web, surfing among various health sites? How do you judge which are trustworthy?

It would be great if a single, perfect indicator of quality existed—or even a small group of such indicators that you could check off one at a time when examining a site. But unfortunately, the information on the Internet does not lend itself to a short checklist of quality indicators. Instead, when assessing a document you must consider a whole assortment of factors, and decide which are applicable—and most important—in a particular case. Here are just some of the issues you may want to keep in mind:

- Is it clear who operates the site? In some cases, the suffix on a site's address provides clues. For example, a site whose address ends ".edu" is operated by an educational institution, ".gov" indicates a government site, ".org" signals a site run by an organization (usually a nonprofit group of some kind), and ".com" indicates a site run by a commercial firm. If you can't figure out who's responsible for a site, be wary.

- Is the site's operator reputable? Sometimes this is easy to determine. For example, the American Heart Association has a long-standing reputation as a fine organization, so you can assume the information on its Internet site is reliable. But what

What Others Are Saying

The issue of whether the Internet provides quality health information is drawing attention from consumer activists, medical professionals, and government officials, among others. Here are some recent comments:

Much of the information we retrieved is, our medical consultants confirm, as good as any you'll find in a good medical library—and in some cases more complete than the information your own physician could provide. But the Internet is still a wild frontier. All sorts of health information—good and bad, true and false, complete and dangerously incomplete—is jostling around together in cyberspace.

—*Consumer Reports*

. . . (W)hen it comes to medical information, the Internet too often resembles a cocktail conversation rather than a tool for effective health care communication and decision making. The problem is not too little information but too much, vast chunks of it incomplete, misleading, or inaccurate, and not only in the medical arena.

—Editorial in the *Journal of the American Medical Association*

My advice to consumers about information on the Internet is the same as it is for other media: You can't believe everything you see, whether it's in a newspaper, on TV, or on a computer screen.

—Bill Rados, director of the communications staff
at the U.S. Food and Drug Administration

about a site operated by an organization or individual you've never heard of? The site's information isn't necessarily bad—just be a bit more careful when looking it over. Many great health sites are operated by private individuals with no formal medical training but a strong personal interest in a particular disease.

- Is the site operated by a pharmaceutical company or other business that's really using it to push a particular product? If so, be aware that the information may be biased.

- Does a site operated by a legitimate, nonprofit organization receive funding from a pharmaceutical company or other firm? Many do, and this money can lead to conflicts of interest.

- Does the site list a postal address, e-mail address, and phone number where you can get more information? If these contact details are missing, watch out.

- Who wrote the specific document you're reading? What are the author's credentials, affiliation, or background? If author information isn't provided, be extra careful.

- What was the author's likely motivation for placing the information online? Was it simply to educate, or was it to promote a particular point of view or sell a product or service?

- Does the information you're reading conflict with commonly accepted medical knowledge? If so, is there strong evidence supporting its claims?

- Do other sources confirm the accuracy of what you've found online? Confirmation can be provided by other Web sites, your doctor or other medical professional, recognized medical journals, and other sources. However, keep in mind that just because you find the same information in two places doesn't prove it's true.

- Does the information appear to be thorough and complete? Sources that only provide a partial picture are especially dangerous when dealing with health information.

- When was the document written, and when was it placed on the Web site? With medical knowledge advancing so quickly, out-of-date information can be incomplete or even dangerous.

- Is the site updated regularly? If the last update occurred months or even years ago, be careful.

- Does the site exhibit the common signs of quackery? There are many signs: testimonials ("I've never seen anything like it—it's simply amazing!"), guarantees ("We absolutely guarantee that you'll lose one inch of fat in 24 hours!"), and claims of persecution ("The medical establishment doesn't want you to know about this!"), among others.

Special care is required when using Internet mailing lists, newsgroups, and chat rooms. All of them can be wonderful sources for support and information, but they're also very popular with hucksters and con artists. Newsgroups and chat rooms are especially popular targets, since they're usually not moderated. When reading messages from mailing lists, newsgroups, or chat rooms, always keep in mind that frequently no one "polices" the postings, people who post can claim to be anyone they wish, and any advice posted is just one person's opinion. In other words, take anything you read with a big grain of salt. You can't be too careful.

Of course, it pays to assess carefully the quality of medical information you get from *any* source—the Internet, popular magazines, newspapers, medical journals, government publications, and so on. Internet information isn't inherently more or less reliable than information from other sources. In every case, the most reliable way to check the accuracy of health information you find—whether from the Internet or elsewhere—is to discuss it with your doctor or other medical professional.

HON Code of Conduct

In an effort to create quality standards for health-related Internet sites, the nonprofit Health on the Net Foundation (HON) developed a Code of Conduct. Internet sites are allowed to display the HON logo by voluntarily complying with the following code:

Principle 1   Any medical/health advice provided and hosted on this site will only be given by medically/health trained and qualified professionals unless a clear statement is made that a piece of advice offered is from a non-medically/health qualified individual/organization.

Principle 2   The information provided on this site is designed to support, not replace, the relationship that exists between a patient/site visitor and his/her existing physician.

Principle 3   Confidentiality of data relating to individual patients and visitors to a medical/health Website, including their identity, is respected by this Website. The Website owners undertake to honor or exceed the legal requirements of medical/health information privacy that apply in the country and state where the Website and mirror sites are located.

Principle 4   Where appropriate, information contained on this site will be supported by clear references to source data and, where possible, have specific HTML links to that data. The date when a clinical page was last modified will be clearly displayed (for example, at the bottom of the page).

Principle 5   Any claims relating to the benefits/performance of a specific treatment, commercial product or service will be supported by appropriate, balanced evidence in the manner outlined in Principle 4 above.

Principle 6   The designers of this Website will seek to provide information in the clearest possible manner and provide contact addresses for visitors that seek further information or support. The Webmaster will display his/her E-mail address clearly throughout the Website.

Principle 7   Support for this Website will be clearly identified, including the identities of commercial and noncommercial organizations that have contributed funding, services, or material for the site.

Principle 8   If advertising is a source of funding it will be clearly stated. A brief description of the advertising policy adopted by the Website owners will be displayed on the site. Advertising and other promotional material will be presented to viewers in a manner and context that facilitates differentiation between it and the original material created by the institution operating the site.

HOW TO USE THIS BOOK

How to Find Health Information on the Internet is divided into four sections:

- Directories, Search Engines, and Reference Sources—The specialized health directories and search engines described in this section are great places to start a search for health information on the Internet. Other highlights in the section include listings for general health sites, medical journals and news sources, and reference sources.

- Conditions, Diseases, and Illnesses—Sites in this section provide specialized information about specific health problems ranging from AIDS to substance abuse.

- Prevention and Treatment—This section focuses primarily on staying well. The sites target such topics as children's health, fitness and exercise, men's health, nutrition and diet, travel medicine, and women's health. Sites that discuss specific treatment methods, such as prescription drugs and transplantation, also are included.

- Health Care Issues—Health care is one of the hottest topics being debated today, and sites in this section offer information about such issues as death and dying, environmental health, ethics and fraud, health care policy, health insurance, occupational health and safety, and smoking.

Within each section, chapters are arranged alphabetically by subject. However, you should check the index for topics of interest because sites frequently have files about numerous subjects.

Basic access information is provided for each site. This information varies from site to site, but you will find the following whenever it's applicable:

- Access method(s)   The tool(s) you can use to access the site, such as the World Wide Web, Gopher, FTP, Telnet, and E-mail.

- To access   The site's address(es) on the Internet.

- Mirror   Other Internet addresses where the same material is maintained.

- E-mail   The e-mail address where you can send questions about the site.

Two other pieces of access information are provided for mailing lists:

- Subject line   The word(s) you must type on an e-mail message's subject line to subscribe to a mailing list. The words you must type are in **bold type.** If this line is blank in the instructions, leave it blank in your message as well.

- Message   The word(s) you must type in an e-mail message's message area to subscribe to a mailing list. The words you must type are in **bold type.** Any words that are in *italics* you must replace with the correct information. For example, if the message in the instructions reads **subscribe *listname firstname lastname*** you must type **subscribe** followed by the list's name, your first name, and your last name.

A FINAL WORD

According to the National Health Information Center, half of all deaths in the United States are caused by factors that people, either individually or as a society, can control. But to take control of your health, you first must be educated about a wide variety of issues. What better education source than the Internet, where you can quickly and easily download articles from medical journals, reports from the National Institutes of Health, and other high-quality material? And where, if you're so inclined, you can find a forum for virtually every medical condition where you can exchange information, questions, and support with other people?

Yet you must remember that the Internet is only one tool in your quest to become a well-informed health consumer. Many other tools also exist—paper journals, books, commercial databases—and you must use them all if your goal is to become truly educated about health issues. And most importantly, you must discuss what you learn with your doctors so that they and you, working together, can make educated decisions that help you take control of your health and your life.

DIRECTORIES, SEARCH ENGINES, AND REFERENCE SOURCES

DIRECTORIES AND SEARCH ENGINES

Achoo Healthcare Online

Achoo is a so-so directory of health-related Internet sites. Despite its links to more than 7,000 sites, Achoo is amazingly skimpy in many categories. The site is operated by MNI Systems Corp., a Canadian firm.

The main directory is divided into three sections: human health and disease, business of health, and organizations and sources. Each listing is very briefly annotated, but the annotations usually aren't very helpful.

Vital Stats:

Access method:	WWW
To access:	http://www.achoo.com
E-mail:	info@achoo.com

BioSites

BioSites is a directory of selected Internet resources in the biomedical sciences. The site listings, which are divided by dozens of topics, are furnished by library staff in the Pacific Southwest Region of the National Network of Libraries of Medicine.

BioSites' coverage is quite limited, although it's still under construction. As the coverage broadens, BioSites could become very useful.

Vital Stats:

Access method:	WWW
To access:	http://www.library.ucsf.edu/biosites
E-mail:	biosites@library.ucsf.edu

CliniWeb

CliniWeb is a searchable directory of nearly 10,000 Internet documents, images, and other resources about clinical medicine. Although its primary audience is physicians, some consumers also may find it useful. The site is operated by the Oregon Health Sciences University.

If you prefer, you can browse the site listings instead of searching them. The listings are indexed under terms from the Medical Subject Headings (MeSH) Anatomy and Disease trees, which were created by the National Library of Medicine.

Vital Stats:

Access method: WWW
To access: http://www.ohsu.edu/cliniweb

Doctor's Guide to the Internet

The highlights of the Doctor's Guide to the Internet are the sections devoted to specific condition and illnesses. Each section typically has dozens of news articles, in addition to links to related newsgroups and Web sites. Some of the medical topics covered include AIDS, allergies, Alzheimer's disease, anxiety, breast cancer, depression, ear infections, elevated cholesterol, epilepsy, hypertension, insomnia, menopause, migraine, obesity, prostate cancer, schizophrenia, stroke, and ulcers and other gastric disorders, among others.

The site also offers daily medical news stories, information about new health-related Internet sites, and hundreds of articles about new drugs or new indications for previously available drugs. It's operated by the P\S\L Consulting Group Inc.

Vital Stats:

Access method: WWW
To access: http://www.docguide.com
E-mail: webmaster@pslgroup.com

Hardin Meta Directory of Internet Health Sources

If you're looking for health information on the Internet, one of the best ways is to find a site that lists lots of other sites about your topic. These directory sites are a godsend, but tracking them down can be difficult.

Hardin solves this problem, at least in the health field. It's a meta directory—a directory of directories, in this case directories about health topics. Looking for cancer information? Start at Hardin, which provides links to nineteen cancer directories that in turn link to hundreds of cancer-related Internet sites, mailing lists, and newsgroups.

Hardin contains links to directories covering about three dozen health subjects—everything from allergy to toxicology. For each subject, there are typically links to ten to twenty directories. Hardin also offers links to a selection of new health sites on the Internet.

The Hardin Meta Directory is operated by the Hardin Library for the Health Sciences at the University of Iowa, which deserves three cheers for creating this wonderful resource.

Vital Stats:

Access method:	WWW
To access:	http://www.lib.uiowa.edu/hardin/md/index.html
E-mail:	hardin-webmaster@uiowa.edu

Health on the Net Foundation

The highlight of this site is MedHunt, a superb search engine that helps you find health documents, Web sites, mailing lists, and Usenet newsgroups across the Internet. You can search the database in English, Danish, German, Spanish, French, Italian, Dutch, and Portuguese. Each listing is rated by the Health on the Net Foundation (HON), a nonprofit organization headquartered in Geneva, Switzerland.

The site also has a Code of Conduct for medical and health Web sites (p. 7), a searchable database of medical movies and images, and information about HON projects and initiatives.

Vital Stats:

Access method:	WWW
To access:	http://www.hon.ch
E-mail:	webmaster@hon.co

HealthAtoZ

HealthAtoZ is a wonderful search engine to help you find health and medical information on the Internet. It's operated by Medical Network Inc., a private company.

HealthAtoZ's database lists thousands of health-related Internet sites, mailing lists, and newsgroups. Many of the best sites in the database carry brief, helpful annotations. If you prefer to browse instead of search, the database entries are broken out into dozens of directories.

HealthAtoZ also provides free access to Medline, a database containing millions of abstracts from the medical literature. You can search Medline by subject, author, keywords, journal, institution, and unique identifier.

Vital Stats:

Access method: WWW
To access: http://healthatoz.com
E-mail: info@healthatoz.com

Healthfinder

Healthfinder provides links to hundreds of federal government publications about health topics and to hundreds of consumer health sites on the Internet. All of the sites have been evaluated for quality by the U.S. Department of Health and Human Services.

Vital Stats:

Access method: WWW
To access: http://www.healthfinder.gov
E-mail: dbaker@hhs-custos.dhhs.gov

HealthWeb

Medical librarians at universities throughout the Midwest collaborated to create HealthWeb, which provides links to thousands of evaluated health-related Web sites, mailing lists, and newsgroups.

The links are divided into dozens of subjects, and each subject page was created by a particular medical library. Pages are currently available for cardiology, consumer health, dentistry, diabetes, gastroenterology, genetics, geriatrics and gerontology, infectious diseases, minority health, neurology, nutrition, oncology, ophthalmology, pediatrics, physical medicine and rehabilitation, primary care and family practice, psychiatry, public health, rheumatology, rural health, substance abuse, transplantation, and women's health, among other topics. Pages for additional subjects will be added in the future.

Since pages were developed independently by various libraries, they vary in their depth of coverage. However, most are quite extensive, and provide excellent starting points for searches on particular medical topics.

Vital Stats:

Access method: WWW
To access: http://healthweb.org
E-mail: healthweb@umich.edu

Index to HSLS Internet Resources

This site offers an excellent collection of links to hundreds of health-related Internet sites, mailing lists, and Usenet newsgroups. The links are divided by dozens of subjects. The site is operated by the Health Sciences Library System (HSLS) at the University of Pittsburgh.

Vital Stats:

Access method: WWW
To access: http://www.hsls.pitt.edu/intres/alphi.html
E-mail: falkweb+@pitt.edu

The Internet Sleuth—Health Indexes

This database lets you search nearly a dozen top directories of Internet health sites using a single interface. Some of the directories included are Achoo, HealthAtoZ, MedExplorer, and Six Senses Review.

You must search each directory separately. The database is part of The Internet Sleuth search engine.

Vital Stats:

Access method:	WWW
To access:	http://www.isleuth.com/heal-index.html
E-mail:	sleuth@isleuth.com

Medical Matrix

This extraordinary resource provides annotated, ranked listings for more than 3,000 health-related Internet sites. It focuses on clinical sites of interest to physicians, but also is of tremendous use to consumers. Medical Matrix is operated by HealthTel Corp.

Most of the listings are categorized by disease. However, there are also sections on clinical trials, ethnic medicine, rural medicine, full text clinical journals, hypertext books, major journals, Medline, news, health care management and policy, health care meta directories, and medical Internet directories and guides, among other subjects.

Vital Stats:

Access method:	WWW
To access:	http://www.medmatrix.org
E-mail:	gmalet@healthtel.com

Medical World Search

This powerful search engine hunts through health-related Internet sites that have been chosen for their quality. If you're searching for health information, it's far more efficient to use Medical World Search than a general search engine such as Altavista, Infoseek, or Webcrawler.

To help with your search, Medical World Search employs a thesaurus of more than half a million medical terms that lets it search automatically for related terms. The site is operated by TLC Information Services, a private company founded by researchers at Polytechnic University in Brooklyn, N.Y.

Vital Stats:

Access method:	WWW
To access:	http://www.mwsearch.com
E-mail:	mwsearch@mwsearch.com

Michigan Electronic Library

The Health Information Resources page of the Michigan Electronic Library (MEL) provides thousands of links to health-related documents and Internet sites. Each resource included in the database has been selected and evaluated by librarians.

The links are arranged under dozens of topics, and you also can search the entire MEL database. MEL is a joint project of the University of Michigan, the Library of Michigan, and Merit Inc.

Vital Stats:

Access method:	WWW
To access:	http://mel.lib.mi.us/health/health-index.html
E-mail:	lansdale@tln.lib.mi.us

National Institutes of Health Server

The National Institutes of Health (NIH) Server is a gateway to the dozens of Internet sites operated by NIH offices and institutes.

The server also has a searchable index of diseases currently being investigated at NIH or by NIH-supported scientists, a list of toll-free phone numbers for NIH information hotlines, a searchable NIH telephone book, a map of the NIH campus, a calendar of events, and much more.

Vital Stats:

Access methods: WWW
To access: http://www.nih.gov
E-mail: webmaster@www.nih.gov

Search NIH Web-Space

Search NIH Web-Space provides a search engine that looks for documents on more than 150 Web sites and Gophers operated by various components of the National Institutes of Health (NIH). You can search by numerous variables, and both basic and complex queries are available.

Vital Stats:

Access method: WWW
To access: http://search.info.nih.gov
E-mail: webmaster@www.nih.gov

Tile.Net

Tile.Net provides links to more than 150 Internet mailing lists devoted to health and medical topics. For each list, Tile.Net lists the sponsor, the subscription address, subscription instructions, and the e-mail address for the list administrator.

Vital Stats:

Access method: WWW
To access: http://tile.net/lists/medicine.html
E-mail: info@shelby.com

Yahoo!

Yahoo!'s health page provides links to thousands of health and medical Internet sites. The links are divided into more than forty top-level subjects, many of which have subdivisions.

Some of the top-level subjects include alternative medicine, death and dying, disabilities, first aid, fitness, mental health, news and media, nutrition, public health and safety, reference, reproductive health, sexuality, weight issues, and women's health.

Yahoo! also has links to chat rooms devoted to health topics and health-related news stories from Reuters.

Vital Stats:

Access method:	WWW
To access:	http://www.yahoo.com/Health

DOCTORS AND HOSPITALS

AMA Physician Select

AMA Physician Select is a database containing basic information about more than 650,000 doctors of medicine and doctors of osteopathy or osteopathic medicine in the United States and its possessions. The site is operated by the American Medical Association.

To search the database, you must know the state where the physician is located. For now you can search by name or medical specialty, and in the near future you'll be able to search for physicians who treat a particular illness or condition.

For each physician, the database lists an office address and phone number, primary practice specialty, year graduated from medical school, medical schools attended, location of medical residency, and whether the doctor is board certified.

Vital Stats:

Access method:	WWW
To access:	http://www.ama-assn.org/aps/amahg.htm
E-mail:	AMAMDSelect@ama-assn.org

DocFinder

This site provides licensing information for doctors in many states. It's operated by the Association of State Medical Board Executive Directors.

When this book was being written, records were available for doctors in Arizona, California, Iowa, Kansas, Maine, Maryland, Massachusetts, Minnesota, North Carolina, Oklahoma, Texas, and Vermont. More states will be added in the future. You must search each state's licenses separately.

The information available for each doctor varies by state, but typically includes medical license status, address, date original license issued, medical school, and year graduated from medical school. Where applicable, the system also lists any hospital disciplinary actions, malpractice awards, or arbitration awards against the doctor.

The site also offers contact information for medical licensing boards in every state.

Vital Stats:

Access method:	WWW
To access:	http://www.docboard.org
E-mail:	docboard@madriver.com

Hospital Select

Hospital Select's database provides basic information about nearly every hospital in the United States. It's operated by the American Medical Association and Medical-Net Inc., a commercial firm.

You can search the database by hospital name, state, city, county, and Zip Code. For each hospital, the database lists the address, telephone number, name of the chief executive officer, services provided, and accreditations.

Even more interesting are the annual bed and utilization statistics listed for each hospital. Data are provided on numbers of beds, intensive care unit beds, admissions, emergency room visits, inpatient surgeries, and outpatient surgeries. The database also supplies annual occupancy percentages for the entire hospital and the intensive care unit.

Vital Stats:

Access method:	WWW
To access:	http://www.hospitalselect.com
E-mail:	jeanne@mednetweb.com

GENERAL HEALTH RESOURCES

Agency for Health Care Policy and Research

The Agency for Health Care Policy and Research site has numerous consumer publications, including *Choosing and Using a Health Plan, Prescription Medicines and You, What You Should Know About Stroke Prevention,* and *Be Informed: Questions to Ask Your Doctor Before You Have Surgery.*

It also has consumer publications about various medical topics, including acute pain management, chronic incontinence, cataracts, depression, management of cancer pain, mammography, acute low back problems, and poststroke rehabilitation, among others.

In addition, the site has various health care statistics, news about upcoming conferences, speeches and congressional testimony by AHCPR officials, announcements about grants and job vacancies, and information about the National Advisory Council for Health Care Policy, Research, and Evaluation.

Vital Stats:
Access method: WWW
To access: http://www.ahcpr.gov
E-mail: info@ahcpr.gov

alt.health

The alt.health newsgroup is devoted to discussions of a wide range of health issues.

Vital Stats:

Access method: Usenet newsgroup
To access: news:alt.health

---

alt.med

Discussions in the alt.med newsgroup cover a wide range of medical topics.

Vital Stats:

Access method: Usenet newsgroup
To access: news:alt.med

AMA Health Insight

AMA Health Insight, which is operated by the American Medical Association, offers a smorgasbord of health information. It has everything from tips on choosing a health care plan to recent medical stories from Reuters to special sections on women's health and adolescent health.

One of the site's highlights is its collection of detailed articles about specific medical conditions. There are articles about arthritis, asthma, blood pressure, depression, type II diabetes, heart attack, HIV/AIDS, and migraine headache.

The site also has an atlas of the human body, strategies for becoming physically fit, a medical glossary, a personal health history record that can be filled out online, recipes, advice on travel health, nutrition information, and lots more.

Vital Stats:

Access method: WWW
To access: http://www.ama-assn.org/consumer.htm
E-mail: insight@ama-assn.org

Brochure Resource Library

This site has dozens of brochures from various sources about alcohol and other drugs, cold care, cold and canker sores, diet and nutrition, eating disorders, fitness, infectious diseases, mental health, reproductive health, sexually transmitted diseases, stress management, and other subjects. It's operated by the Fronske Health Center at Northern Arizona University.

Vital Stats:

Access method:	WWW
To access:	http://www.nau.edu/~fronske/broch.html
E-mail:	Elizabeth.Applebee@nau.edu

CDC Servers

The CDC Servers offer an incredible collection of health-related databases, books, and documents. They're operated by the Centers for Disease Control and Prevention (CDC).

The servers offer *Physical Activity and Health: A Report of the Surgeon General;* the full text of the *Morbidity and Mortality Weekly Report;* brochures from the National Center for Health Statistics about lead poisoning, preventing birth defects, and other topics; *Emerging Infectious Diseases,* a journal published by the National Center for Infectious Diseases; and brochures about chronic fatigue syndrome, Lyme disease, and malaria.

They also provide access to CDC WONDER, a huge database system that provides CDC reports, guidelines, and public health data; numerous publications from the National Center for Health Statistics; extensive health-related information for international travelers, including details about vaccine requirements and health recommendations for specific regions of the world; the *HIV/AIDS Surveillance Report,* a report published semiannually by the CDC that contains tabular and graphic information about AIDS and HIV case reports in the United States; and lots, lots more.

Vital Stats:

Access methods:	WWW, FTP
To access:	http://www.cdc.gov *or* ftp://ftp.cdc.gov
Login (FTP only):	**anonymous**
Password (FTP only):	your e-mail address
E-mail:	netinfo@cdc.gov

Consumer Information Center

The Consumer Information Center (CIC) offers the full text of dozens of federal government publications about nutrition and general health topics. The CIC is part of the U.S. General Services Administration.

Here are the titles of some of the available publications in the site's food and nutrition section:

- A Consumer's Guide to Fats

- Dietary Guidelines for Americans

- Eat Right to Help Lower Your High Blood Pressure

- How to Buy Fresh Fruits

- How to Help Avoid Foodborne Illness in the Home

- Taking the Fat Out of Food

- Vegetarian Diets

The site's health section offers the following titles, among others:

- A Guide to Contraceptive Choices

- Alzheimer's Disease

- Attention Deficit Hyperactivity Disorder

- Anxiety Disorders

- Cancer Tests You Should Know About

- Chronic Fatigue Syndrome

- Controlling Asthma

- Dizziness

- Eating Disorders

- Fitness and Exercise

- Getting Fit Your Way

- Guide to Choosing a Nursing Home

- Headaches

- Helping the Depressed Person Get Treatment

- Menopause

- Overcoming Infertility

- Personal Health Guide

- Preventing Stroke

- Questions to Ask Your Doctor Before You Have Surgery

- The Healthy Heart Handbook for Women

- Urinary Tract Infections in Adults

- What You Need to Know About Skin Cancer

Vital Stats:

Access method:	WWW
To access:	http://www.pueblo.gsa.gov
E-mail:	catalog.pueblo@gsa.gov

Diagnostic Test Information Server

This experimental site offers a searchable database with information about diagnostic tests. The data are taken from the 1996 book *Pocket Guide to Diagnostic Tests,* and the site is provided by the Department of Medicine at the University of California-San Francisco.

For now, you can only search for laboratory tests. In the future, the developers plan to add microbiology and radiology tests. For each test, the database provides a clinical description, data on the normal range for results, and the cost.

Vital Stats:

Access method:	WWW
To access:	http://dgim-www.ucsf.edu/TestSearch.html
E-mail:	bdetmer@virginia.edu

Go Ask Alice!

Go Ask Alice! is a question-and-answer service provided by Columbia University Health Services. Users can submit questions about sexuality, sexual health, relationships, general health, fitness and nutrition, emotional well-being, and alcohol and other drugs, or they can search through hundreds of previous questions and answers on those topics.

VItal Stats:

Access method: WWW
To access: http://www.columbia.edu/cu/healthwise/alice.html

Health Information for Patients

This site provides brief patient information handouts about more than 200 health topics. Some of the subjects covered include migraine headaches, sleep apnea, pain relief after surgery, the female reproductive system, allergies, gastrointestinal disorders, psychological disorders, sleep disorders, addictions, bioethics, infections, pregnancy, and exercise, among many others. The site is operated by the American Academy of Family Physicians.

Vital Stats:

Access method: WWW
To access: http://home.aafp.org/family/patient
E-mail: fp@aafp.org

Healthy Lives

This site has more than a dozen brochures about various medical conditions. Some of the topics covered include asthma, bronchitis, chicken pox, depression, ear infections, herpes, migraines, nasal allergies, shingles, and ulcers, among others. The site is operated by Glaxo Wellcome, a pharmaceutical company.

Vital Stats:

Access method: WWW
To access: http://www.healthylives.com

InfoNet

InfoNet offers phone numbers for dozens of organizations that people can call to get information about medical conditions. Some of the organizations listed include the Elder Care Locator Service, National AIDS Information Clearinghouse, Well Spouse Foundation, American Chronic Pain Association, American Association of Disabled Persons, National Headache Foundation, and the National Organization for Rare Disorders, among many others.

InfoNet also provides links to Web sites operated by these organizations. InfoNet is provided by the Johns Hopkins Medical Institutions.

Vital Stats:

Access method:	WWW
To access:	http://infonet.welch.jhu.edu/advocacy.html
E-mail:	www@infonet.welch.jhu.edu

Internet FDA

A wide range of information about the Food and Drug Administration (FDA) and its regulation of food, drugs, medical devices, and the blood supply is available on Internet FDA.

The site has information about the FDA's efforts to regulate tobacco; the weekly *FDA Enforcement Report,* which lists FDA-regulated products that are being recalled; *FDA Consumer,* a consumer magazine; telephone numbers for many FDA offices and officials; brief summaries of laws that the FDA enforces; information about how to report problems with foods, drugs, and other products that the FDA regulates; lists of FDA publications; the full text of selected speeches and testimony by FDA officials; press releases; links to other FDA Internet sites; and much more.

Vital Stats:

Access method:	WWW
To access:	http://www.fda.gov

The Internet Sleuth—Health

This database lets you search more than a dozen of the best general health sites on the Internet using a single interface. You must search each site separately. The database is part of The Internet Sleuth search engine.

Vital Stats:

Access method:	WWW
To access:	http://www.isleuth.com/heal.html
E-mail:	sleuth@isleuth.com

Mayo Health O@sis

Mayo Health O@sis, which is operated by the Mayo Clinic, provides thousands of articles about virtually every medical topic you can imagine. It's one of the premier medical sites on the Internet.

The site is particularly strong in the subjects of diet and nutrition, pregnancy and child health, cancer, heart wellness, women's health, and medicine. But it also has extensive materials about various diseases, mental health, first aid, fitness, food and diet, health care options, how the body works, medical tests and procedures, natural healing, prevention and wellness, rehabilitation, and sexuality, among many other topics.

One of the site's most interesting features provides detailed information about more than 8,000 prescription and over-the-counter drugs. Another interesting feature lets you submit questions to Mayo doctors. And the site has a handy glossary of medical terms.

Vital Stats:

Access method:	WWW
To access:	http://www.mayohealth.org

Med Help International

Med Help International offers a superb database containing all kinds of medical information. If you type in the name of a disease or condition, the database will return articles from such sources as the National Institutes of Health and The Johns Hopkins University, relevant entries from a medical glossary, news items about the subject, a list of patient support groups, and links to other articles at selected medical sites. The site is operated by Med Help International, a nonprofit organization.

Another useful feature is a set of forums where users can submit questions to doctors. Questions in the Gastroenterology and Liver Disease Forum and the Urology Forum are answered by doctors from the Henry Ford Health System in Detroit, and questions in the Heart Forum and the Neurology and Neurosurgery Forum are answered by doctors from The Cleveland Clinic Foundation. Additional forums will be added in the future.

Another highlight is the Patient Network, where users can search for other people who share their medical conditions and who wish to share information and support by e-mail. Users also can register so others can contact them.

Vital Stats:

Access method:	WWW
To access:	http://www.medhelp.org
E-mail:	staff@medhelp.org

MedicineNet

MedicineNet has articles and links related to hundreds of diseases and medical conditions. It's operated by a group of board-certified physicians.

One interesting feature lets you submit questions to the doctors. You also can search through answers to 6,000 previous questions.

The site also has brief articles about hundreds of prescription drugs, a medical dictionary, basic first aid information, and contact information for poison control centers around the country.

Vital Stats:

Access method: WWW
To access: http://www.medicinenet.com
E-mail: mniceo@fia.net

Mediconsult.com

This site provides extensive information about more than sixty diseases and health issues. Some of the topics covered include Alzheimer's disease, arthritis, chronic pain, colostomy, contraception, depression, fitness, headache, incontinence, infertility, inflammatory bowel disease, melatonin, palliative care, pregnancy complications, skin disorders, stress, travel vaccinations, vasectomy, and vitamins and nutrition. The site is operated by a marketing company.

For each topic, the site offers articles and brochures from government agencies and other sources, a moderated support group, news items, summaries of journal articles, drug information, and links to related Web sites.

Vital Stats:

Access method: WWW
To access: http://www.mediconsult.com
E-mail: ask_barb@mediconsult.com

Medscape

Medscape offers thousands of full-text articles from various sources. Many are from more than two dozen medical journals, including *The AIDS Reader, American Heart Journal, Cancer Control, Clinical Psychiatry News, Emerging Infectious Diseases, Hippocrates, Oncology Issues, Pediatric News,* and *Skin & Allergy News,* among others. You must register to read the articles and other resources, but registration is free.

Medscape also offers free access to three databases created by the National Library of Medicine:

- MEDLINE, which provides bibliographic information and abstracts for nearly nine million articles from medical journals.

- AIDSLINE, which provides bibliographic information and abstracts for journal articles, government reports, newspaper articles, and other items about HIV/AIDS published from 1980 to the present.

- TOXLINE, which has more than four million citations for materials about the pharmacological, biochemical, physiological, and toxicological effects of drugs and other chemicals.

Medscape also provides daily medical news, a medical dictionary, and lots more.

Vital Stats:

Access method:	WWW
To access:	http://www.medscape.com
E-mail:	stephen_smith@mail.medscape.com

misc.health

A wide variety of health issues are discussed in the newsgroup misc.health.

Vital Stats:

Access method:	Usenet newsgroup
To access:	news:misc.health

National Academy Press

Dozens of books about behavioral sciences, food and nutrition, health care, and related subjects are available in full text at this site. The National Academy Press is the publishing arm of the National Academy of Sciences, a nonprofit organization that was chartered by Congress in 1863 to advise the federal government on scientific and technical matters.

Some of the available titles include *Women and Health Research, Broadening the Base of Treatment for Alcohol Problems, Child Health and Human Rights, Pesticides in the Diets of Infants and Children, Nutrition During Pregnancy, Expanding Access to Investigational Therapies for HIV Infection and AIDS*, and *Possible Health Effects of Exposure to Residential Electric and Magnetic Fields.*

Some of the other titles provided include *Preparing for the 21st Century: Focusing on Quality in a Changing Health Care System; AIDS and Behavior: An Integrated Approach; Risking the Future: Adolescent Sexuality, Pregnancy, and Childbearing;*

Tinnitus: Facts, Theories, and Treatments; Eat for Life: The Food and Nutrition Board's Guide to Reducing Your Risk of Chronic Disease; 2020 Vision: Health in the 21st Century; Health Data in the Information Age: Use, Disclosure, and Privacy; Telemedicine: A Guide to Assessing Telecommunications for Health Care; Approaching Death: Improving Care at the End of Life; and *Primary Care: America's Health in a New Era.*

Vital Stats:

Access method:	WWW
To access:	http://www.nap.edu
E-mail:	mgriskey@nas.edu

NIH Clinical Research Studies

This site provides detailed information about more than 1,000 medical studies being conducted at the National Institutes of Health (NIH) Clinical Center. You can search the studies using keywords or browse them by institute or disease category. Although the site is aimed at physicians, it provides a fascinating look at some of the research being conducted at NIH.

Vital Stats:

Access method:	WWW
To access:	http://www.cc.nih.gov/nihstudies

Office of Disease Prevention

The Office of Disease Prevention site offers dozens of reports that evaluate scientific information on various medical topics. The reports, known as Consensus Development Statements, result from National Institutes of Health conferences.

There are reports about genetic testing for cystic fibrosis, interventions to prevent HIV risk behaviors, breast cancer screening for women ages forty to forty-nine, physical activity and cardiovascular health, optimal calcium intake, mortality and morbidity of dialysis, early identification of hearing impairment in infants and young children, impotence, diagnosis and treatment of early melanoma, diagnosis and treatment of depression in late life, and treatment of panic disorder, among other subjects.

The site also has background information about the Women's Health Initiative, a huge national study aimed at reducing coronary heart disease, breast and colorectal cancer, and osteoporotic fractures among postmenopausal women.

Vital Stats:

Access method:	WWW
To access:	http://odp.od.nih.gov
E-mail:	webmaster@www.nih.gov

Office of Disease Prevention and Health Promotion

This site offers a list of federal health information centers and clearinghouses, a list of health-related organizations that have toll-free hotlines, and a calendar of national health observances.

The site also has the report *Nutrition and Your Health: Dietary Guidelines for Americans,* information about the Healthy People 2000 initiative, and the *Catalog of Federal Domestic Assistance,* which describes more than 1,300 federal programs that provide grants, loans, services, information, training, and other assistance to the public.

Vital Stats:

Access method:	WWW
To access:	http://www.odphp.osophs.dhhs.gov
E-mail:	dbaker@osophs.dhhs.gov

Office of Minority Health Resource Center

The Office of Minority Health Resource Center offers the *Minority Health Resource Pocket Guide,* which lists federal and state minority health officials, federal health information centers and clearinghouses, national minority organizations, and sources of health materials for minority populations.

The site also has information about services available from the center, legislative news, grant information, a calendar of events and conferences, a bimonthly newsletter titled *Closing the Gap,* searchable databases containing bibliographic information for publications about minority health, and the *Funding Guide,* which has information about grants and funding resources, state resources, the top twenty-five foundations, and writing proposals.

In addition, the site has a list of seventy health-related federal information centers and clearinghouses, lists of health professionals who volunteer to provide technical assistance to community-based organizations that are active in minority health issues, and a publication titled *Breast Cancer and Minorities: A Resource Guide.*

Vital Stats:

Access method: WWW
To access: http://www.omhrc.gov
E-mail: lmosby@omhrc.gov

Office of Rare Diseases

The Office of Rare Diseases site has a list of about 2,000 rare diseases, a searchable database of current clinical trials involving rare diseases, news about research results, a calendar of events, and links to other Internet sites that provide information about rare diseases. The office is part of the National Institutes of Health.

Vital Stats:

Access method: WWW
To access: http://rarediseases.info.nih.gov/ord
E-mail: ordcomments@icic.nci.nih.gov

sci.med

This very active newsgroup, which averages nearly 100 messages daily, covers a wide range of medical topics.

Vital Stats:

Access method: Usenet newsgroup
To access: news:sci.med

Thrive

Thrive has everything from medical news stories by Reuters to files about dozens of specific illnesses and conditions, including AIDS, anxiety, back pain, chronic fatigue, depression, head pain, incontinence, insomnia, and sleep apnea, among many others.

Thrive, which is a joint venture between America Online and Time Inc., also offers:

- A searchable database with summaries of thousands of articles on health topics from consumer magazines, medical publications, and newspapers.
- Message boards on general health, fitness, asthma, osteoporosis, endometriosis, menopause, sex, and health books.
- Scheduled chats on depression, fitness, stress, pregnancy loss, menopause, breast cancer, alternative medicine, sleep disorders, walking, asthma, transplants, and other subjects.
- A feature where you can ask questions about eating, fitness, general health, women's health, psychology, sex, and asthma.

Vital Stats:

Access method:	WWW
To access:	http://www.thriveonline.com
E-mail:	help@pathfinder.com

The Virtual Hospital

The Virtual Hospital, which is operated by the University of Iowa College of Medicine, has hundreds of consumer pamphlets about a variety of medical topics.

Some sample titles include *Warning Signs of Breast Cancer, What Are Clinical Trials All About?, Taking Time: Support for People with Cancer and the People Who Care About Them, Action Guide for Healthy Eating, How to Protect Your Skin from Sun Damage, How to Increase the Amount of Fiber in Your Diet, Recommended Heart-Healthy Cookbooks, Cast Care, Learning to Live with Diabetes, Exercises for Your Sore Shoulder, What to Do When You Can't Sleep, Continuous Hormone Replacement Therapy After Menopause, How to Prevent Foodborne Illness, Smell & Taste Disorders, Parents' Guide to Children's Eating Problems,* and *Advance Directives for Health Care.*

The pamphlets are from a variety of sources—the National Cancer Institute, University of Iowa Cancer Center, American Academy of Family Physicians, American Academy of Pediatrics, Massachusetts Department of Public Health, Boston Children's Hospital, and the American Academy of Otolaryngology-Head and Neck Surgery, among others.

Another site highlight is a collection of articles, lectures, and books for physicians about various health issues. Some of the topics covered include travel-related diseases, the human brain, dermatology, emergency medicine, primary care medicine, lung cancer, acute low back problems in adults, infectious diseases of the central nervous system, fatal child abuse and neglect in the United States, back pain in children, asthma in children, preventive medicine, and clinical psychopharmacology.

Vital Stats:

Access method:	WWW
To access:	http://www.vh.org
E-mail:	librarian@vh.org

MEDICAL JOURNALS, NEWSPAPERS, AND OTHER NEWS SOURCES

Archives Specialty Journals

Abstracts from nine specialty journals published by the American Medical Association are provided on this site. Abstracts are available for articles published back to July 1995. A few full-text articles also are provided.

The journals abstracted include the *Archives of Internal Medicine, Archives of Dermatology, Archives of Family Medicine, Archives of Otolaryngology-Head & Neck Surgery, Archives of Neurology, Archives of General Psychiatry, Archives of Ophthalmology, Archives of Surgery,* and the *Archives of Pediatrics & Adolescent Medicine.*

Vital Stats:
Access method: WWW
To access: http://www.ama-assn.org/public/journals

British Medical Journal

The highlight of this site is a book that introduces nonexperts to finding medical articles and assessing their value. The book, *How to Read a Paper: The Basics of Evidence-Based Medicine,* is provided in full text.

Several other books also are provided in full text: *Statistics at Square One, Epidemiology for the Uninitiated, ABC of Medical Computing,* and *A Guide to the Internet for Medical Practitioners.*

The site also has selected articles from the weekly *British Medical Journal* published from March 1995 to the present.

Vital Stats:

Access method:	WWW
To access:	http://www.bmj.com
E-mail:	bmj@bmj.com

CNN Health

This site offers daily stories on a wide variety of health topics. It's operated by the Cable News Network (CNN).

Besides the daily stories, the site has an archive containing thousands of past stories. They're separated by topic, including abortion, Alzheimer's disease, cancer, diabetes, euthanasia, fitness, obesity, parenting, pregnancy, sleeping, and women's health, among many others.

Vital Stats:

Access method:	WWW
To access:	http://www.cnn.com/HEALTH
E-mail:	cnn.feedback@cnn.com

Docnet MediS Search

MediS is a search engine that indexes articles from dozens of major medical journals. Each "hit" links to an abstract or article at the journal publisher's Web site. Docnet is operated by a group of physicians in England.

Some of the journals indexed include the *British Medical Journal, New England Journal of Medicine, Journal of the American Medical Association, Archives of Psychiatry, Archives of Women's Health, Age and Aging, American Journal of Preventive Medicine, Alcohol and Alcoholism, Anti-Cancer Drug Design, Health Policy and Planning, Stroke, The Journal of Psychopharmacology,* and *The Journal of Neuroscience.*

Vital Stats:

Access method:	WWW
To access:	http://www.docnet.org.uk/medisn/search.html
E-mail:	webmaster@docnet.org.uk

The Internet Sleuth—Journals

This database lets you search sites operated by a dozen medical journals using a single interface. You must search each site separately. The database is part of The Internet Sleuth search engine.

Vital Stats:

Access method:	WWW
To access:	http://www.isleuth.com/medi-jour.html
E-mail:	sleuth@isleuth.com

The Internet Sleuth—News

This database lets you search a half-dozen sites that offer health and medical news using a single interface. You must search each site separately. The database is part of The Internet Sleuth search engine.

Vital Stats:

Access method:	WWW
To access:	http://www.isleuth.com/medi-news.html
E-mail:	sleuth@isleuth.com

JAMA

This site has abstracts of most articles published in *JAMA,* also known as the *Journal of the American Medical Association,* since July 1995. A few articles are available in full text.

Vital Stats:

Access method:	WWW
To access:	http://www.ama-assn.org/public/journals/jama
E-mail:	jama-comments@ama-assn.org

Medical Tribune Online

Each edition of the *Medical Tribune* published online has more than a dozen feature articles, many reporting the results of studies published in medical journals. Some recent article titles include "Easing Up on Obesity Not the Way to Go," "New Pediatric Guidelines Take Aim at Antibiotic Resistance," "Researchers Reaffirm Depression-CVD Link," "Clinton Proposes Medicare Benefits for Those Under 65," and "Advocacy Groups Urge More Screening for Colorectal Cancer."

Issues are archived online dating back to November 1996. The archives are fully searchable.

The Medical Tribune is published twenty-one times annually by Jobson Publishing, which supplies medical news to the New York Times Syndicate.

Vital Stats:

Access method:	WWW
To access:	http://www.medtrib.com
E-mail:	sbutsch@jobson.com

MMWR Mailing Lists

The Centers for Disease Control and Prevention operates three mailing lists that distribute portions or the complete text of the *Morbidity and Mortality Weekly Report* (MMWR). The MMWR has articles about public health topics such as emerging infectious diseases, immunizations, and environmental health. The three lists are:

- MMWR distributes the full text in a PDF file that includes charts, tables, and graphs.
- MMWR-ASC distributes the full text in ASCII text, with no charts, tables, or graphs.
- MMWR-TOC distributes the table of contents and instructions about how to download the full articles electronically.

Vital Stats:

Access method:	E-mail
To access:	Send an e-mail message to listserv@listserv.cdc.gov
Subject line:	
Message:	**subscribe *listname***
E-mail (questions):	mmwrq@epo.em.cdc.gov

New England Journal of Medicine

This site has abstracts of all articles published in the *New England Journal of Medicine* since January 1993. A limited number of articles are available in full text. The journal is published weekly by the Massachusetts Medical Society.

The following features from each issue are available online in full text: Images in Clinical Medicine, Case Records of the Massachusetts General Hospital, Editorials, Sounding Board articles, Correspondence, and Book Reviews. Original Articles, which report clinical research results, and Special Articles, which report on health policy research, are only provided in abstracts.

In addition, the site has the full text of selected articles on specific subjects. The topics change periodically, but when this book was being written they included kidney disease, breast cancer, molecular medicine, and asthma.

Another useful feature is a searchable calendar of medical meetings.

The Massachusetts Medical Society also operates the TOC-L mailing list (p. 45), which each week distributes the table of contents for the *New England Journal of Medicine.*

Vital Stats:

Access method:	WWW
To access:	http://www.nejm.org
E-mail:	comments@massmed.org

Newswise

Each month, dozens of press releases from leading medical research institutions are posted on the Newswise site. Newswise is aimed at reporters, but anyone interested in current medical research will find it valuable.

Press releases are available from the American College of Physicians, Mayo Clinic, Johns Hopkins Medical Institutions, UCLA, University of Pittsburgh, Cleveland Clinic, Cornell University, American Heart Association, Yale University, Temple University, American Academy of Dermatology, and American Psychiatric Association, among other institutions.

Vital Stats:

Access method:	WWW
To access:	http://www.newswise.com/menu-sm.htm
E-mail:	rjohnson@newswise.com

PR Newswire Health/Biotech

This site archives press releases from more than 100 pharmaceutical, biotechnology, and health care companies. The releases are separated by company. For some companies, there also are links to stock quotes and home pages. The site is operated by PR Newswire, a company that distributes press releases.

Vital Stats:

Access method:	WWW
To access:	http://www.prnewswire.com/healthcare_news.html
E-mail:	todd_grossman@prnewswire.com

PsychArticle Search

This search engine lets you search more than 1,100 psychology, psychiatry, and social science journals. You can search individual journals or groups of journals. Depending on the journal, the search engine returns a table of contents, abstract, or full-text article.

It also has annotated links to the journals. You can browse the links alphabetically, by subject, by language, and by other variables.

Vital Stats:

Access method:	WWW
To access:	http://telehealth.net/armin/jsearch.html
Mirror:	http://www.shef.ac.uk/~psysc/journals/jsearch.html
E-mail:	Armin.Guenther@WiSo.Uni-Augsburg.DE

TOC-L

The TOC-L mailing list distributes the weekly table of contents for the *New England Journal of Medicine.* The list is operated by the Massachusetts Medical Society, which also operates the New England Journal of Medicine Web site (p. 44).

Vital Stats:

Access method:	E-mail
To access:	Send an e-mail message to listserv@massmed.org

Subject line:
Message: **SUBSCRIBE TOC-L *firstname lastname***
E-mail: TOC-L-request@massmed.org

WebMedLit

WebMedLit is a searchable index of abstracts and articles published in nearly two dozen major medical journals. When you conduct a search, each "hit" links you to the original abstract or article at the publisher's Web site. WebMedLit, which is operated by Web Medical Literature Services, only indexes articles published in the last six weeks.

If you prefer, instead of searching you can browse through listings in ten subject categories: AIDS/virology, cancer/oncology, cardiology, dermatology, diabetes/endocrinology, gastroenterology, immunology, medical economics, neurology, and women's health.

Some of the journals indexed include the *Journal of the American Medical Association, New England Journal of Medicine, British Medical Journal, American Journal of Epidemiology, Archives of General Psychiatry, Archives of Ophthalmology, Archives of Internal Medicine, Journal of the National Cancer Institute, Journal of Clinical Oncology, Cancer, Diabetes Care,* and *Brain.*

Vital Stats:

Access method: WWW
To access: http://www.webmedlit.com
E-mail: feedback@webmedlit.com

www.reutershealth.com

This site provides about a dozen medical stories for consumers each day. It's operated by Reuters Health Information.

Some recent headlines include "1959 Blood Yields Earliest Known HIV Case," "Gene Therapy May Help Heart Failure," "Antibiotics Won't Help Most Colds," "Suicides Rise After Natural Disasters," and "Congress Unites to Oppose Cloning."

Although it costs nothing to read the daily stories, accessing a searchable archive and other site features requires an annual subscription payment.

Vital Stats:

Access method:	WWW
To access:	http://www.reutershealth.com
E-mail:	webmaster@reutershealth.com

Your Health Daily

Your Health Daily provides about a half-dozen articles concerning health issues each day. It's operated by The New York Times Syndicate.

Some recent headlines include "'Keyhole' Surgery May Cure Severe Heartburn," "Disaster Survivors at Greater Risk of Suicide," "New Heart Devices May Conquer 'Last Frontier,'" "Researchers Try to 'Turn On' Resting HIV Cells," "Cocaine Link to Brain Damage is Studied," "Article on Saccharin Leaves Bitter Taste," and "Earliest-Known Case of AIDS Detected."

All articles are archived for about six weeks. In addition, articles about two dozen specific topics are archived for several months.

The site also provides nearly two dozen discussion groups on various health topics. However, when this book was being written, they weren't very active.

Vital Stats:

Access method:	WWW
To access:	http://yourhealthdaily.com
E-mail:	vancepw@nytimes.com

MEDICAL LIBRARIES

bit.listserv.medlib-l, MEDLIB-L

The newsgroup bit.listserv.medlib-l, which is mirrored on the MEDLIB-L mailing list, is aimed at medical and health sciences librarians. It's operated by the Medical Library Association.

Vital Stats:

Access methods:	Usenet newsgroup, E-mail
To access (Usenet):	news:bit.listserv.medlib-l
To access (mailing list):	Send an e-mail message to listserv@listserv.acsu.buffalo.edu
Subject line:	
Message:	**subscribe MEDLIB-L *firstname lastname***
E-mail:	MEDLIB-L-request@listserv.acsu.buffalo.edu

DENTALIB

The DENTALIB mailing list is a discussion forum for dental librarians. It's operated by the dental section of the Medical Library Association.

Vital Stats:

Access method:	E-mail
To access:	Send an e-mail message to listproc@usc.edu
Subject line:	
Message:	**subscribe DENTALIB *firstname lastname***
E-mail:	fmason@hsc.usc.edu

Medical/Health Sciences Libraries on the Web

This site has links to Internet sites operated by more than 100 medical libraries around the world. The United States listings are divided by state, and the foreign listings by country. The site is part of the Hardin Meta Directory of Internet Health Sources (p. 15), which is operated by the Hardin Library for the Health Sciences at the University of Iowa.

Vital Stats:

Access method:	WWW
To access:	http://www.arcade.uiowa.edu/hardin-www/hslibs.html
E-mail:	eric-rumsey@uiowa.edu

National Institutes of Health Library Catalog

This site provides access to the online catalog at the National Institutes of Health Library. The catalog, which lists books and journals in the library's collection, can be searched by author, title, words in the title, subject, and call number.

Vital Stats:

Access method:	Telnet
To access:	telnet://nih-library.ncrr.nih.gov

National Library of Medicine

The National Library of Medicine site has dozens of bibliographies on such topics as medical treatment of heroin addiction, acupuncture, malaria, thalidomide, genetic testing for cystic fibrosis, interventions to prevent HIV risk behaviors, breast cancer screening in women ages forty to forty-nine, public health informatics, dietary supplements, cervical cancer, and confidentiality of electronic health data, among many others.

It also has links to National Library of Medicine sites that provide free access to the MEDLINE database of references to medical journal articles, Grateful Med software to use in accessing MEDLINE, descriptions of more than forty databases offered by the library, information for visitors and researchers, a sample of images and animation from the Visible Human Project, information about telemedicine projects around the country, a staff directory, and much more.

A mailing list called nlmfiles (below) distributes weekly announcements about new and updated files on the site.

Vital Stats:

Access method:	WWW
To access:	http://www.nlm.nih.gov
E-mail:	hyperdoc@nlm.nih.gov

NLM Locator

NLM Locator is the online catalog at the National Library of Medicine, which is the world's largest biomedical library. The library's collection includes 4.9 million items.

The site offers separate catalogs of the library's books, audiovisual materials, and journal titles; information about the library's hours and services; and a searchable database of organizations that provide health information.

Vital Stats:

Access method:	Telnet
To access:	telnet://locator.nlm.nih.gov
Login:	**locator**
E-mail:	ref@nlm.nih.gov

nlmfiles

The nlmfiles mailing list distributes weekly announcements about new and updated files on the National Library of Medicine Web site (p. 49).

Vital Stats:

Access method:	E-mail
To access:	Send an e-mail message to lists@mailserv.nlm.nih.gov
Subject line:	
Message:	**subscribe nlmfiles**
E-mail:	www.nlm@nlm.nih.gov

REFERENCE SOURCES

CDC WONDER

CDC WONDER lets you analyze data maintained by the Centers for Disease Control and Prevention (CDC) on such subjects as mortality, cancer incidence, hospital discharges, AIDS, behavioral risk factors, diabetes, and other topics. The system also provides access to reports and guidelines prepared by the CDC. While CDC WONDER is aimed at public health professionals, anyone from journalists to academic researchers should find it enormously useful.

You must register online to access the data sets.

Vital Stats:
Access method:	WWW
To access:	http://wonder.cdc.gov
E-mail:	cwus@cdc.gov

Combined Health Information Database

The Combined Health Information Database (CHID) offers more than a dozen databases that provide bibliographic information about journal articles, directories, videotapes, books, bibliographies, newsletters, and reports about various diseases and conditions. The site is a joint effort of the National Institutes of Health and the Centers for Disease Control and Prevention.

The site has separate databases with references to materials about AIDS education, Alzheimer's disease, arthritis and musculoskeletal and skin diseases, cancer patient education, cancer prevention and control, comprehensive school health, deafness and communication disorders, diabetes, digestive diseases, disease prevention and health promotion, epilepsy education and prevention, health promotion and education, kidney and urologic diseases, maternal and child health, medical genetics and rare disorders, oral health, prenatal smoking cessation, and weight control.

You can search an individual database or all the databases together. Each database record provides a title, abstract, and availability information.

Vital Stats:

Access method:	WWW
To access:	http://chid.nih.gov
E-mail:	CHID@aerie.com

Complete Home Medical Guide

This site provides the full text of *The Columbia University College of Physicians and Surgeons Complete Home Medical Guide.* Following is a list of the chapter titles:

• How to Get the Care You Need

• Meeting the Health Care Needs of the Aged and Disabled

• Medical Decision Making: Ethical Considerations

• The Fundamentals of Good Health

• The Basics of Good Nutrition

• Smoking, Alcohol, and Substance Abuse

• Health Concerns During Infancy and Childhood

• The Adolescent Years

• Special Health Concerns of Women

• Health Concerns of Men

• Symptoms and the Diagnostic

• Diagnostic Tests and Procedures

• Basics of CPR and Life Support

• Common First-Aid Procedures

• The Basics of Safety

• Heart and Blood Vessel Diseases

• Cancer

• Infectious Diseases

- HIV Infection and AIDS
- Respiratory Diseases and Lung Health
- Diabetes and Other Endocrine Disorders
- Disorders of the Digestive System
- Blood Disorders
- Disorders of the Musculoskeletal System
- Arthritis
- Brain, Nerve, and Muscle Disorders
- Kidney and Urinary Tract Disorders
- Skin Diseases
- Allergies
- The Eyes
- Diseases of the Ear, Nose, and Throat
- Maintaining Oral Health
- Mental and Emotional Health
- Proper Use of Medications
- Commonly Prescribed Drugs
- Directory of Health Organizations and Resources
- Directory of Regional Poison Control Centers
- Family Medical Records

Vital Stats:

Access method:	WWW
To access:	http://cpmcnet.columbia.edu/texts/guide/all.html
E-mail:	Webmaster@cpmcnet.columbia.edu

Dr. Felix's Free MEDLINE Page

This site provides links to all of the Internet sites that offer free access to MEDLINE. MEDLINE is a database created by the National Library of Medicine that contains references to nearly nine million articles from medical journals.

Besides the links, Dr. Felix provides brief summaries of what's provided at each MEDLINE site. Where available, these summaries include the site name, a list of the available databases, dates of database coverage, frequency of updates, registration requirements, usage restrictions, and details about available document delivery services.

The site also has links to MEDLINE tutorials from various sources, links to other sites that list free MEDLINE sources, and links to papers about MEDLINE.

Vital Stats:

Access method:	WWW
To access:	http://www.docnet.org.uk/felix-frames.html
Mirror:	http://www.beaker.iupui.edu/drfelix
E-mail:	medline@grhlib.demon.co.uk

HealthGate

The centerpiece of HealthGate is a series of databases created by the National Library of Medicine. HealthGate provides free access to the databases, although some other areas of the site are fee-based. The site is operated by HealthGate Data Corp., a private company.

The National Library of Medicine databases include:

- MEDLINE, which contains bibliographic information for more than eight million journal articles about medicine. Abstracts are available for some of the articles. Coverage is from 1966 to the present, and the database is updated weekly.

- CANCERLIT, which offers bibliographic information and abstracts for journal articles, meeting abstracts, government reports, and other documents about cancer. Coverage is from 1976 to the present, and the database is updated monthly.

- AIDSDRUGS, which has information about drugs and other agents that are currently being tested, or that have previously been tested, in AIDS-related clinical trials. Coverage is from 1980 to the present, and the database is updated bimonthly.

- AIDSLINE, which contains bibliographic information and abstracts for journal articles, technical reports, meetings, books, and other materials about HIV/AIDS. Coverage is from 1980 to the present, and the database is updated bimonthly.

- AIDSTRIALS, which provides information about active and closed clinical trials for drugs and other agents being tested for use with AIDS patients. Coverage is from 1980 to the present, and the database is updated bimonthly.

- BIOETHICSLINE, which has bibliographic information and abstracts for articles about ethical, legal, and policy issues affecting health care. Some of the subjects covered in the database include human experiments, abortion, and euthanasia. Coverage is from 1973 to the present, and the database is updated bimonthly.

- HealthSTAR, which provides bibliographic information and abstracts for journal articles about nonclinical aspects of health care. Some of the subjects covered in the database include health care administration, insurance, and accreditation. Coverage is from 1975 to the present, and the database is updated monthly.

Another useful HealthGate feature not created by the National Library of Medicine is a database that has information on nearly 300 diagnostic procedures. For each procedure, the database provides information about the indications and contraindications, patient preparation, how the procedure is performed, and interpretation of results, among other details. The database was created in 1995 by Lexi-Comp inc., and is updated quarterly.

Finally, for free HealthGate also provides articles and other materials about women's health, men's health, food and nutrition, parenting, and sexuality.

Vital Stats:

Access method:	WWW
To access:	http://www.healthgate.com
E-mail:	support@healthgate.com

HealthSquare

HealthSquare provides the full text of three books: *PDR Family Guide to Prescription Drugs, PDR Family Guide to Women's Health,* and *PDR Family Guide Encyclopedia of Medical Care.* The site is operated by New Media Systems, a private company.

The *PDR Family Guide to Prescription Drugs* has more than twenty chapters, covering heart disease, high blood pressure, arthritis, osteoporosis, digestive disorders, cancer, pain, birth control, allergies, kidney disease, and urinary disorders, among other topics.

The more than three dozen chapters in the *PDR Family Guide to Women's Health* cover a wide range of women's health issues. Some of the topics discussed include PMS, fibroids, urinary tract infections, sexually transmitted diseases, the reproductive system, infertility, contraceptives, pregnancy, prenatal testing, labor and delivery, miscarriage, headaches, diet and health, plastic surgery, breast cancer, cervical cancer, ovarian cancer, stress, mood disorders, eating disorders, sexual assaults, and menopause, among others.

And finally, the *PDR Family Guide Encyclopedia of Medical Care* has hundreds of articles covering everything from abdominal pain to wrist injuries.

Vital Stats:

Access method:	WWW
To access:	http://www.healthsquare.com
E-mail:	newmediaso@aol.com

Human Anatomy On-line

Human Anatomy On-line presents dozens of anatomy illustrations. You can click on hot spots on the images to get brief descriptions of each body system. The site also has animations of some body systems, such as the heart pumping. Informative Graphics Corp., a developer of educational software and other products, created the site.

Vital Stats:

Access method:	WWW
To access:	http://www.innerbody.com/indexbody.html

Internet Grateful Med

Internet Grateful Med provides access to eleven databases prepared by the National Library of Medicine that are part of the MEDLARS system. Most of the databases provide bibliographical information for articles published in the medical literature. To help with your searches, the site provides a detailed user's manual.

The premier database is MEDLINE, which has bibliographic information for more than 8.5 million articles published from 1966 to the present. Almost three-quarters of the listings also have an abstract. The data cover more than 3,700 biomedical journals about medicine, nursing, dentistry, veterinary medicine, and the preclinical sciences. The database is updated daily.

Following are brief descriptions of the other databases:

• AIDSDRUGS has records about more than 240 chemical and biological agents that are currently being evaluated in AIDS clinical trials. Each entry includes standard chemical names, synonyms and trade names, CAS Registry Numbers, protocol ID numbers, pharmacological action, adverse reactions and contraindications, physical and chemical properties, and manufacturer's name. The database also contains a bibliography of relevant articles.

- AIDSLINE offers bibliographic citations for more than 124,000 journal articles, government reports, technical reports, books, audiovisual items, and other materials about AIDS published from 1980 to the present. The database is updated weekly.

- AIDSTRIALS has records about more than 700 open and closed clinical trials of substances being tested for use against AIDS, HIV infection, and AIDS-related opportunistic diseases. Each record has information about the title and purpose of the trial, diseases studied, patient eligibility criteria, contact persons, agents tested, and trial locations. The database is updated biweekly.

- DIRLINE contains records about more than 17,000 health and biomedical information sources. The records cover organizations, government agencies, information centers, professional societies, voluntary associations, support groups, academic and research institutions, and research facilities. Each record has the resource name, address, and telephone number, along with descriptions of services, publications, and holdings.

- HealthSTAR provides bibliographic citations for more than 2.5 million journal articles, technical and government reports, meeting papers, and books published from 1975 to the present. The items cover both clinical and nonclinical aspects of medicine, including such topics as evaluation of patient outcomes, effectiveness of procedures and programs, health care administration, and health care planning. The database is updated monthly.

- HISTLINE offers about 155,000 bibliographic records for monographs, journal articles, books, and other materials about the history of health related professions. The database covers publications from 1964 to the present, and it's updated weekly.

- HSRPROJ provides about 3,000 records concerning research in progress that's funded by federal and private grants and contracts. The types of information available for each project vary, but frequently include a project summary, the names of performing and sponsoring agencies, the name and address of the principal investigator, the beginning and ending years of the project, and the study design and methodology. The database is updated quarterly.

- OLDMEDLINE has bibliographic information for articles published in international biomedical journals from 1964 to 1965. The database contains more than 307,000 records.

- PREMEDLINE is a database started in August 1996 that provides basic bibliographic information and abstracts for new materials that are in the process of being indexed for MEDLINE. The database is updated every weekday. Once a record is fully indexed, it's added to MEDLINE and deleted from PREMEDLINE.

- SDILINE has bibliographic information for all materials added to MEDLINE in the most recent complete month. The database is updated monthly, and usually offers about 31,000 new citations each month.

Vital Stats:

Access method:	WWW
To access:	http://igm.nlm.nih.gov
E-mail:	access@nlm.nih.gov

Merck & Co.

This site provides the full text of *The Merck Manual of Diagnosis and Therapy,* a widely used textbook that's more commonly known simply as *The Merck Manual.* You can browse through individual chapters or search the entire book.

The online version is the sixteenth edition, which was published in 1992. A new edition is scheduled to be published in early 1999.

The manual's twenty-three chapters cover infectious disease, immunology and allergic disorders, cardiovascular disorders, pulmonary disorders, gastrointestinal disorders, hepatic and biliary disorders, nutritional and metabolic disorders, endocrine disorders, hematology and oncology, musculoskeletal and connective tissue disorders, neurologic disorders, psychiatric disorders, genitourinary disorders, gynecology and obstetrics, pediatrics and genetics, otolaryngology, ophthalmologic disorders, dermatologic disorders, dental and oral disorders, disorders due to physical agents, special subjects, clinical pharmacology, and poisoning and bites.

The site also has the full text of two chapters from *The Merck Manual of Medical Information—Home Edition,* a book aimed at consumers that is based on the textbook. The chapters cover women's health and heart and blood vessel disorders.

Vital Stats:

Access method:	WWW
To access:	http://www.merck.com

National Health Information Center

Databases at this site tell how to contact more than 1,000 organizations and government offices that offer health information. The databases also have links to Web sites operated by those groups that have them. The site also has a calendar of national health observances that includes contact information for each event.

Vital Stats:

Access method: WWW
To access: http://nhic-nt.health.org
E-mail: nhicinfo@health.org

OneLook Dictionaries

OneLook provides links to more than two dozen medical dictionaries and glossaries on the Internet. The site is operated by Study Technologies.

If you prefer, instead of browsing through individual dictionaries you can search all 220 dictionaries and glossaries indexed by OneLook. This is a very handy feature if you want to quickly compare how various dictionaries define a word.

Vital Stats:

Access method: WWW
To access: http://www.onelook.com/browse.shtml
E-mail: bware@onelook.com

PubMed

PubMed provides free searching of all nine million citations in MEDLINE, a database that provides bibliographical information for the biomedical literature. It also contains citations that have not yet been entered in MEDLINE.

MEDLINE is a database created by the National Library of Medicine that covers the fields of medicine, nursing, dentistry, veterinary medicine, the health care system, and the preclinical sciences. The database has citations from more than 3,800 biomedical journals published in the United States and seventy foreign countries. Records are available dating back to 1966.

PubMed is operated by the National Center for Biotechnology Information at the National Library of Medicine.

Vital Stats:

Access method: WWW
To access: http://www.ncbi.nlm.nih.gov/PubMed
E-mail: info@ncbi.nlm.nih.gov

Social Statistics Briefing Room

The health page at the Social Statistics Briefing Room has links to various national health statistics. The briefing room is part of the Welcome to the White House Web site.

The links lead to statistics on the birth rate, infant mortality rate, life expectancy, use of health services, proportion of women over age fifty who have had a mammogram within the previous two years, firearm-related deaths, Lyme disease, and health insurance coverage. The statistics were compiled by the National Center for Health Statistics and the Centers for Disease Control and Prevention.

Vital Stats:

Access method: WWW
To access: http://www.whitehouse.gov/fsbr/health.html
E-mail: feedback@www.whitehouse.gov

CONDITIONS, DISEASES, AND ILLNESSES

AIDS AND HIV

AEGIS (AIDS Education Global Information System)

AEGIS is amazing. The site bills itself as "the largest HIV/AIDS database in the world," and it's hard to argue otherwise. The site is operated by a nonprofit charitable and education corporation and supported by grants from the National Library of Medicine and Roxanne Laboratories.

The heart of the site is its searchable database containing more than 340,000 documents about HIV and AIDS from sources around the world. The database contains documents about avoiding HIV infection, living with HIV, treatment for AIDS, and other issues, in addition to news articles about AIDS from 1986 to the present. You can search the entire database, search just selected parts of it, or browse the most popular materials by subject.

AEGIS also offers links to daily news stories about AIDS from various publications, a huge database containing detailed information about current clinical trials of AIDS drugs, conferences about various AIDS issues, and links to hundreds of related Internet sites.

Vital Stats:

Access method: WWW
To access: http://www.aegis.com
E-mail: webmaster@aegis.com

AIDS, sci.med.aids

This is a moderated mailing list/newsgroup for people with AIDS, their loved ones, AIDS service providers, educators, researchers, and the public. Some of the topics frequently discussed include causes of AIDS, vaccines, treatments for AIDS and opportunistic infections, and AIDS prevention and education.

Vital Stats:

Access methods:	E-mail, Usenet newsgroup
To access (mailing list):	Send an e-mail message to majordomo@wubios.wustl.edu
Subject line:	
Message:	**subscribe aids *e-mail address***
To access (Usenet):	news:sci.med.aids
E-mail:	aids-moderators@wubios.wustl.edu

AIDS Book Review Journal

The AIDS Book Review Journal reviews books, videos, journals, and other materials about AIDS, safe sex, and sexually transmitted diseases. It's published by the University of Illinois at Chicago Library.

Vital Stats:

Access method:	E-mail
To access:	Send an e-mail message to listserv@uicvm.uic.edu
Subject line:	
Message:	**sub AIDSBKRV *firstname lastname***
E-mail:	aidsbkrv@uicvm.uic.edu

AIDS Clinical Trials Information Service

The AIDS Clinical Trials Information Service has detailed information about clinical trials of HIV/AIDS drugs that are open for enrollment. The site is a joint project of the Centers for Disease Control and Prevention, National Institute of Allergy and Infectious Diseases, Food and Drug Administration, and National Library of Medicine.

The site also has a database of bibliographic references for journal articles about the interim or final results of HIV/AIDS-related clinical trials, a fact sheet about AIDS clinical trials, a list of FDA-approved drugs for HIV infection and AIDS-related conditions, press releases about clinical trials, and links to other Internet sites that have information about AIDS clinical trials.

Vital Stats:

Access method:	WWW
To access:	http://www.actis.org
E-mail:	actis@cdcnac.org

AIDS-L

AIDS educators exchange information and tips on the AIDS-L mailing list.

Vital Stats:

Access method:	E-mail
To access:	Send an e-mail message to listserv@siu.edu
Subject line:	
Message:	**subscribe AIDS-L _firstname lastname_**
E-mail:	AIDS-L-request@siu.edu

AIDS Research Information Center

This site has an eclectic mix of useful AIDS information, ranging from numerous articles about medical topics to lists of mail and telephone contacts for buyer's clubs, AIDS hotlines, government and professional organizations, advocacy groups, and AIDS lobbying groups. It's operated by the AIDS Research Information Center, a nonprofit AIDS medical information service in Baltimore.

The site also has summaries of financial statements submitted to the IRS by many national AIDS groups, AIDS images, a quarterly newsletter, links to dozens of other AIDS sites on the Internet, and lots of local information, including a list of Baltimore-area AIDS service providers and a local bulletin board.

Access method: WWW
To access: http://www.critpath.org/aric
E-mail: aricinc@clark.net

AIDSACT

Subscribers to the AIDSACT mailing list discuss political aspects of the AIDS crisis. The list is aimed at AIDS activists.

Vital Stats:

Access method: E-mail
To access: Send an e-mail message to listproc@critpath.org
Subject line:
Message: **subscribe AIDSACT *firstname lastname***
E-mail: kiyoshi@critpath.org

AIDSNews

AIDSNews is a mailing list that distributes AIDS-related documents from the Centers for Disease Control and Prevention and other federal agencies.

Documents distributed through the list include the CDC's *AIDS Daily Summary*, selected articles from the *Morbidity and Mortality Weekly Report*, information about clinical trials, conference announcements, and news about funding opportunities.

Vital Stats:

Access method: E-mail
To access: Send an e-mail message to listproc@cdcnac.com
Subject line:
Message: **subscribe aidsnews *firstname lastname***
E-mail (for questions): aidsinfo@cdcnac.com

The Body: A Multimedia AIDS and HIV Information Resource

The Body is one of the best Internet sites about AIDS. It offers hundreds of publications, both original and from other sources, about such topics as AIDS demographics, safe sex, treatment options, infections and complications, experimental drugs, diet and nutrition, mental health issues, financial and legal issues, and political action, among many others. The Body is operated by Body Health Resources Corporation, with support from several drug companies.

One of the site's most useful features is its forums where you can ask questions of experts about treatment, safe sex and prevention, AIDS and HIV in the workplace, HIV and mental health, and spiritual support. Another helpful feature is a collection of links to Web sites operated by some of the leading AIDS hospitals in the United States.

The Body also has a discussion group where people can exchange their stories about HIV/AIDS, political action alerts, news from recent conferences, links to Web sites operated by many major AIDS organizations, and lots more.

Vital Stats:

Access method:	WWW
To access:	http://www.thebody.com
E-mail:	BGoldman@thebody.com

CDC National AIDS Clearinghouse

Operated by the Centers for Disease Control and Prevention (CDC), the CDC National AIDS Clearinghouse site offers lots of useful information about HIV/AIDS and numerous links to other Internet sites about the subject.

The site offers a database that has descriptions of more than 19,000 HIV/AIDS service organizations, a database that provides information about private and government funding opportunities for community-based and HIV/AIDS service organizations, articles about AIDS from the CDC's *Morbidity and Mortality Weekly Report,* and the CDC's *AIDS Daily Summary,* which summarizes articles about AIDS from newspapers, wire services, magazines, and journals.

It also has the full text and selected tables about AIDS prevalence from the *HIV/AIDS Surveillance Report,* a CDC publication titled *Glossary of HIV/AIDS-Related Terms,* numerous bibliographies of AIDS-related materials, the CDC *Guide to Selected HIV/AIDS Related Internet Resources,* a bookmark file you can download with links to HIV/AIDS and health sites on the Internet, and numerous fact sheets, brochures, and other publications.

Vital Stats:

Access method:	WWW
To access:	http://www.cdcnac.org
E-mail:	aidsinfo@cdcnac.com

Critical Path AIDS Project

The Critical Path AIDS Project site is a tremendous resource about AIDS—one of the very best on the Internet. The project is a Philadelphia-based organization founded by persons with AIDS.

The site's greatest strength is its links to other AIDS sites, which are arranged by subject. Great care has been taken to annotate the links, so you have a good idea of what you'll get when you click on one. Some of the available subjects include prevention, research, clinical trials, treatment, alternative treatment, publications, and AIDS organizations.

The site also offers news bulletins, links to Web pages of more than forty AIDS organizations hosted by Critical Path, and lots of local information, including lists of health care providers in the Philadelphia region who are experienced in treating HIV/AIDS.

Vital Stats:

Access method:	WWW
To access:	http://www.critpath.org
E-mail:	kiyoshi@critpath.org

Doctor's Guide to AIDS Information & Resources

This site has more than 100 news stories about HIV and AIDS, links to other AIDS-related sites, and information about relevant Usenet newsgroups. It's part of the Doctor's Guide to the Internet (p. 14), which is sponsored by P/S/L NuMedia.

Vital Stats:

Access method:	WWW
To access:	http://www.pslgroup.com/AIDS.HTM
E-mail:	webmaster@pslgroup.com

HIV InSite

HIV InSite offers a superb collection of original information and HIV/AIDS resources collected from organizations around the world. It's operated by the University of California-San Francisco AIDS Research Institute, the UCSF AIDS Program at San Francisco General Hospital, the Center for AIDS Prevention Studies, and the Henry J. Kaiser Family Foundation.

It has hundreds of files about everything from prevention to social issues, a database listing all HIV-related clinical trials in the United States that are open for enrollment, a database containing information about medications commonly used in treating HIV/AIDS, and the *AIDS Daily Summary* from the Centers for Disease Control and Prevention.

HIV InSite also has detailed information about AIDS in each state, including statistics, lists of clinical trials and trial sites, and contact information for AIDS service organizations and government offices; *The AIDS Knowledge Base,* a textbook about HIV/AIDS; annotated links to sites offering AIDS newsletters, journals, and other publications; and much more.

Vital Stats:

Access method:	WWW
To access:	http://hivinsite.ucsf.edu
E-mail:	hivinsite@sfaids.ucsf.edu

HIV-Support

HIV-Support is a mailing list where people with HIV or AIDS share emotional support and medical information. The list is solely aimed at people with HIV/AIDS and their caregivers. Researchers, observers, and others are asked not to subscribe.

Vital Stats:

Access method:	E-mail
To access:	Send an e-mail message to lists@web-depot.com
Subject line:	
Message:	**subscribe hiv-support**
E-mail:	davon@web-depot.com

HIV/AIDS Treatment Information Service

This site has numerous articles, brochures, and other publications about the treatment of HIV and AIDS. It's sponsored by six U.S. Public Health Service agencies.

Some of the available titles include *HIV Protease Inhibitors & You, Caring for Someone with AIDS at Home, FDA Approved Drugs for HIV Infection and AIDS-Related Conditions,* and *Eating Defensively: Food Safety Advice for Persons with AIDS.* The site also has numerous links to other Internet sites that offer treatment information.

Vital Stats:

Access method:	WWW
To access:	http://www.hivatis.org
E-mail:	atis@cdcnac.org

International Association of Physicians in AIDS Care

This site offers dozens of excellent articles about various aspects of HIV/AIDS, many written by physicians. Some of the topics covered include antiviral therapies, nutrition, pediatrics, minority issues, conferences, opportunistic diseases, women's health issues, and vaccines. It also has reviews of books about AIDS. The site is operated by the International Association of Physicians in AIDS Care.

Vital Stats:

Access method:	WWW
To access:	http://www.iapac.org
E-mail:	journal@iapac.org

The Internet Sleuth—AIDS

This database lets you search ten Internet sites about AIDS using a single interface. You can search up to six of the sites simultaneously. The database is part of The Internet Sleuth search engine.

Vital Stats:

Access method:	WWW
To access:	http://www.isleuth.com/dise-ai.html
E-mail:	sleuth@isleuth.com

JAMA HIV/AIDS Information Center

This site offers a wide range of useful information, including abstracts and the full text where available of articles about HIV/AIDS from the *Journal of the American Medical Association (JAMA)* and other medical journals. The site is sponsored by *JAMA,* with financial assistance from the drug company Glaxo Wellcome.

Other offerings include daily news briefings, articles from conferences, ethics guidelines for treating AIDS patients, physician guidelines from various sources for preventing and managing HIV/AIDS, a glossary of HIV/AIDS drugs, contact information for national HIV/AIDS organizations and state and local hotlines, and links to dozens of other AIDS-related Internet sites.

Vital Stats:

Access method: WWW
To access: http://www.ama-assn.org/special/hiv/hivhome.htm
E-mail: hiv-comments@ama-assn.org

---

misc.health.aids

Most of the messages in this very active newsgroup, which averages several dozen posts daily, focus on how to provide support for AIDS patients.

Vital Stats:

Access method: Usenet newsgroup
To access: news:misc.health.aids

National AIDS Treatment Advocacy Project

The National AIDS Treatment Advocacy Project site offers an excellent booklet titled *Protease Inhibitor User's Guide,* position papers, articles about drug development, conference reports, and a newsletter. The project is a nonprofit organization.

Vital Stats:

Access method: WWW
To access: http://www.natap.org
E-mail: julev@aol.com

National Institute of Allergy and Infectious Diseases (NIAID)

The National Institute of Allergy and Infectious Diseases (NIAID) site specializes in information about AIDS. It has a searchable glossary of AIDS-related terms, news about vaccine studies, details about study recruitment, information about nursing and HIV/AIDS, the *AIDS Daily Summary* from the Centers for Disease Control, information about opportunistic infections, and reports from the National Commission on AIDS.

The site also offers information about asthma, allergies, chronic fatigue syndrome, fungal research, malaria, sexually transmitted diseases, transplantation, Lyme disease, tuberculosis, colds and flu, emerging infectious diseases, and many other diseases and medical conditions.

Vital Stats:

Access method: WWW
To access: http://www.niaid.nih.gov
E-mail: ocpostoffice@flash.niaid.nih.gov

---

sci.med.aids

The sci.med.aids newsgroup, which is moderated, is one of the most popular newsgroups about AIDS.

Vital Stats:

Access method: Usenet newsgroup
To access: news:sci.med.aids

USPTO Patent Databases

This site provides access to the International AIDS Patent Database, which contains the full text and images of patents related to AIDS issued in the United States, Europe, and Japan. The database contains more than 5,000 patents. The site is a joint project of the Center for Networked Information Discovery and Retrieval, U.S. Patent and Trademark Office, and National Science Foundation.

Vital Stats:

Access method:	WWW
To access:	http://aids.uspto.gov
E-mail:	patenthelp@cnidr.org

---

www.aidsnyc.org

This site hosts Web pages created by more than two dozen community based AIDS organizations in New York City, including the AIDS in Prison Project, the Orphan Project, the PWA Health Group, and the Treatment Action Group. It also has links to dozens of other AIDS-related Internet sites around the country.

Vital Stats:

Access method:	WWW
To access:	http://www.aidsnyc.org
E-mail:	aidsnyc@earthlink.net

ALLERGIES

ALLERGY

Members of the ALLERGY mailing list discuss human allergies of all types. Some of the topics discussed include how allergies affect lifestyles, treatments, self-help prevention of allergy symptoms, and allergy self-care.

Vital Stats:

Access method:	E-mail
To access:	Send an e-mail message to listserv@listserv.tamu.edu
Subject line:	
Message:	**subscribe ALLERGY *firstname lastname***
E-mail:	ALLERGY-Request@listserv.tamu.edu

Allergy Basics Center

This site provides no original information, but it has links to dozens of Internet sites devoted to allergies and asthma. Some of the topics covered by the links include food allergies, kids' allergies, latex allergy, hay fever and other seasonal allergies, skin allergies, and insect stings. It also has information about mailing lists and Usenet newsgroups about allergies.

Vital Stats:

Access method: WWW
To access: http://www.Immune.Com/allergy/allabc.html
E-mail: allergylinks@Immune.Com

---

alt.med.allergy

The alt.med.allergy newsgroup has discussions about treatment and other issues involving all types of allergies.

Vital Stats:

Access method: Usenet newsgroup
To access: news:alt.med.allergy

---

alt.support.food-allergies

All types of food allergies are discussed in the newsgroup alt.support.food-allergies.

Vital Stats:

Access method: Usenet newsgroup
To access: news:alt.support.food-allergies

American Academy of Allergy, Asthma & Immunology

This site has basic patient publications about allergies and asthma, articles about allergies and asthma from various news sources, information about how to find an allergy and immunology specialist, and links to federal health care legislation. It's operated by the American Academy of Allergy, Asthma & Immunology, a physician group.

Vital Stats:

Access method:	WWW
To access:	http://www.aaaai.org
E-mail:	info@aaaai.org

CEL-KIDS

The CEL-KIDS mailing list is devoted to discussions of celiac disease in children. The disease makes people unable to digest gluten from some grains. A sister list, CELIAC (below), is devoted to general discussions of celiac disease.

Vital Stats:

Access method:	E-mail
To access:	Send an e-mail message to listserv@maelstrom.stjohns.edu
Subject line:	
Message:	**SUB CEL-KIDS *firstname lastname***
E-mail:	CEL-KIDS-Request@maelstrom.stjohns.edu

CELIAC

Members of the CELIAC mailing list/newsgroup exchange information about celiac disease, which makes people unable to digest gluten from some grains. A sister list, CEL-KIDS (above), focuses on celiac disease in children.

Vital Stats:

Access methods:	E-mail, Usenet newsgroup
To access (mailing list):	Send an e-mail message to listserv@maelstrom.stjohns.edu
Subject line:	
Message:	**SUB CELIAC *firstname lastname***
To access (Usenet):	news:bit.listserv.celiac
E-mail:	CELIAC-Request@maelstrom.stjohns.edu

Doctor's Guide to Allergies Information & Resources

This site has dozens of news stories about allergies, links to other allergy-related documents and sites, and information about relevant Usenet newsgroups and mailing lists. It's part of the Doctor's Guide to the Internet (p. 14), which is sponsored by P/S/L NuMedia.

Vital Stats:

Access method:	WWW
To access:	http://www.pslgroup.com/ALLERGIES.HTM
E-mail:	webmaster@pslgroup.com

Rubber

Subscribers to the Rubber mailing list discuss all aspects of rubber and latex allergies.

Vital Stats:

Access method:	E-mail
To access:	Send an e-mail message to listserv@listserv.tamu.edu
Subject line:	
Message:	**subscribe Rubber *firstname lastname***
E-mail:	RUBBER-Request@listserv.tamu.edu

ARTHRITIS

alt.support.arthritis

The newsgroup alt.support.arthritis provides support for people with arthritis.

Vital Stats:

Access method: Usenet newsgroup
To access: news:alt.support.arthritis

American College of Rheumatology

The American College of Rheumatology site offers more than two dozen brief patient fact sheets about such topics as back pain, exercise and arthritis, fibromyalgia, gout, Lyme disease, osteoporosis, and rheumatoid arthritis, among others. It also has answers to basic questions about arthritis and rheumatic diseases, abstracts from the journals *Arthritis & Rheumatism* and *Arthritis Care and Research*, a directory of ACR members, a newsletter, and legislative updates.

Vital Stats:

Access method: WWW
To access: http://www.rheumatology.org
E-mail: webmaster@rheumatology.org

Arthritis Foundation

The Arthritis Foundation site has answers to frequently asked questions about arthritis, numerous articles about juvenile arthritis, a list of local offices around the country, information about brochures and books that can be ordered from the foundation, a list of state and federal legislative priorities, and legislative updates.

Vital Stats:

Access method:	WWW
To access:	http://www.arthritis.org
E-mail:	webmaster@arthritis.org

Doctor's Guide to Arthritis Information & Resources

This site has dozens of news stories about arthritis, a good collection of links to other arthritis-related documents and sites, and information about relevant Usenet newsgroups. It's part of the Doctor's Guide to the Internet (p. 14), which is sponsored by P/S/L NuMedia.

Vital Stats:

Access method:	WWW
To access:	http://www.pslgroup.com/ARTHRITIS.HTM
E-mail:	webmaster@pslgroup.com

---

misc.health.arthritis

All aspects of treating and living with arthritis are discussed in this newsgroup.

Vital Stats:

Access method:	Usenet newsgroup
To access:	news:misc.health.arthritis

National Institute of Arthritis and Musculoskeletal and Skin Diseases

This site provides brochures about arthritis and exercise, hip replacement, Lyme disease, lupus, psoriasis, and other topics. It's operated by the National Institute of Arthritis and Musculoskeletal and Skin Diseases, which is part of the National Institutes of Health (NIH).

The site also has NIH consensus statements about optimal calcium intake and total hip replacement, information about research being conducted at the institute, workshop summaries, a calendar of events, and press releases.

Vital Stats:

Access method: WWW
To access: http://www.nih.gov/niams
E-mail: NIAMSweb@od.niams.nih.gov

ASTHMA

alt.support.asthma

Discussions in the alt.support.asthma newsgroup focus on living with and getting relief from asthma.

Vital Stats:

Access method: Usenet newsgroup
To access: news:alt.support.asthma

Doctor's Guide to Asthma Information & Resources

This site has dozens of news stories about asthma, a good collection of links to other asthma-related documents and sites, and information about relevant Usenet newsgroups. It's part of the Doctor's Guide to the Internet (p. 14), which is sponsored by P/S/L NuMedia.

Vital Stats:

Access method: WWW
To access: http://www.pslgroup.com/ASTHMA.HTM
E-mail: webmaster@pslgroup.com

JAMA Asthma Information Center

Operated by the *Journal of the American Medical Association (JAMA)*, this site has a small collection of patient education publications, stories about asthma from Reuters Health Information Service, and clinical treatment guidelines for physicians.

The site also offers the full text of articles about asthma from *JAMA* and other medical journals, summaries from major professional meetings, a report from the National Institutes of Health titled *Asthma Management and Prevention (A Pocket Guide for Physicians and Nurses)*, drug information, contact information for organizations for asthma patients, and links to nearly two dozen asthma sites on the Internet.

Vital Stats:

Access method:	WWW
To access:	http://www.ama-assn.org/special/asthma
E-mail:	asthma@ama-assn.org

BLOOD DISORDERS

alt.support.hemophilia

Participants in the newsgroup alt.support.hemophilia provide information and support for each other.

Vital Stats:
Access method: Usenet newsgroup
To access: news:alt.support.hemophilia

alt.support.scleroderma

People who have scleroderma are the primary audience for this newsgroup.

Vital Stats:
Access method: Usenet newsgroup
To access: news:alt.support.scleroderma

BONE AND MUSCLE DISORDERS

GENERAL

alt.support.ataxia

The alt.support.ataxia newsgroup is for people who have difficulty controlling their muscle movements.

Vital Stats:

Access method: Usenet newsgroup
To access: news:alt.support.ataxia

alt.support.dystonia

Participants in this newsgroup exchange information and support about dystonia, which involves impairment of muscle tone.

Vital Stats:

Access method: Usenet newsgroup
To access: news:alt.support.dystonia

alt.support.jaw-disorders

Various types of jaw problems are discussed in this newsgroup.

Vital Stats:

Access method: Usenet newsgroup
To access: news:alt.support.jaw-disorders

alt.support.marfan

Messages in this newsgroup focus on Marfan's syndrome.

Vital Stats:

Access method: Usenet newsgroup
To access: news:alt.support.marfan

alt.support.spina-bifida

Various aspects of living with spina bifida are discussed in this newsgroup.

Vital Stats:

Access method: Usenet newsgroup
To access: news:alt.support.spina-bifada

Doctor's Guide to ALS (Lou Gehrig's Disease) Information & Resources

This site has more than a dozen news stories about amyotrophic lateral sclerosis (ALS), more commonly known as Lou Gehrig's Disease. It also has links to other ALS-related documents and sites and information about relevant Usenet newsgroups and mailing lists. It's part of the Doctor's Guide to the Internet (p. 14), which is sponsored by P/S/L NuMedia.

Vital Stats:

Access method: WWW
To access: http://www.pslgroup.com/ALS.HTM
E-mail: webmaster@pslgroup.com

---

sci.med.diseases.als

Discussions in this newsgroup focus on amyotrophic lateral sclerosis (ALS), more commonly known as Lou Gehrig's disease.

Vital Stats:

Access method: Usenet newsgroup
To access: news:sci.med.diseases.als

---

sci.med.orthopedics

Orthopedic surgery and related issues are discussed in this newsgroup.

Vital Stats:

Access method: Usenet newsgroup
To access: news:sci.med.orthopedics

OSTEOPOROSIS

Doctor's Guide to Osteoporosis Information & Resources

This site has dozens of news stories about osteoporosis, a small collection of links to other osteoporosis-related documents and sites, and information about relevant Usenet newsgroups. It's part of the Doctor's Guide to the Internet (p. 14), which is sponsored by P/S/L NuMedia.

Vital Stats:

Access method:	WWW
To access:	http://www.pslgroup.com/OSTEOPOROSIS.HTM
E-mail:	webmaster@pslgroup.com

Osteoporosis and Related Bone Diseases National Resource Center

This site provides information about osteoporosis, Paget's disease, osteogenesis imperfecta, hyperparathyroidism, fibrous dysplasia, and hypophosphatasia. It's operated by the Osteoporosis and Related Bone Diseases National Resource Center, which is supported by the National Institute of Arthritis and Musculoskeletal and Skin Diseases.

One of the site's highlights is a collection of two dozen fact sheets about alcohol and bone disorders, African American women and osteoporosis, biochemical markers of bone metabolism, depression and bone loss, fall prevention for older adults, peak bone mass in women, psychosocial consequences of osteoporosis, and women in clinical trials, among other subjects.

The site also provides more than two dozen bibliographies. They cover such topics as bone density and bone mass, calcium, eating disorders and bone density, estrogen and bone loss, exercise and postmenopausal women, female athletes and bone health, and men and osteoporosis.

Vital Stats:

Access method: WWW
To access: http://www.osteo.org
E-mail: orbdnrc@nof.org

---

sci.med.diseases.osteoporosis

Participants in this newsgroup exchange information and support about osteoporosis.

Vital Stats:

Access method: Usenet newsgroup
To access: news:sci.med.diseases.osteoporosis

BRAIN DISEASES AND INJURIES

alt.support.cerebral-palsy

This newsgroup provides support for people who have cerebral palsy.

Vital Stats:

Access method:	Usenet newsgroup
To access:	news:alt.support.cerebral-palsy

American Brain Tumor Association

The American Brain Tumor Association site offers extensive information about brain tumors and their treatment. It has a booklet titled *A Primer of Brain Tumors,* information about state-of-the-art treatment, a list of publications available from the association, a list of physicians who offer investigative treatments for brain tumor patients, and a calendar of association events.

Vital Stats:

Access method:	WWW
To access:	http://www.abta.org
E-mail:	info@abta.org

BRAINTMR

Subscribers to the BRAINTMR mailing list discuss brain tumor research and provide support for each other.

Vital Stats:

Access method:	E-mail
To access:	Send an e-mail message to listserv@mitvma.mit.edu
Subject line:	
Message:	**subscribe BRAINTMR**
E-mail:	samajane@sasquatch.com

DISCUSS-TBI

This mailing list is aimed at survivors of traumatic brain injuries.

Vital Stats:

Access method:	E-mail
To access:	Send an e-mail message to listserv@maelstrom.stjohns.edu
Subject line:	
Message:	**subscribe DISCUSS-TBI** *firstname lastname*
E-mail:	DISCUSS-TBI-request@maelstrom.stjohns.edu

The National Parkinson Foundation

This site offers basic information about Parkinson's disease and several online publications. Some of the available titles include *Adjustment, Adaptation, and Accommodation: Psychosocial Approaches to Living with Parkinson's Disease, Introduction to Speech and Swallowing Problems Associated with Parkinson's Disease, Nutritional Considerations of Parkinson's Disease,* and *Practical Pointers for Parkinsonians.* The site is operated by the National Parkinson Foundation.

Vital Stats:

Access method:	WWW
To access:	http://www.parkinson.org
E-mail:	gizak@npf.med.miami.edu

PARKINSN

The PARKINSN mailing list is a discussion group about Parkinson's disease. It's aimed at people with Parkinson's, their loved ones, and medical professionals who are interested in the disease.

Vital Stats:

Access method:	E-mail
To access:	Send an e-mail message to listserv@listserv.utoronto.ca
Subject line:	
Message:	**subscribe PARKINSN *firstname lastname***
E-mail:	PARKINSN-request@listserv.utoronto.ca

TBI-FAM

This mailing list provides support for family members of people suffering from traumatic brain injuries.

Vital Stats:

Access method:	E-mail
To access:	Send an e-mail message to listserv@maelstrom.stjohns.edu
Subject line:	
Message:	**subscribe TBI-FAM *firstname lastname***
E-mail:	TBI-FAM-request@maelstrom.stjohns.edu

TBI-SPRT

This mailing list/newsgroup provides support and information for people affected by traumatic brain injury.

Vital Stats:

Access methods:	E-mail, Usenet newsgroup
To access (mailing list):	Send an e-mail message to listserv@maelstrom.stjohns.edu
Subject line:	
Message:	**subscribe TBI-SPRT *firstname lastname***
To access (Usenet):	news:bit.listserv.tbi-support
E-mail:	TBI-SPRT-request@maelstrom.stjohns.edu

CANCER

BREAST CANCER

BCN-FLASH

BCN-FLASH is a daily newsletter that summarizes news articles about the prevention, screening, and treatment of breast cancer. It also lists URLs that point to the full articles. The newsletter is distributed twice daily, and each issue generally contains six to eight items.

Vital Stats:

Access method:	E-mail
To access:	Send an e-mail message to majordomo@redbank.net
Subject line:	
Message:	**subscribe bcn-flash**
E-mail:	owner-bcn-flash@redbank.net

BREAST-CANCER

Members of the BREAST-CANCER mailing list discuss any issues relating to breast cancer. The list is aimed at patients, family and friends of patients, researchers, and physicians.

Vital Stats:

Access method:	E-mail
To access:	Send an e-mail message to listserv@morgan.ucs.mun.ca
Subject line:	
Message:	**subscribe breast-cancer**
E-mail:	jchurch@morgan.ucs.mun.ca

Breast Cancer Information Clearinghouse

The Breast Cancer Information Clearinghouse is exactly what its name implies. It has a large collection of electronic publications about breast cancer from various sources, in addition to links to publications at other Internet sites. The site is operated by the New York State Education and Research Network, a nonprofit organization.

The publications and links are arranged two ways: by creating agency and by subject. Some of the subjects covered include prevention, risk factors, diagnosis, treatment, breast reconstruction, pain management, diet, appearance, survivorship, insurance and legal issues, and breast cancer advocacy.

Besides the publications and links, the site has archives of the BREAST-CANCER mailing list (p. 92), a list of telephone hotline numbers, and a calendar of upcoming events and conferences.

Vital Stats:

Access method:	WWW
To access:	http://nysernet.org/bcic
E-mail:	kennett@nysernet.org

Community Breast Health Project

The Community Breast Health Project offers useful articles about understanding pathology reports, patient rights under the Family Medical Leave Act, breast reconstruction, the drug Tamoxifen, bone marrow transplants, cancer pain, and related issues. The site also has reviews of books about breast cancer and links to dozens of Internet sites related to breast cancer, cancer in general, and general medicine. The CBHP is a nonprofit organization, and server space is provided by the Stanford Medical Center.

Vital Stats:

Access method:	WWW
To access:	http://www-med.stanford.edu/CBHP
E-mail:	ldieguez@best.com

Doctor's Guide to Breast Cancer Information & Resources

This site has dozens of news stories about breast cancer and a small collection of links to other breast cancer-related documents and sites. It's part of the Doctor's Guide to the Internet (p. 14), which is sponsored by P/S/L NuMedia.

Vital Stats:

Access method:	WWW
To access:	http://www.pslgroup.com/BREASTCANCER.HTM
E-mail:	webmaster@pslgroup.com

MALEBC

Subscribers to the MALEBC mailing list exchange information about breast cancer in men.

Vital Stats:

Access method:	E-mail
To access:	Send an e-mail message to listserv@listserv.acor.org
Subject line:	
Message:	**subscribe MALEBC *firstname lastname***
E-mail:	MALEBC-request@listserv.acor.org

National Action Plan on Breast Cancer

This site has fact sheets about such topics as hereditary susceptibility and clinical trials, press releases, and calendars of events related to breast cancer. The National Action Plan on Breast Cancer is a public/private partnership that's coordinated by the U.S. Department of Health and Human Services.

The site also has grant information, links to Internet sites about clinical trials, and links to dozens of Internet sites that have information about breast cancer.

Vital Stats:

Access method:	WWW
To access:	http://www.napbc.org
E-mail:	info@napbc.org

National Alliance of Breast Cancer Organizations

This site offers a basic collection of information about breast cancer. Perhaps the most notable features are its articles about clinical trials and directory of breast cancer trials. The site is operated by the National Alliance of Breast Cancer Organizations, a network of more than 375 groups.

Other features of particular interest include a lengthy list of books and pamphlets about various aspects of breast cancer, a list of breast cancer support groups around the country, and fact sheets about obtaining low-cost mammograms, getting quality mammograms, managed care and breast cancer, genetic testing, young women and breast cancer, detection of breast cancer, the risk of developing breast cancer, and related topics.

Vital Stats:

Access method:	WWW
To access:	http://www.nabco.org
E-mail:	NABCOinfo@aol.com

National Breast Cancer Coalition

Political advocacy to eradicate breast cancer is this site's focus. It has a list of current congressional bills endorsed by the National Breast Cancer Coalition, along with information about the coalition's training program for breast cancer advocates, annual advocacy training conference, and clinical trials project.

Vital Stats:

Access method:	WWW
To access:	http://www.natlbcc.org
E-mail:	clhain@natlbcc.org

Y-ME National Breast Cancer Organization

The Y-ME National Breast Cancer Organization site has information about how to perform breast self-examinations, survivor stories, answers to frequently asked questions, a list of books about breast cancer, and a newsletter. It also offers a list of free publications that can be ordered from Y-ME, a list of Y-ME chapters, stories written by children whose mothers have breast cancer, and a booklet for husbands or partners of women diagnosed with breast cancer. Y-ME was founded by two breast cancer patients in 1978.

Vital Stats:

Access method:	WWW
To access:	http://www.y-me.org
E-mail:	help@y-me.org

DIRECTORIES AND SEARCH ENGINES

Cancer News on the Net

Cancer News on the Net has dozens of links to cancer-related sites on the Internet. Of particular interest are links to sites created by cancer patients. Cancer News on the Net is operated by K. J. Brown, M.D.

Vital Stats:

Access method:	WWW
To access:	http://www.cancernews.com
E-mail:	webmaster@cancernews.com

The Internet Sleuth—Cancer

This database lets you search more than twenty Internet sites about cancer using a single interface. You can search up to six of the sites simultaneously. The database is part of The Internet Sleuth search engine.

Vital Stats:

Access method:	WWW
To access:	http://www.isleuth.com/dise-ca.html
E-mail:	sleuth@isleuth.com

GENERAL RESOURCES

alt.support.cancer

The newsgroup alt.support.cancer provides support for people who have any type of cancer.

Vital Stats:

Access method:	Usenet newsgroup
To access:	news:alt.support.cancer

American Cancer Society

The American Cancer Society site offers extensive information about cancer prevention, detection, and treatment for patients and their family members. It provides background about specific types of cancers, information about alternative therapies, dietary and other guidelines, and cancer statistics.

The site also has information about the settlement between the tobacco companies and the federal government, details about research supported by the society, links to other cancer-related Internet sites, and lots more.

Vital Stats:

Access method:	WWW
To access:	http://www.cancer.org
E-mail:	webmaster@cancer.org

American Institute for Cancer Research Online

This site focuses on the link between diet and cancer. It has dozens of recipes for healthier eating, information about recent research findings, grant listings, lists of free publications that can be ordered from the institute, and newspaper columns by the institute about cooking, healthy eating, and nutrition.

Vital Stats:

Access method: WWW
To access: http://www.aicr.org
E-mail: aicrweb@aicr.org

ASCO Online

This site has publications about cancer pain, the breast cancer gene test, and clinical trials. Each publication offers links to other Internet sites with information about the topic. The site is operated by the American Society of Clinical Oncology (ASCO).

Other offerings include news about pending legislation affecting cancer treatment, guidelines for treatment following breast cancer surgery, lists of national cancer support organizations, and abstracts from the society's annual meeting.

Vital Stats:

Access method: WWW
To access: http://www.asco.org

CA: A Cancer Journal for Clinicians

CA: A Cancer Journal for Clinicians is a peer-reviewed journal published for the American Cancer Society by Lippincott-Raven Publishers. The Web site offers the full text of all issues published from January/February 1996 to the present.

Some sample article titles include "Quality-of-Life Management of Patients with Colorectal Cancer," "American Cancer Society Guideline for the Early Detection of Prostate Cancer," "American Cancer Society Guidelines for the Early Detection of Breast Cancer," and "Tumor-Related Prognostic Factors for Breast Cancer."

Vital Stats:

Access method: WWW
To access: http://www.ca-journal.org

CANCER-L

Subscribers to the CANCER-L mailing list discuss patient experiences, research, clinical trials, treatment practices, treatment alternatives, and related issues. The list is aimed at patients, family, friends, researchers, and physicians.

Vital Stats:

Access method: E-mail
To access: Send an e-mail message to listserv@wvnvm.wvnet.edu
Subject line:
Message: **subscribe CANCER-L**
E-mail: cancer-l-request@wvnvm.wvnet.edu

CancerGuide

CancerGuide offers a superb collection of practical information for cancer patients. The aim of the site, which is operated by cancer patient Steve Dunn, is to help cancer patients research their options.

The site offers an eclectic collection of resources, including a guide to reading biopsy reports, basic information about cancer staging and tumors, a list of recommended books about cancer, stories of cancer patients, a guide to clinical trials, details about how to find and research clinical trials, extensive information about how to research the medical literature, information about bone marrow transplants, advice on obtaining second opinions, links to other cancer-related Internet sites, and much more.

Vital Stats:

Access method: WWW
To access: http://cancerguide.org
E-mail: dunns@h2net.net

CancerNet

CancerNet, which is operated by the National Cancer Institute, offers hundreds of files about prevention, diagnosis, and treatment of cancer. There are documents about risk factors and possible causes of cancer, unconventional treatment methods, side effects frequently experienced by cancer patients, coping with cancer, caring for cancer patients, clinical trials of new cancer drugs, and sources of cancer information. Many of the documents are available in Spanish versions.

The site also has abstracts of recent journal articles about cancer and links to more than two dozen other cancer sites on the Internet.

Vital Stats:

Access method:	WWW
To access:	http://cancernet.nci.nih.gov
E-mail:	comments@icic.nci.nih.gov

CancerWire

CancerWire is a mailing list that distributes general news about cancer and specific news about clinical trials, support groups, Internet resources, and other topics. The list, which is operated by a private individual, is aimed at cancer patients, caregivers, and professionals.

Vital Stats:

Access method:	E-mail
To access:	Send an e-mail message to listserv@rwneill.com
Subject line:	
Message:	**subscribe cancerwire**

CAREGIVERS

The CAREGIVERS mailing list is a support forum for caregivers of people diagnosed with cancer.

Vital Stats:

Access method:	E-mail
To access:	Send an e-mail message to listserv@listserv.acor.org
Subject line:	
Message:	**subscribe CAREGIVERS** *firstname lastname*
E-mail:	CAREGIVERS-request@listserv.acor.org

Journal of Clinical Oncology

This site offers a searchable database containing abstracts of articles published in the *Journal of Clinical Oncology*, the official publication of the American Society of Clinical Oncology. It also has tables of contents of the journal dating back to March 1996.

Vital Stats:

Access method:	WWW
To access:	http://www.jcojournal.org
E-mail:	whippend@jco.asco.org

National Cancer Institute

The National Cancer Institute site has details about how to contact the Cancer Information Service, which provides information about cancer to the public and health professionals. The site also has a calendar of upcoming cancer-related meetings, budget data for NCI, and links to Internet sites operated by NCI branches. In addition, it has a link to CancerNet (p. 100), an NCI Internet site that offers hundreds of documents for cancer patients and physicians.

Vital Stats:

Access method:	WWW
To access:	http://www.nci.nih.gov
E-mail:	msears@nih.gov

NCCS

The NCCS (National Coalition for Cancer Survivorship Cyberspace Town Hall) mailing list is a discussion forum for cancer survivors, caregivers, loved ones, and anyone else interested in the discussions.

Vital Stats:

Access method:	E-mail
To access:	Send an e-mail message to listserv@listserv.aol.com
Subject line:	
Message:	**subscribe NCCS *firstname lastname***

OncoLink

OncoLink is the premier cancer site on the Internet—a must see for both patients and physicians. Through its files and links to other Internet sites, OncoLink presents a huge array of information covering just about everything: dietary factors affecting cancer risk, new cancer treatments, preventing nausea and vomiting, insurance issues for cancer patients, pain management, end of life issues, and many other topics. OncoLink is operated by the University of Pennsylvania Cancer Center.

One of OncoLink's best features is its menus devoted to specific types of cancer. For each type of cancer, the site typically provides information about screening, risk factors and prevention, treatment options, genetic issues, support groups, and news.

Another great feature is a form that lets you sign up for any of several dozen cancer-related mailing lists. OncoLink doesn't operate the lists, but its convenient sign-up form saves you having to search around the Internet for lists of interest.

Vital Stats:

Access method:	WWW
To access:	http://www.oncolink.upenn.edu
E-mail:	editors@oncolink.upenn.edu

ONCONEWS

ONCONEWS is a mailing list that distributes news about cancer to researchers, physicians, and patients.

Vital Stats:

Access method:	E-mail
To access:	Send an e-mail message to listserv@listserv.acor.org
Subject line:	
Message:	**subscribe ONCONEWS *firstname lastname***
E-mail:	ONCONEWS-request@listserv.acor.org

PED-ONC

The PED-ONC mailing list is a support group for parents of children diagnosed with cancer.

Vital Stats:

Access method:	E-mail
To access:	Send an e-mail message to listserv@listserv.acor.org
Subject line:	
Message:	**subscribe PED-ONC *firstname lastname***
E-mail:	PED-ONC-request@listserv.acor.org

SARCOMA

Members of the SARCOMA mailing list discuss various aspects of living with and fighting all forms of sarcomas.

Vital Stats:

Access method:	E-mail
To access:	Send an e-mail message to listserv@listserv.acor.org
Subject line:	
Message:	**subscribe SARCOMA *firstname lastname***
E-mail:	SARCOMA-request@listserv.acor.org

---

sci.med.diseases.cancer

Issues involving various types of cancer are discussed in the newsgroup sci.med.diseases.cancer.

Vital Stats:

Access method:	Usenet newsgroup
To access:	news:sci.med.diseases.cancer

LEUKEMIA AND MYELOMA

BMT-TALK

Members of the BMT-TALK mailing list discuss treatments and other issues involved with bone marrow transplants. The list is aimed at patients, their loved ones, researchers, and physicians.

Vital Stats:

Access method: E-mail
To access: Send an e-mail message to listserv@listserv.acor.org
Subject line:
Message: **subscribe BMT-TALK *firstname lastname***
E-mail: BMT-TALK-request@listserv.acor.org

CLL

Subscribers to the CLL mailing list exchange information and support about chronic lymphocytic leukemia.

Vital Stats:

Access method: E-mail
To access: Send an e-mail message to listserv@listserv.acor.org
Subject line:
Message: **subscribe CLL *firstname lastname***
E-mail: CLL-request@listserv.acor.org

CML-TALK

Subscribers to the CML-TALK mailing list exchange information and support regarding chronic myelogenous leukemia.

Vital Stats:

Access method:	E-mail
To access:	Send an e-mail message to listserv@listserv.aol.com
Subject line:	
Message:	**subscribe CML-TALK *firstname lastname***
E-mail:	CML-TALK-request@listserv.aol.com

HEM-ONC

Subscribers to the HEM-ONC mailing list discuss clinical and nonclinical issues related to leukemia, lymphoma, and multiple myeloma. Some of the subjects discussed include patient experiences, psychosocial issues, research, clinical trials, and treatment practices and alternatives.

Vital Stats:

Access method:	E-mail
To access:	Send an e-mail message to listserv@listserv.acor.org
Subject line:	
Message:	**subscribe HEM-ONC *firstname lastname***

International Myeloma Foundation

The International Myeloma Foundation site has background information about multiple myeloma, news updates, selected articles from the quarterly newsletter *Myeloma Today,* a list of support groups, information about how to start your own support group, stories from myeloma survivors, and links to dozens of other cancer-related Internet sites.

Vital Stats:

Access method:	WWW
To access:	http://www.myeloma.org
E-mail:	TheIMF@aol.com

Leukemia Society of America

The Leukemia Society of America site offers information about leukemia and related cancers—lymphoma, multiple myeloma, and Hodgkin's disease. It has booklets about the diseases, articles about related issues such as therapy choices and bone marrow transplants, a list of support groups, contact information for local chapters around the country, articles about new research, a quarterly newsletter, grant information, a list of professional conferences and meetings, and links to other cancer-related Internet sites.

Vital Stats:

Access method:	WWW
To access:	http://www.leukemia.org
E-mail:	bockf@leukemia.org

OTHER SPECIFIC TYPES OF CANCER

AA-MDS-TALK

This mailing list provides support for patients, family members, friends, and medical providers affected by aplastic anemia and myelodysplastic syndrome.

Vital Stats:

Access method: E-mail
To access: Send an e-mail message to listserv@listserv.aol.com
Subject line:
Message: **sub aa-mds-talk *firstname_lastname***
E-mail: AA-MDS-TALK-request@listserv.aol.com

CARCINOID

Members of the CARCINOID mailing list discuss carcinoid tumors, a low-grade malignancy that starts in cells that are capable of producing hormones.

Vital Stats:

Access method: E-mail
To access: Send an e-mail message to listserv@listserv.acor.org
Subject line:
Message: **subscribe CARCINOID *firstname lastname***
E-mail: CARCINOID-request@listserv.acor.org

COLON

Subscribers to the COLON mailing list exchange messages about a wide range of issues related to colon cancer.

Vital Stats:

Access method:	E-mail
To access:	Send an e-mail message to listserv@listserv.acor.org
Subject line:	
Message:	**subscribe COLON *firstname lastname***
E-mail:	COLON-request@listserv.acor.org

EC-GROUP

The EC-GROUP mailing list is devoted to esophageal cancers. Its primary purpose is to allow members to exchange personal experiences about the medical and psychological aspects of esophageal cancers.

Vital Stats:

Access method:	E-mail
To access:	Send an e-mail message to listserv@listserv.acor.org
Subject line:	
Message:	**subscribe EC-Group *firstname lastname***
E-mail:	EC-Group-request@listserv.acor.org

GYN-ONC

The GYN-ONC mailing list is a support group for people affected by gynecological cancers. These include uterine, endometrial, vaginal, vulvar, and ovarian cancer, among others.

Vital Stats:

Access method:	E-mail
To access:	Send an e-mail message to listserv@listserv.acor.org
Subject line:	
Message:	**subscribe GYN-ONC *firstname lastname***
E-mail:	GYN-ONC-request@listserv.acor.org

KIDNEY-ONC

Members of the KIDNEY-ONC mailing list exchange support and information about kidney cancer.

Vital Stats:

Access method:	E-mail
To access:	Send an e-mail message to listserv@listserv.acor.org
Subject line:	
Message:	**subscribe KIDNEY-ONC *firstname lastname***
E-mail:	KIDNEY-ONC-request@listserv.acor.org

L-M-SARCOMA

Subscribers to L-M-SARCOMA discuss leiomyosarcoma, a tumor that affects smooth muscle cells.

Vital Stats:

Access method:	E-mail
To access:	Send an e-mail message to listserv@listserv.acor.org
Subject line:	
Message:	**subscribe L-M-SARCOMA *firstname lastname***
E-mail:	L-M-SARCOMA-request@listserv.acor.org

LARYNX-C

LARYNX-C is a mailing list whose members exchange messages about larynx cancer.

Vital Stats:

Access method:	E-mail
To access:	Send an e-mail message to listserv@listserv.acor.org
Subject line:	
Message:	**subscribe LARYNX-C *firstname lastname***
E-mail:	LARYNX-C-request@listserv.acor.org

LIVER-ONC

The LIVER-ONC mailing list is a support group for liver cancer patients, their loved ones, researchers, and physicians.

Vital Stats:

Access method: E-mail
To access: Send an e-mail message to listserv@listserv.acor.org
Subject line:
Message: **subscribe LIVER-ONC *firstname lastname***
E-mail: LIVER-ONC-request@listserv.acor.org

LUNG-ONC

The LUNG-ONC mailing list is devoted to discussions of lung cancer.

Vital Stats:

Access method: E-mail
To access: Send an e-mail message to listserv@listserv.acor.org
Subject line:
Message: **subscribe LUNG-ONC *firstname lastname***
E-mail: LUNG-ONC-request@listserv.acor.org

MEL-L

Members of the MEL-L mailing list discuss clinical and nonclinical issues involving melanoma. The list is primarily aimed at patients and their loved ones, although anyone may subscribe.

Vital Stats:

Access method: E-mail
To access: Send an e-mail message to melsub@mwt.net
Subject line:
Message: **subscribe mel-l**
E-mail: ctustis@mwt.net

OVARIAN

The primary purpose of the OVARIAN mailing list is to discuss ovarian cancer, although other ovarian disorders such as ovarian cysts also are discussed. Issues such as reproductive and fertility problems are not appropriate for the list.

Vital Stats:

Access method:	E-mail
To access:	Send an e-mail message to listserv@maelstrom.stjohns.edu
Subject line:	
Message:	**subscribe ovarian *firstname lastname***
E-mail:	OVARIAN-request@maelstrom.stjohns.edu

RARE-CANCER

The RARE-CANCER mailing list is a support group for people suffering from rare forms of cancer.

Vital Stats:

Access method:	E-mail
To access:	Send an e-mail message to listserv@listserv.acor.org
Subject line:	
Message:	**subscribe RARE-CANCER *firstname lastname***
E-mail:	RARE-CANCER-request@listserv.acor.org

STOMACH-ONC

Subscribers to the STOMACH-ONC mailing list discuss stomach cancer.

Vital Stats:

Access method:	E-mail
To access:	Send an e-mail message to listserv@listserv.acor.org
Subject line:	
Message:	**subscribe STOMACH-ONC *firstname lastname***
E-mail:	STOMACH-ONC-request@listserv.acor.org

THYROID-ONC

The THYROID-ONC mailing list is devoted to discussions about thyroid cancer.

Vital Stats:

Access method:	E-mail
To access:	Send an e-mail message to listserv@listserv.acor.org
Subject line:	
Message:	**subscribe THYROID-ONC** *firstname lastname*
E-mail:	THYROID-ONC-request@listserv.acor.org

PANCREAS CANCER

Pancreas Cancer Web

The Pancreas Cancer Web is a great resource about pancreas cancer. It primarily offers information about research and clinical developments involving pancreas cancer at Johns Hopkins Medical Institutions, which sponsors the site.

For example, it has information about current clinical trials at Johns Hopkins and about the National Familial Pancreas Tumor Registry, which is based at Hopkins. In addition, it has a chat room where patients and others can discuss pancreas cancer and links to other Internet sites about the subject.

Vital Stats:
Access method:	WWW
To access:	http://www.path.jhu.edu/pancreas

PANCREAS-ONC

Pancreas cancer is the focus of the PANCREAS-ONC mailing list, which is aimed at patients, their loved ones, physicians, and researchers.

Vital Stats:
Access method:	E-mail
To access:	Send an e-mail message to listserv@listserv.acor.org
Subject line:	
Message:	**subscribe PANCREAS-ONC *firstname lastname***
E-mail:	PANCREAS-ONC-request@listserv.acor.org

PROSTATE CANCER

alt.support.cancer.prostate

Discussions in the alt.support.cancer.prostate newsgroup focus on prostate cancer.

Vital Stats:

Access method:	Usenet newsgroup
To access:	news:alt.support.cancer.prostate

Doctor's Guide to Prostate Cancer Information & Resources

This site has dozens of news stories about prostate cancer, an excellent collection of links to other prostate cancer-related documents and sites, and information about relevant Usenet newsgroups. It's part of the Doctor's Guide to the Internet (p. 14), which is sponsored by P/S/L NuMedia.

Vital Stats:

Access method:	WWW
To access:	http://www.pslgroup.com/PROSTCANCER.HTM
E-mail:	webmaster@pslgroup.com

PROSTATE

The primary focus of the PROSTATE mailing list is prostate cancer, although subscribers also discuss other diseases of the prostate gland.

Vital Stats:

Access method:	E-mail
To access:	Send an e-mail message to listserv@listserv.acor.org
Subject line:	
Message:	**sub PROSTATE *firstname lastname***
E-mail:	prostate-request@listserv.acor.org

Prostate Cancer Home Page

The Prostate Cancer Home Page, which is operated by the University of Michigan Comprehensive Cancer Center, has articles about prostate cancer from medical journals and popular publications. It also offers information about treatment options, a list of prostate cancer clinical trials being conducted at Michigan, details about a Michigan project that's examining possible genetic causes of prostate cancer, and links to other cancer sites on the Internet.

Vital Stats:

Access method:	WWW
To access:	http://www.cancer.med.umich.edu:80/prostcan/prostcan.html

---

Prostate Cancer InfoLink

The Prostate Cancer InfoLink has lots of useful information about prostate cancer, including news items, review articles, details about clinical trials, answers to hundreds of questions, and a dictionary of prostate cancer terms. It's operated by CoMed Communications, which develops medical education programs.

Vital Stats:

Access method:	WWW
To access:	http://comed.com/Prostate
E-mail:	peterm@comed.com

---

sci.med.prostate.cancer

Various aspects of prostate cancer are discussed in the newsgroup sci.med.prostate.cancer.

Vital Stats:

Access method:	Usenet newsgroup
To access:	news:sci.med.prostate.cancer

US TOO International, Inc.

The US TOO International site offers information about prostate cancer, including explanations of various treatments, an extensive glossary of terms, a list of prostate cancer support groups across the country, and results from a Louis Harris survey about doctor and patient attitudes concerning prostate cancer. However, the site's highlight is its excellent collection of annotated links to other Internet sites that offer information about prostate cancer. US TOO International is a nonprofit organization.

Vital Stats:

Access method: WWW
To access: http://www.ustoo.com
E-mail: ustoo@ustoo.com

TESTICULAR CANCER

alt.support.cancer.testicular

Various aspects of testicular cancer are discussed in the newsgroup alt.support.cancer.testicular.

Vital Stats:

Access method: Usenet newsgroup
To access: news:alt.support.cancer.testicular

TC-NET

Members of the TC-NET mailing list exchange messages about testicular cancer.

Vital Stats:

Access method: E-mail
To access: Send an e-mail message to listserv@listserv.acor.org
Subject line:
Message: **subscribe TC-NET *firstname lastname***
E-mail: TC-NET-request@listserv.acor.org

Testicular Cancer Resource Center

This site has everything you ever wanted to know about testicular cancer. It has basic information about the disease, instructions for conducting self-exams, a dictionary of terms, details about various treatments, e-mail addresses of patients with whom you can correspond, helpful hints for patients, and links to hundreds of Internet sites. The site is operated by two testicular cancer patients.

Vital Stats:

Access method: WWW
To access: http://www.acor.org/TCRC
E-mail: canis@stic.net

CHRONIC FATIGUE SYNDROME

alt.health.cfids-action, CFIDS-L

Political issues involving chronic fatigue syndrome (CFS) are discussed in the alt.health.cfids-action newsgroup, which is mirrored on the mailing list CFIDS-L.

Vital Stats:

Access methods:	Usenet newsgroup, E-mail
To access (Usenet):	news:alt.health.cfids-action
To access (mailing list):	Send an e-mail message to listserv@american.edu
Subject line:	
Message:	**SUB CFIDS-L firstname lastname**
E-mail:	CFIDS-L-REQUEST@american.edu

alt.med.cfs, CFS-L

The moderated alt.med.cfs newsgroup, which is mirrored on the CFS-L mailing list, is aimed at people with chronic fatigue syndrome. Some of the topics discussed include medical treatments, disability benefits, and coping.

Vital Stats:

Access methods:	Usenet newsgroup, E-mail
To access (Usenet):	news:alt.med.cfs
To access (mailing list):	Send an e-mail message to listserv@maelstrom.stjohns.edu
Subject line:	
Message:	**SUB CFS-L firstname lastname**
E-mail:	CFS-L-REQUEST@maelstrom.stjohns.edu

alt.med.cfs.open, CFS-OPEN

The unmoderated newsgroup alt.med.cfs.open, which is mirrored in the mailing list CFS-OPEN, offers a wide ranging discussion of chronic fatigue syndrome.

Vital Stats:

Access methods:	Usenet newsgroup, E-mail
To access (Usenet):	news:alt.med.cfs.open
To access (mailing list):	Send an e-mail message to listserv@maelstrom.stjohns.edu
Subject line:	
Message:	**SUB CFS-OPEN *firstname lastname***
E-mail:	CFS-OPEN-REQUEST@maelstrom.stjohns.edu

The CFIDS Association of America

The CFIDS Association of America site has a smattering of information about chronic fatigue and immune dysfunction syndrome (CFIDS), also known as chronic fatigue syndrome, myalgic encephalomyelitis, and other names. The association is a nonprofit organization.

The site has answers to frequently asked questions about CFIDS, news about congressional bills dealing with CFIDS, information about how to file a CFIDS disability claim with the Social Security Administration, numerous articles and other information about pediatric CFIDS, selected articles from the association's quarterly publication titled *The CFIDS Chronicle,* links to other Web sites about CFIDS, and a huge list of books, articles, tapes, and other materials that can be ordered from the association.

Vital Stats:

Access method:	WWW
To access:	http://www.cfids.org
E-mail:	info@cfids.org

CFS-NEWS

This mailing list distributes the CFS-NEWS Electronic Newsletter between one and four times monthly. The newsletter contains articles about research, medical conferences, publications, and other medical issues involving chronic fatigue syndrome.

Vital Stats:

Access method: E-mail
To access: Send an e-mail message to listserv@maelstrom.stjohns.edu
Subject line:
Message: **SUB CFS-NEWS *firstname lastname***
E-mail: CFS-NEWS-REQUEST@maelstrom.stjohns.edu

CFS-Y

This mailing list is aimed at people age twenty-five and under who have chronic fatigue syndrome.

Vital Stats:

Access method: E-mail
To access: Send an e-mail message to listserv@maelstrom.stjohns.edu
Subject line:
Message: **SUB CFS-Y *firstname lastname***
E-mail: CFS-Y-REQUEST@maelstrom.stjohns.edu

Chronic Fatigue Syndrome/Myalgic Encephalomyelitis

This site is a great source for information about chronic fatigue syndrome, which is also known as myalgic encephalomyelitis. It's operated by a person with CFS.

The site has answers to frequently asked questions, newsletters, articles about CFS from various governmental and medical resources, information about CFS mailing lists and Usenet newsgroups, links to CFS-related Web sites around the world, and lots more. It also offers limited information about fibromyalgia, Lyme disease, Gulf War syndrome, and multiple chemical sensitivity.

Vital Stats:

Access method: WWW
To access: http://www.cais.com/cfs-news
E-mail: cfs-news-request@maelstrom.stjohns.edu

CO-CURE

Members of the CO-CURE mailing list discuss efforts toward finding a cure for chronic fatigue syndrome and the related fibromyalgia.

Vital Stats:

Access method:	E-mail
To access:	Send an e-mail message to listserv@listserv.nodak.edu
Subject line:	
Message:	**subscribe CO-CURE *firstname lastname***
E-mail:	CO-CURE-request@listserv.nodak.edu

CHRONIC PAIN

alt.support.chronic-pain

This newsgroup provides support for people who suffer from chronic pain.

Vital Stats:

Access method: Usenet newsgroup
To access: news:alt.support.chronic-pain

American Academy of Pain Management

The American Academy of Pain Management site offers a patient's bill of rights and a database showing results from various pain management treatments. It also has a database of pain management programs nationwide, a directory of academy members, and links to related sites. The academy is a professional association.

Vital Stats:

Access method: WWW
To access: http://www.aapainmanage.org
E-mail: aapm@aapainmanage.org

PAIN-L

The mailing list PAIN-L is an educational forum where members exchange information about chronic physical pain. It is not a chat line. The list is aimed at doctors, other health care professionals, patients, and others interested in chronic pain.

Vital Stats:

Access method:	E-mail
To access:	Send an e-mail message to listserv@maelstrom.stjohns.edu
Subject line:	
Message:	**subscribe PAIN-L *firstname lastname***
E-mail:	PAIN-L-owner@maelstrom.stjohns.edu

DIABETES

adults_cwd

Adults who have diabetes exchange messages on this mailing list. It's operated by the children with DIABETES Web site (p. 127).

Vital Stats:

Access method:	E-mail
To access:	Send an e-mail message to adults.request@childrenwithdiabetes.com
Subject line:	
Message:	**subscribe *e-mail address***
E-mail:	adults.request@childrenwithdiabetes.com

alt.support.diabetes

Discussions in this newsgroup focus on various aspects of diabetes.

Vital Stats:

Access method:	Usenet newsgroup
To access:	news:alt.support.diabetes

alt.support.diabetes.kids

Children with diabetes and their loved ones exchange information and support in this newsgroup.

Vital Stats:

Access method: Usenet newsgroup
To access: news:alt.support.diabetes.kids

American Diabetes Association

The American Diabetes Association site has numerous articles about various types of diabetes, understanding lab tests, medical treatment of diabetes, nutrition and fitness, living with diabetes, and related topics.

It also offers a very basic diabetes risk test, the full text of the journal *Diabetes,* selected articles from the magazine *Diabetes Forecast,* daily recipes for diabetics, a buyer's guide to diabetes supplies, and details about the rights of diabetics.

The site also has information about diabetes research, legislative information, ordering details for dozens of books available from the association, the association's annual report, and links to lots of other Internet sites about diabetes.

Vital Stats:

Access method: WWW
To access: http://www.diabetes.org/default.htm

CDC Diabetes Home Page

This site has publications about diabetes for patients, physicians, and public health researchers. It's operated by the Centers for Disease Control and Prevention.

Some of the highlights include a brochure titled *Diabetes At-A-Glance,* a lengthy patient guide titled *Take Charge of Your Diabetes,* a report for physicians titled *The Prevention and Treatment of Complications of Diabetes Mellitus: A Guide for Primary Care Practitioners,* diabetes prevalence and mortality data for each state, and information about diabetes control programs in each state.

Vital Stats:

Access method:	WWW
To access:	http://www.cdc.gov/nccdphp/ddt/ddthome.htm
E-mail:	cdcinfo@cdc.gov

children with DIABETES

This fantastic site is aimed at children with diabetes and their parents, but anyone affected by diabetes will find it valuable. It's operated by the father of a child with diabetes.

The site has basic information about subjects like insulin and hypoglycemia, details about how to care for diabetes while in school, reviews of products for children with diabetes, dozens of recipes, a dictionary containing definitions of hundreds of diabetes-related terms, information about camps for children with diabetes, news about research and legislative issues, links to regional sources for diabetes information, and much more.

One of the site's most useful features allows you to post questions, which are answered online by a panel of experts. Another great feature is a database of thousands of children and teens with diabetes, parents, adults with diabetes, and others who are willing to exchange mail or e-mail about diabetes. And don't miss the chat rooms, which are among the site's most visited pages. There are separate chat rooms for parents, kids, teens, adults, and adults with Type 2 diabetes.

Vital Stats:

Access method:	WWW
To access:	http://www.castleweb.com/diabetes
E-mail:	diabetes@castleweb.com

Diabetes in America

This site provides the full text of *Diabetes in America,* a 733-page book published by the National Institute of Diabetes and Digestive and Kidney Diseases.

The book's thirty-six chapters cover such subjects as diagnostic criteria and screening for diabetes, the prevalence and incidence of various types of diabetes, physical and metabolic characteristics of persons with diabetes, risk factors, complications of diabetes, therapy for diabetes, health insurance and diabetes, pregnancy in preexisting diabetes, and diabetes in special populations.

Each chapter of the book is provided in a separate PDF (Portable Document Format) file. You must have the Adobe Acrobat Reader software to view them, and this site links to an Adobe site where you can download the software for free.

Vital Stats:

Access method:	WWW
To access:	http://diabetes-in-america.s-3.com

Diabetes Information Center

The Diabetes Information Center has a nice collection of information about diabetes, most of it provided by links to other sites. It offers background information about diabetes, articles from a few medical publications, information about drugs used in treating diabetes, research news from medical meetings, and links to Usenet newsgroups, mailing lists, and Web sites about diabetes. The center is part of PharmInfoNet (p. 237).

Vital Stats:

Access method:	WWW
To access:	http://pharminfo.com/disease/diabetes/diab_info.html
E-mail:	johnmack@virsci.com

Diabetes Mall

The Diabetes Mall has a small collection of articles about diabetes, along with a good selection of links to Internet sites related to diabetes. It also has an online catalog of books, software, scales, and other products for people with diabetes.

Vital Stats:

Access method:	WWW
To access:	http://www.diabetesnet.com
E-mail:	jwalsh@diabetesnet.com

Diabetes Monitor

This superb site is a must-see for anyone affected by diabetes. It's operated by the Midwest Diabetes Care Center Inc.

One of the site's highlights is the Diabetes Registry. It's a collection of links—but with a great twist. Instead of linking to sites, the registry links to specific documents about diabetes throughout the Internet. The links are arranged by subject, making it easy to zero in quickly on specific information instead of rummaging through site after site.

Another highlight is an excellent collection of articles. They cover such topics as using an insulin pump, diabetes quackery, new diabetes medications, sugarfree sweets, exercise, the cost of diabetes, diabetes advocacy, classification and diagnostic criteria for diabetes, symptoms of diabetes, family planning for young women with diabetes, and many others.

The site also has information regarding journals and magazines about diabetes, links to sites that provide news about diabetes, contact information for medical boards in each state, a list of diabetes support groups in western Missouri and eastern Kansas, and much more.

Vital Stats:

Access method:	WWW
To access:	http://www.diabetesmonitor.com
E-mail:	monitor@diabetesmonitor.com

---

diabetic

Members of the diabetic mailing list exchange information about all aspects of living with diabetes.

Vital Stats:

Access method:	E-mail
To access:	Send an e-mail message to listserv@lehigh.edu
Subject line:	
Message:	**subscribe diabetic *firstname lastname***

Doctor's Guide to Diabetes Information & Resources

This site has dozens of news stories about diabetes, a good collection of links to other diabetes-related documents and sites, and information about relevant Usenet newsgroups. It's part of the Doctor's Guide to the Internet (p. 14), which is sponsored by P/S/L NuMedia.

Vital Stats:

Access method: WWW
To access: http://www.pslgroup.com/DIABETES.HTM
E-mail: webmaster@pslgroup.com

The Internet Sleuth—Diabetes

This database lets you search a half-dozen Internet sites about diabetes using a single interface. You must search each site separately. The database is part of The Internet Sleuth search engine.

Vital Stats:

Access method: WWW
To access: http://www.isleuth.com/dise-di.html
E-mail: sleuth@isleuth.com

Juvenile Diabetes Foundation International

This site has testimony by Juvenile Diabetes Foundation officials before Congress, legislative alerts, information about publications that can be ordered from the foundation, contact information for chapters around the world, and links to other diabetes sites on the Internet.

Vital Stats:

Access method: WWW
To access: http://www.jdfcure.org
E-mail: info@jdfcure.org

kids_cwd

This mailing list is aimed at children with diabetes. It's operated by the children with DIABETES Web site (p. 127).

Vital Stats:

Access method:	E-mail
To access:	Send an e-mail message to kids.request@childrenwithdia-betes.com
Subject line:	
Message:	**subscribe *e-mail address***
E-mail:	kids.request@childrenwithdiabetes.com

---

misc.health.diabetes

This very active newsgroup, which averages more than fifty messages daily, covers all aspects of diabetes.

Vital Stats:

Access method:	Usenet newsgroup
To access:	news:misc.health.diabetes

National Diabetes Information Clearinghouse

The clearinghouse provides the Diabetes Database, which has titles, abstracts, and availability information for diabetes publications and health education materials. It's operated for the National Institute of Diabetes and Digestive and Kidney Diseases, which also operates the NIDDK WWW Server (p. 135).

Vital Stats:

Access method:	WWW
To access:	http://www.aerie.com/nihdb/ndic/dmdbase.html
E-mail:	ndic@aerie.com

On-line Diabetes Resources

This site attempts to catalog every Internet or online resource pertaining to diabetes, making it a great place to start a search for diabetes information. And even better, each listing is carefully annotated. It's operated by a medical writer.

The site has links to more than 200 Web sites, mailing lists, Usenet newsgroups, Internet Relay Chat channels, commercial online services, and bulletin board systems that provide diabetes information. All in all, it's quite a tribute to what a dedicated individual can achieve with the Internet.

Vital Stats:

Access method:	WWW
To access:	http://www.mendosa.com/faq.htm
E-mail:	mendosa@mendosa.com

---

teens_cwd

This mailing list is aimed at teenagers who have diabetes. It's operated by the children with DIABETES Web site (p. 127).

Vital Stats:

Access method:	E-mail
To access:	Send an e-mail message to teens.request@childrenwithdia-betes.com
Subject line:	
Message:	**subscribe *e-mail address***
E-mail:	teens.request@childrenwithdiabetes.com

DIGESTIVE DISEASES

alt.support.crohns-colitis

Discussions in this newsgroup focus on problems with the digestive system, especially Crohn's disease and colitis.

Vital Stats:

Access method: Usenet newsgroup
To access: news:alt.support.crohns-colitis

alt.support.ostomy

Various aspects of living with ostomies are discussed in this newsgroup.

Vital Stats:

Access method: Usenet newsgroup
To access: news:alt.support.ostomy

Doctor's Guide to Gastric Disorders Information & Resources

This site has dozens of news stories about gastric problems, a small collection of links to other gastric-related documents and sites, and information about relevant Usenet newsgroups. It's part of the Doctor's Guide to the Internet (p. 14), which is sponsored by P/S/L NuMedia.

Vital Stats:

Access method:	WWW
To access:	http://www.pslgroup.com/ULCERS.HTM
E-mail:	webmaster@pslgroup.com

GERD Information Resource Center

This site has basic information about gastroesophageal reflux disease (GERD). Among the site's highlights are a multimedia primer about GERD and answers to numerous frequently asked questions about the disease. It's operated by Astra Merck, a pharmaceutical company.

Vital Stats:

Access method:	WWW
To access:	http://www.gerd.com
E-mail:	information.center@astramerck.com

National Digestive Diseases Information Clearinghouse

This site provides the Digestive Diseases Database, which has titles, abstracts, and availability information for digestive disease publications and health education materials. It's operated for the National Institute of Diabetes and Digestive and Kidney Diseases, which also operates the NIDDK WWW Server (below).

Vital Stats:

Access method:	WWW
To access:	http://www.aerie.com/nihdb/nddic/dddbase.html
E-mail:	nddic@aerie.com

NIDDK WWW Server

The NIDDK WWW Server is operated by the National Institute of Diabetes and Digestive and Kidney Diseases (NIDDK), which is part of the National Institutes of Health.

The site has dozens of publications about diabetes, digestive diseases, endocrine disorders, hematologic disorders, kidney disorders, nutrition, obesity, and urologic disorders. It also has information about services available from the National Digestive Diseases Information Clearinghouse.

Vital Stats:

Access method:	WWW
To access:	http://www.niddk.nih.gov
E-mail:	kranzfeldk@hq.niddk.nih.gov

United Ostomy Association

This site provides information for people with intestinal or urinary diversions. It's operated by the United Ostomy Association, a patient organization.

The site offers answers to frequently asked questions following ostomy surgery, definitions of key terms, information about insurance and Medicare, ordering information for brochures and care manuals published by the UOA, links to Web sites operated by UOA chapters around the country, advice about finding ostomy equipment and suppliers, phone numbers for distributors of ostomy equipment, and an excellent collection of links to related health sites.

Vital Stats:

Access method: WWW
To access: http://www.uoa.org
E-mail: stuart@gulf.net

DISABILITIES AND REHABILITATION

ABLEDATA

ABLEDATA offers a database containing detailed information about more than 23,000 products designed for people with disabilities, ranging from white canes to voice output programs. The database contains descriptions of each product, along with price and company information. ABLEDATA is funded by the National Institute of Disability and Rehabilitation Research, which is part of the Education Department.

The site also has links to hundreds of Web sites with disabilities-related information, fact sheets about assistive technology devices ranging from wheelchairs to winter sports equipment, and consumer guides about wheelchair selection, office equipment for people with visual disabilities, accessible housing, and assistive technology for people with spinal cord injuries.

Vital Stats:

Access method:	WWW
To access:	http://www.abledata.com
E-mail:	KABELKNAP@aol.com

alt.support.attn-deficit

The alt.support.attn-deficit newsgroup, which frequently averages seventy-five messages each day, is aimed at people with attention deficit disorder and their loved ones.

Vital Stats:

Access method: Usenet newsgroup

To access: news:alt.support.attn-deficit

alt.support.disabled.caregivers

Caregivers of people with disabilities exchange information and support in this newsgroup.

Vital Stats:

Access method: Usenet newsgroup

To access: news:alt.support.disabled.caregivers

alt.support.disabled.sexuality

This newsgroup focuses on sexual issues involving people with disabilities.

Vital Stats:

Access method: Usenet newsgroup

To access: news:alt.support.disabled.sexuality

alt.support.learning-disab

People with learning disabilities and their loved ones are the primary audience for this newsgroup.

Vital Stats:

Access method: Usenet newsgroup

To access: news:alt.support.learning-disab

American Foundation for the Blind

This site has a wide range of useful information for the blind and visually impaired, much of it dealing with public policy. For example, it has reports about adding audio and video descriptions to television programs, articles about the blind and the Americans with Disabilities Act, recommendations for employers on how to accommodate an applicant or employee who is blind is visually impaired, congressional testimony, and information about legislative developments.

It also has fact sheets and reports about Braille, articles about assistive technology devices, bibliographies on various issues related to blindness and visual impairments, a guide for parents to obtaining education services for a blind or visually impaired child, press releases, newsletters, a catalog of books and videos published by the AFB Press, and dozens of photographs of Helen Keller, whose papers are deposited with the AFB.

Vital Stats:

Access method:	WWW
To access:	http://www.afb.org
E-mail:	afbinfo@afb.org

DIS-SPRT

This mailing list is an online support group for families that are coping with disabilities.

Vital Stats:

Access method:	E-mail
To access:	Send an e-mail message to listserv@maelstrom.stjohns.edu
Subject line:	
Message:	**subscribe DIS-SPRT _firstname lastname_**
E-mail:	DIS-SPRT-request@maelstrom.stjohns.edu

DISABLED

Members of the DISABLED mailing list discuss the social aspects of disabilities, with a special focus on the emotional aspects of living with disabilities. Some of the topics discussed include therapeutic work, self-help, social empowerment, and challenging assumptions about what makes a person "normal" or "different."

Vital Stats:

Access method:	E-mail
To access:	Send an e-mail message to listserv@maelstrom.stjohns.edu
Subject line:	
Message:	**subscribe DISABLED *firstname lastname***
E-mail:	DISABLED-request@maelstrom.stjohns.edu

Family Village

Family Village bills itself as "a global community of disability-related resources," which is an accurate description. It provides little original information, but has an amazing collection of disability-related links neatly organized by disease or subject. The site is operated by the Waisman Center at the University of Wisconsin-Madison.

One of the site's many highlights is its collection of separate pages for hundreds of disabilities—everything from Aarskog Syndrome to X-Linked Myotubular Myopathy. Each page has links to patient associations, chat areas, documents, and Web sites related to a particular disability.

Another nice feature is a set of message boards where parents of a child with a disability or an adult with a disability can find others in similar circumstances with whom to correspond.

Finally, don't miss the subject pages. They provide links to a huge array of Internet sites about:

- Assistive technology and adaptive products—everything from adaptive toys to adaptive clothing to scooters to wheelchairs.

- Education of children with disabilities.

- Recreation and leisure for people with disabilities.

- Advocacy and public policy.

- Caregiver resources.

- Employment of people with disabilities.

- Independent living.

- Worship resources for people with disabilities and their families.
- Adoptive families, Native Americans, single parents, grandparents, foster parents, African Americans, fathers, and military fathers.
- Disability related books and videos.
- Disability research programs.

Vital Stats:

Access method:	WWW
To access:	http://www.familyvillage.wisc.edu
E-mail:	rowley@waisman.wisc.edu

Internet Resources for Special Children

This site provides no original information, but has hundreds of links to useful sites about children and disabilities. It's operated by the parent of a child with cerebral palsy, epilepsy, and moderate retardation.

The links are arranged by subject. Some of the topics covered include adaptive clothing, amputees, arthritis, brain injury, deafness and hearing impairment, employment resources, fetal alcohol syndrome, learning disabilities, mental retardation, paralysis and spinal cord injury, parenting and support resources, recreation and sports, and special education, among many others.

Vital Stats:

Access method:	WWW
To access:	http://www.irsc.org
E-mail:	julio_c@one.net

JAN on the Web

Extensive information about the Americans with Disabilities Act (ADA) is available from JAN on the Web, which is operated by the Job Accommodation Network (JAN). The site, which is a service of the President's Committee on Employment of People with Disabilities, has the text of the ADA, regulations, technical assistance manuals, information about how to file ADA complaints, publications about how to work with employees who have various disabilities, information about reasonable accommodation under the ADA, links to other Internet sites that offer disability and health information, and much more.

Vital Stats:

Access method:	WWW
To access:	http://janweb.icdi.wvu.edu
E-mail:	jan@jan.icdi.wvu.edu

---

misc.handicap

Discussions in this newsgroup are aimed at people with disabilities.

Vital Stats:

Access method:	Usenet newsgroup
To access:	news:misc.handicap

MOBILITY

Subscribers to the MOBILITY mailing list discuss mobility disabilities.

Vital Stats:

Access method:	E-mail
To access:	Send an e-mail message to listserv@maelstrom.stjohns.edu
Subject line:	
Message:	**subscribe MOBILITY *firstname lastname***
E-mail:	MOBILITY-request@maelstrom.stjohns.edu

National Council on Disability

This site has more than twenty reports published by the National Council on Disability, an independent federal agency that makes recommendations to the president and Congress about disability issues.

Some sample titles include *Access to the Information Superhighway and Emerging Information Technologies by People with Disabilities, ADA Watch: A Report to the President and the Congress on Progress in Implementing the Americans with Disabilities Act, Achieving Independence: The Challenge for the 21st Century, Inclusionary Education for Students with Disabilities: Keeping the Promise, Meeting the Unique Needs of Minorities with Disabilities,* and *Wilderness Accessibility for People with Disabilities.*

Vital Stats:

Access method:	WWW
To access:	http://www.ncd.gov
E-mail:	mquigley@ncd.gov

National Rehabilitation Information Center

This site offers extensive information about disabilities and rehabilitation, including details about how to design accessible Web pages, a calendar of events, annotated links to hundreds of Internet sites related to disabilities and rehabilitation, *The Americans with Disabilities Act (ADA): A NARIC Resource Guide,* and a database that contains summaries of 14,000 disabilities-related textbooks, journal articles, resource guides, videos, and technical reports.

The National Rehabilitation Information Center is funded by the National Institute on Disability and Rehabilitation Research (NIDRR), which is part of the U.S. Education Department.

Vital Stats:

Access method:	WWW
To access:	http://www.naric.com/naric
E-mail:	wendling@macroint.com

Project Enable

Project Enable has more than 5,000 files about disabilities and rehabilitation, searchable databases, and more than 100 conferences. Project Enable is operated by the West Virginia University Rehabilitation Research and Training Center, with funding from the U.S. Department of Education.

Here are some highlights of what's available:

- Thousands of files about all types of disabilities, education for people with disabilities, legal issues related to disabilities, regulations under the Family and Medical Leave Act, the Americans with Disabilities Act, Internet mailing lists about disabilities, online disability information, and much more.

- Databases, most of which allow you to search large documents using keywords. For example, you can search the Americans with Disabilities Act, the Rehabilitation Act of 1973 and related regulations, and the Randolph Sheppard Act and related regulations. Another database allows you to check your eligibility for food stamps, Aid to Families with Dependent Children, Medicaid, and other federal programs.

- More than 100 conferences where people exchange messages about disabilities, rehabilitation, employment, and education. Many are "echoes" from international networks such as FidoNet and QuickLink. There are conferences about sports for people with disabilities, artists with disabilities, occupational disabilities, disability rights, Alzheimer's disease, arthritis, blindness and other visual impairments, cancer, chronic fatigue syndrome, diabetes, environmental illness, nutrition, rare conditions and diseases, stress management, and coping with terminally ill relatives, among many other subjects.

Vital Stats:

Access methods:	WWW, Telnet, FTP, dial-in
To access:	http://www.icdi.wvu.edu/enable.htm *or*
	telnet://enable.wvnet.edu *or* ftp://ftp.icdi.wvu.edu
Login (FTP only):	**anonymous**
Password (FTP only):	your e-mail address
E-mail:	enable@rtc2.icdi.wvu.edu
Dial-in access:	304-766-2690

Special Olympics International

This site provides background information about Special Olympics, an international sports training and competition program for people with mental retardation. It has information about upcoming events, details about volunteer and coaching opportunities, links to Web sites operated by Special Olympics chapters around the United States, and contact information for Special Olympics programs around the world.

Vital Stats:

Access method:	WWW
To access:	http://specialolympics.org
E-mail:	mikejanes@juno.com

Trace Research & Development Center

The Trace Research & Development Center site has extensive information about disabilities and creating an accessible world for people with disabilities. The center, which is located at the University of Wisconsin-Madison, is supported by the National Institute on Disability and Rehabilitation Research of the U.S. Department of Education.

The site has an especially strong collection of information about computer access for people with disabilities, including guidelines for designing accessible Web sites, information about major ongoing programs addressing Web access issues, information about accessibility software and hardware, a calendar of events, and much more.

The site also has databases containing descriptions of thousands of assistive technology products, toys and computers for kids with disabilities, assistive technology funding resources, articles and publications about disabilities and rehabilitation, and rehabilitation training materials. In addition, it offers numerous documents about creating access for people with disabilities, the American with Disabilities Act and other laws, financing assistive technology, and telecommunications access.

Vital Stats:

Access methods:	WWW, Gopher
To access:	http://trace.waisman.wisc.edu *or*
	gopher://trace.waisman.wisc.edu
E-mail:	info@trace.wisc.edu

EAR, NOSE, AND THROAT CONDITIONS

alt.support.hearing-loss

Various aspects of hearing loss are discussed in the newsgroup alt.support.hearing-loss.

Vital Stats:

Access method: Usenet newsgroup
To access: news:alt.support.hearing-loss

alt.support.sinusitis

Various types of sinus problems are discussed in this newsgroup.

Vital Stats:

Access method: Usenet newsgroup
To access: news:alt.support.sinusitis

alt.support.tinnitus

People who have tinnitus (ringing in the ears) are the primary audience for this newsgroup.

Access method: Usenet newsgroup
To access: news:alt.support.tinnitus

American Speech-Language-Hearing Association

This site offers brochures about recognizing communication disorders, communication disorders and aging, how to buy a hearing aid, voice problems, stuttering, tinnitus, assistive listening devices, noise and hearing loss, and related issues. It also has contact information for patient organizations related to speech and language disabilities and hearing loss.

Vital Stats:

Access method: WWW
To access: http://www.asha.org
E-mail: webmaster@asha.org

beyond-hearing

The beyond-hearing mailing list is aimed at people with a hearing loss who seek to overcome the barriers that the loss creates.

Vital Stats:

Access method: E-mail
To access: Send an e-mail message to majordomo@acpub.duke.edu
Subject line:
Message: **subscribe beyond-hearing**
E-mail: beyond-hearing-owner@acpub.duke.edu

Ear, Nose, and Throat Information Center

This site offers dozens of brochures about various sinus, hearing, throat, and neck problems. It's operated by a doctor, although most of the brochures were originally produced by the American Academy of Otolaryngology-Head and Neck Surgery.

Some of the subjects covered include the common cold, tonsils and adenoids, ears and airplane travel, snoring, smell and taste disorders, postnasal drip, cochlear implants, dizziness and motion sickness, sore throats, reflux, warning signs for head and neck cancer, noise pollution, facial nerve problems, facial sports injuries, and fever blisters and canker sores, among many others.

Vital Stats:

Access method: WWW
To access: http://www.netdoor.com/com/entinfo

National Institute on Deafness and Other Communication Disorders Information Clearinghouse

This site provides the Deafness and Communication Disorders Database, which has titles, abstracts, and availability information for publications and health education materials. The institute is part of the National Institutes of Health.

Vital Stats:

Access method: WWW
To access: http://www.aerie.com/nihdb/nidcd/dctest.html
E-mail: nidcd@aerie.com

EYE CARE

alt.support.glaucoma

People with glaucoma are the primary audience for the newsgroup alt.support.glaucoma.

Vital Stats:

Access method: Usenet newsgroup
To access: news:alt.support.glaucoma

American Society of Cataract & Refractive Surgery

This site has patient guides to cataract surgery and refractive surgery, along with video clips of both procedures. It also offers a glossary of eye care terms and links to dozens of Internet sites about eye care and other health issues. The site is operated by the American Society of Cataract & Refractive Surgery.

Vital Stats:

Access method: WWW
To access: http://www.ascrs.org
E-mail: ascrs@ascrs.org

EyeNet

EyeNet provides articles about eye safety for children, computers and eye strain, preventing eye injuries in sports, cataracts, glaucoma, macular degeneration, learning disabilities and vision, refractive errors, and related subjects. It's operated by the American Academy of Ophthalmology.

It also has contact information for support groups and consumer organizations, a database containing contact information for ophthalmologists around the country, and links to dozens of mailing lists and Internet sites devoted to eye care.

Vital Stats:

Access method:	WWW
To access:	http://www.eyenet.org
E-mail:	webmaster@aao.org

Glaucoma Research Foundation

This site has a booklet titled *Understanding & Living with Glaucoma,* news about recent research, and fact sheets about cataracts and glaucoma, microsurgery, and laser surgery. The site also has a quarterly newsletter, information about the Glaucoma Support Network, and details about current foundation research grants. It's operated by the Glaucoma Research Foundation, a nonprofit organization.

Vital Stats:

Access method:	WWW
To access:	http://www.glaucoma.org
E-mail:	info@glaucoma.org

National Eye Institute

The National Eye Institute site has brochures about age-related macular degeneration, cataracts, glaucoma, and diabetic eye disease, among other subjects. The institute is part of the National Institutes of Health.

The site also has information about clinical trials that are currently recruiting patients, research being conducted or supported by the National Eye Institute, grants and contracts, and visiting the institute.

In addition, it offers a directory of more than thirty national eye health-related organizations, a list of resources for people with visual impairments, information about financial assistance for eye care available through national organizations, tips for finding an eye care professional, an eye diagram, a glossary of eye-related terms, and lesson plans for fourth through eighth grades.

Vital Stats:

Access method:	WWW
To access:	http://www.nei.nih.gov
E-mail:	2020@b31.nei.nih.gov

Prevent Blindness America

This site provides answers to frequently asked questions about age-related macular degeneration, cataracts, computers and your eyes, diabetic retinopathy, and glaucoma. It's operated by Prevent Blindness America, a nonprofit organization.

Other highlights include an article titled *Living with Low Vision? 10 Steps to Ensure Your Independence,* articles about eye problems in children, eye safety tips, eye tests for children and adults, selected articles from *Prevent Blindness News,* a calendar of eye health and safety observances, and a catalog of publications and videos that can be ordered from Prevent Blindness America.

Vital Stats:

Access method:	WWW
To access:	http://www.prevent-blindness.org
E-mail:	info@preventblindness.org

---

sci.med.vision

Various aspects of caring for eyes are discussed in this newsgroup.

Vital Stats:

Access method:	Usenet newsgroup
To access:	news:sci.med.vision

GULF WAR SYNDROME

The Missing GulfLINK Files

This site has several hundred U.S. Defense Department documents about the possible release of Iraqi chemical and biological weapons during the 1991 Persian Gulf War. It's operated by Insignia Publishing Company, a private firm.

The documents are part of a larger group that the Defense Department originally posted on its GulfLINK Internet page in July 1995. After the CIA complained that some of the documents were released too quickly and provided sensitive information, the Defense Department removed more than 300 of them. After another review, the department reposted nearly 100 of the documents in August 1996.

In November 1996, Insignia posted the full text of the more than 300 original documents on its Web site. You can read the documents individually or download the entire collection at once.

Vital Stats:

Access method:	WWW
To access:	http://www.insigniausa.com/Gulflink.htm
E-mail:	102350.3213@compuserve.com

Presidential Advisory Committee on Gulf War Veterans' Illnesses

The Presidential Advisory Committee on Gulf War Veterans' Illnesses site has the committee's interim and final reports, transcripts of committee hearings, and background information about the committee and its members.

Vital Stats:

Access method:	WWW
To access:	http://www.gwvi.gov
E-mail:	lashofjc@gwvi.gov

HEADACHES

alt.support.headaches.migraine

Participants in the alt.support.headaches.migraine newsgroup exchange information about preventing, treating, and living with migraine headaches. The group is very active, averaging several dozen messages daily.

Vital Stats:

Access method:	Usenet newsgroup
To access:	news:alt.support.headaches.migraine

American Council for Headache Education

This site has descriptions of various types of headaches and background about what causes headaches. It's operated by the American Council for Headache Education, a nonprofit organization.

The site also offers a guide to over-the-counter pain relievers, a list of recommended books, and links to other Internet sites that provide headache information.

Vital Stats:

Access method:	WWW
To access:	http://www.achenet.org
E-mail:	achehq@ache.smarthub.com

Doctor's Guide to Migraine Information & Resources

This site has more than a dozen news stories about migraines, a good collection of links to other migraine-related documents and sites, and information about relevant Usenet newsgroups. It's part of the Doctor's Guide to the Internet (p. 14), which is sponsored by P/S/L NuMedia.

Vital Stats:

Access method:	WWW
To access:	http://www.pslgroup.com/MIGRAINE.HTM
E-mail:	webmaster@pslgroup.com

JAMA Migraine Information Center

This site's highlight is a collection of patient education articles about migraine headaches. Some of the topics covered include the types of headaches, the causes of migraines, managing migraines, treating tension headaches, drugs for migraines, and children and migraines. The site is operated by the *Journal of the American Medical Association (JAMA)*.

The site also has news stories about migraine headaches from Reuters, summaries of presentations at major professional meetings, articles from *JAMA* and other medical journals, contact information for support groups, and clinical treatment guidelines.

Vital Stats:

Access method:	WWW
To access:	http://www.ama-assn.org/special/migraine
E-mail:	migraine@ama-assn.org

National Headache Foundation

This site has articles about dozens of topics, including allergy and headache, cluster headaches, depression and headache, environmental and physical factors, headaches in children, hormones and migraine, stress, tension headaches, visual disturbances, and headache medications, among others. It's operated by the National Headache Foundation, a nonprofit organization.

The site also offers selected articles from the quarterly publication *NHF Head Lines*, information about support groups in various states, and a list of books and videotapes that can be ordered from the foundation.

Vital Stats:

Access method:	WWW
To access:	http://www.headaches.org

HEART AND CARDIOVASCULAR SYSTEM

American College of Cardiology

The highlight of this site is a collection of policy statements on issues such as access to cardiovascular care, clinical trials, preventive cardiology and atherosclerotic disease, same-day surgical admission, smoking as a health hazard, and student loan repayment, among others. It's operated by the American College of Cardiology.

The site also has clinical practice guidelines for the treatment of various cardiovascular diseases, position statements on everything from the use of animals in research to cardiovascular rehabilitation, background information about cardiovascular specialists, news releases, and links to other Web sites that offer information about cardiovascular health care.

Vital Stats:

Access method: WWW
To access: http://www.acc.org

American Heart Association

The American Heart Association site offers a wealth of information about heart disease and stroke. It has everything from a list of the warning signs for heart disease and stroke to dozens of articles about physical activity, diet and nutrition, risk factors for heart disease and stroke, and talking with your doctor.

One of the site's highlights is its collection of dozens of scientific statements about heart-related topics. Some of the topics covered include alcohol and heart disease, aspirin as a therapeutic agent in cardiovascular disease, cardiovascular screening of competitive athletes, nutrition and children, obesity in youth, public screening for blood cholesterol, fiber, dietary guidelines for adults, fish consumption, exercise, and selection and treatment of candidates for heart transplantation.

Other statements discuss obesity and heart disease, preventing heart attack and death in patients with coronary disease, primary prevention of cardiovascular diseases, cardiac rehabilitation programs, cigarette smoking, minimally invasive heart surgery, cardiovascular disease in women, and trans fatty acids, among other subjects.

The site also has the *Heart and Stroke A-Z Guide,* an interactive coronary heart disease risk assessment, responses to new scientific studies, dozens of consumer and professional news articles from Reuters, recipes, information about books and videotapes produced by the association, and lots more.

Vital Stats:

Access method:	WWW
To access:	http://www.amhrt.org
E-mail:	dstokes@amhrt.org

Doctor's Guide to Elevated Cholesterol Information & Resources

This site has dozens of news stories about cholesterol, an excellent collection of links to other cholesterol-related documents and sites, and information about relevant Usenet newsgroups. It's part of the Doctor's Guide to the Internet (p. 14), which is sponsored by P/S/L NuMedia.

Vital Stats:

Access method:	WWW
To access:	http://www.pslgroup.com/ELEVCHOL.HTM
E-mail:	webmaster@pslgroup.com

Doctor's Guide to Stroke Information & Resources

This site has dozens of news stories about strokes, a good collection of links to other stroke-related documents and sites, and information about relevant Usenet newsgroups. It's part of the Doctor's Guide to the Internet (p. 14), which is sponsored by P/S/L NuMedia.

The Heart: An Online Exploration

Just about anything you might want to know about the heart is available here—everything from tips about how to have a healthy heart to a video of heart bypass surgery. Some of the topics covered include heart surgery, various methods for monitoring the heart, blood vessels, the pulmonary system, blood cells, heart disease, and blood pressure, among many others. The site is operated by the Franklin Institute Science Museum in Philadelphia.

Vital Stats:

Access method:	WWW
To access:	http://www.fi.edu/biosci
E-mail:	webteam@www.fi.edu

HeartInfo

If you're looking for information about heart disease, turn on your answering machine, put on a pot of coffee, and prepare to spend awhile with HeartInfo. The site, which was founded by a heart patient and a physician who specializes in heart disease, is a wondrous resource about any and all aspects of heart disease.

It would be faster to list what the site *doesn't* have than what it does have. Among the highlights, it offers hundreds of articles about heart diseases, CPR instructions, news articles, answers to nearly 1,000 questions submitted by users, a listing of 140 lipid clinics in the United States, dozens of stories by heart patients, and reviews and links to 500 sites related to cardiovascular issues.

HeartInfo also has reports about new drugs and procedures, results of recent clinical trials, an extensive nutrition guide, images of blocked coronary arteries, an animation of an angioplasty, and lots, lots more.

Vital Stats:

Access method:	WWW
To access:	http://www.heartinfo.org
E-mail:	webmaster@heartinfo.org

HEARTTALK-L

All aspects of living with heart disease are discussed on the HEARTTALK-L mailing list, which is primarily aimed at people with heart disease and their families and friends.

Vital Stats:

Access method:	E-mail
To access:	Send an e-mail message to listserv@maelstrom.stjohns.edu
Subject line:	
Message:	**subscribe HEARTTALK-L *firstname lastname***
E-mail:	HEARTTALK-L-REQUEST@maelstrom.stjohns.edu

The Internet Sleuth—Cardiology

This database lets you search a half-dozen Internet sites about cardiology using a single interface. You must search each site separately. The database is part of The Internet Sleuth search engine.

Vital Stats:

Access method:	WWW
To access:	http://www.isleuth.com/medi-card.html
E-mail:	sleuth@isleuth.com

The Internet Sleuth—Heart Disease

This database lets you search several Internet sites about heart disease using a single interface. You must search each site separately. The database is part of The Internet Sleuth search engine.

Vital Stats:

Access method:	WWW
To access:	http://www.isleuth.com/dise-hd.html
E-mail:	sleuth@isleuth.com

National Heart, Lung, and Blood Institute

The National Heart, Lung, and Blood Institute (NHLBI) site has publications about high blood pressure, obesity, asthma, smoking, coronary heart disease, sleep apnea, insomnia, sickle cell disease, heart and lung transplants, and hormone replacement therapy and heart disease, among other subjects. Some of the publications are aimed at the public, while others are geared toward health professionals.

The site also has a catalog of NHLBI education materials, a staff directory, details about studies that are seeking patients, press releases, and brief descriptions of NHLBI research laboratories.

Vital Stats:

Access method:	WWW
To access:	http://www.nhlbi.nih.gov/nhlbi/nhlbi.htm
E-mail:	pl29i@nih.gov

---

sci.med.cardiology

Discussions in the sci.med.cardiology newsgroup cover all aspects of cardiology.

Vital Stats:

Access method:	Usenet newsgroup
To access:	news:sci.med.cardiology

STROKE-L

People affected by strokes are the primary audience for the STROKE-L mailing list.

Vital Stats:

Access method:	E-mail
To access:	Send an e-mail message to listserv@lsv.uky.edu
Subject line:	
Message:	**subscribe STROKE-L *firstname lastname***
E-mail:	STROKE-L-request@lsv.uky.edu

INFECTIOUS DISEASES

GENERAL RESOURCES

alt.support.post-polio

People affected by polio are the primary audience for this newsgroup.

Vital Stats:

Access method: Usenet newsgroup
To access: news:alt.support.post-polio

Outbreak

Outbreak provides reports about current outbreaks of infectious diseases around the world. It's a great place to check before you travel overseas. The site is operated by Pragmatica, an Internet software company.

One highlight is a collection of detailed information about specific emerging diseases. Some of the topics covered include chemical and biological agents, dengue, ebola, hantavirus, malaria, plague, smallpox, and yellow fever, among others.

The site also has an overview of emerging diseases, information about historical outbreaks, a glossary of terms, a list of books about emerging infectious diseases, and links to related Web sites.

Vital Stats:

Access method: WWW
To access: http://www.outbreak.org

HEPATITIS

HEPV-L

The HEPV-L mailing list is a support group for people with hepatitis.

Vital Stats:

Access method:	E-mail
To access:	Send an e-mail message to listserv@maelstrom.stjohns.edu
Subject line:	
Message:	**subscribe HEPV-L *firstname lastname***
E-mail:	HEPV-L-request@maelstrom.stjohns.edu

---

sci.med.diseases.hepatitis

Treatment, research, and related issues regarding hepatitis are discussed in this newsgroup.

Vital Stats:

Access method:	Usenet newsgroup
To access:	news:sci.med.diseases.hepatitis

LYME DISEASE

LymeNet

LymeNet has abstracts of more than 4,000 medical and scientific articles about Lyme disease. The site also has news about research results, information about legal issues involving Lyme disease, a message board, listings for support groups, and links to other Internet sites about Lyme disease. It's operated by the Lyme Disease Network, a nonprofit organization.

Vital Stats:

Access method:	WWW
To access:	http://www.lymenet.org
E-mail:	carol_stolow@lymenet.org

LymeNet-L

LymeNet-L is a newsletter that presents information about new treatments, research, and political events related to Lyme disease. It's published about twenty times annually by the Lyme Disease Network, which also operates a Web site (above).

Vital Stats:

Access method:	E-mail
To access:	Send an e-mail message to listserv@lehigh.edu
Subject line:	
Message:	**subscribe LymeNet-L *firstname lastname***
E-mail:	carol_stolow@lymenet.org

sci.med.diseases.lyme

Various aspects of Lyme disease are discussed in this newsgroup. It's very active, averaging several dozen messages daily.

Vital Stats:

Access method:	Usenet newsgroup
To access:	news:sci.med.diseases.lyme

SEXUALLY TRANSMITTED DISEASES

alt.support.herpes

People with herpes are the primary audience for this newsgroup.

Vital Stats:

Access method: Usenet newsgroup
To access: news:alt.support.herpes

JAMA Sexually Transmitted Disease Information Center

Produced by the *Journal of the American Medical Association (JAMA)*, this site's highlight is a collection of fact sheets about various types of sexually transmitted diseases published by the National Institute of Allergy and Infectious Diseases.

The site also has daily news articles about sexually transmitted diseases from Reuters Health Information and the Centers for Disease Control and Prevention, articles from *JAMA* and other medical journals, treatment guidelines, contact information for patient support groups, statistics about sexually transmitted diseases, and links to related Internet sites.

Vital Stats:

Access method: WWW
To access: http://www.ama-assn.org/special/std
E-mail: std@ama-assn.org

KIDNEY DISEASES

AAKP Renal Flash

The AAKP Renal Flash is a monthly electronic newsletter for kidney patients. It's published by the American Association of Kidney Patients, which also operates a Web site (p. 168).

Vital Stats:

Access method: E-mail
To access: Send an e-mail message to aakpflash@aol.com
Subject line: **subscribe**
Message:
E-mail: AAKPnat@aol.com

alt.support.kidney-failure

People suffering from kidney failure are the primary audience for this newsgroup.

Vital Stats:

Access method: Usenet newsgroup
To access: news:alt.support.kidney-failure

American Association of Kidney Patients

This site offers numerous brochures for kidney patients, explanations of treatment options, and a statement of patient rights and responsibilities. It's operated by the American Association of Kidney Patients.

The site also has a list of books for kidney patients, links to online support groups, patient stories, an electronic newsletter, information about regional chapters, and links to lots of related Internet sites.

The association also produces the AAKP Renal Flash electronic newsletter (p. 167).

Vital Stats:

Access method:	WWW
To access:	http://www.aakp.org/aakpteam.html
E-mail:	AAKPnat@aol.com

National Kidney and Urologic Diseases Information Clearinghouse

The clearinghouse provides the Kidney and Urologic Diseases Database, which has titles, abstracts, and availability information for publications and health education materials. It's operated for the National Institute of Diabetes and Digestive and Kidney Diseases, which also operates the NIDDK WWW Server (p. 135).

Vital Stats:

Access method:	WWW
To access:	http://www.aerie.com/nihdb/nkudic/kudbase.html
E-mail:	nkudic@aerie.com

National Kidney Foundation

This site has fact sheets about kidney disease and related illnesses, a monthly electronic newsletter, and information about donating kidneys. It's operated by the National Kidney Foundation.

The site also has information about the foundation's programs, contact information for foundation affiliates around the country, press releases, and links to related sites.

Vital Stats:

Access method: WWW
To access: http://www.kidney.org
E-mail: webmaster@kidney.org

The Nephron Information Center

Although this site offers little original information, it has an excellent collection of links to sites that provide information about dialysis, transplantation, diet, vitamins, health insurance, the Americans with Disabilities Act, and other topics of interest to kidney patients. The Nephron Information Center is operated by a doctor who is the medical director for the Houston Kidney Center Integrated Service Network.

Vital Stats:

Access method: WWW
To access: http://nephron.com
E-mail: fadem@nephron.com

MENTAL HEALTH

ALZHEIMER'S DISEASE

ALZHEIMER

The ALZHEIMER mailing list is aimed at patients, caregivers, researchers, policy makers, students, and anyone else interested in Alzheimer's disease or related disorders in older adults. The list is operated by the Washington University Alzheimer's Disease Research Center and supported by a grant from the National Institute on Aging.

Vital Stats:

Access method:	E-mail
To access:	Send an e-mail message to majordomo@wubios.wustl.edu
Subject line:	
Message:	**subscribe ALZHEIMER**
E-mail (for questions):	ALZHEIMER-owner@wubios.wustl.edu

ALZHEIMER Page

The ALZHEIMER Page has an archive of messages posted to the ALZHEIMER mailing list (above), links to dozens of other Internet sites about aging and dementia, and information about new Internet sites on the subject. It's operated by the Washington University Alzheimer's Disease Research Center and supported by a grant from the National Institute on Aging.

Alzheimer Research Forum

Although the Alzheimer Research Forum is aimed at researchers, it also offers lots of interest to educated consumers. The site is operated by a nonprofit organization.

One of the site's highlights is a collection of information about drugs that are currently in clinical trials for the treatment of Alzheimer's disease. It also has abstracts of recent journal articles about Alzheimer's, abstracts (and in some cases the full text) of "milestone" journal articles about Alzheimer's, a directory of genes that have been studied for their possible role in Alzheimer's, six newsgroups about various aspects of Alzheimer's, links to Web sites operated by Alzheimer's research institutes and laboratories, links to electronic journals, and links to Web sites about Alzheimer's for consumers.

Alzheimers.com

This site has dozens of useful articles about Alzheimer's disease. Some of the topics covered include how to stay mentally sharp for life, the warning signs of early Alzheimer's disease, treatments, risk factors, the biology of Alzheimer's, the stages of Alzheimer's, diagnostic criteria, household modifications, managing behavior problems, caregiver distress, support groups, and other forms of dementia. The site is operated by a doctor and the publisher NetHealth.

Alzheimers.com also provides news stories, a bulletin board, an excellent collection of annotated links to dozens of related sites, contact information for the twenty-eight national Alzheimer Disease Centers at medical schools, and a list of selected books, videos, and organizations.

Alzheimer's Association

This site's highlight is a collection of brochures for caregivers of Alzheimer's patients. Some of the available titles include *Is It Alzheimer's? Warning Signs You Should Know, 10 Ways to Help an Alzheimer Family, Financial and Health Care Benefits You May Need, Caregiving at Home,* and *Caregiver Stress.* The site is operated by the Alzheimer's Association.

The site also has background information about Alzheimer's disease, contact information for association chapters around the country, information about drugs used in treating Alzheimer's, selected articles from the association's newsletter, and information about the Safe Return program for Alzheimer's patients who wander.

Some other highlights include a glossary of terms related to Alzheimer's disease, information about how to get involved in advocacy, details about recent federal government developments related to Alzheimer's, two dozen bibliographies about various aspects of Alzheimer's, and links to related Web sites.

Vital Stats:

Access method:	WWW
To access:	http://www.alz.org
E-mail:	webmaster@alz.org

Alzheimer's Disease Education & Referral Center

This National Institute on Aging site provides extensive information about Alzheimer's disease and related dementias.

The site has background information about Alzheimer's, reports about progress in unraveling the mysteries of Alzheimer's, information about Alzheimer's Disease Centers around the country that are conducting research, press releases about recent research results, a quarterly newsletter from the center, a list of publications that can be ordered from the center, a calendar of events, links to other federal Internet sites that provide information about Alzheimer's, and a link to another federal Internet site that has a database containing references to more than 4,000 books, articles, and other items about Alzheimer's.

Vital Stats:

Access method:	WWW
To access:	http://www.alzheimers.org
E-mail:	adearweb@alzheimers.org

Alzheimer's Disease Review

This site offers the full text of the *Alzheimer's Disease Review*, a peer-reviewed journal that contains articles about research on Alzheimer's disease and related disorders. The journal is published annually by the Sanders-Brown Center on Aging at the University of Kentucky.

The site also tells how to receive future issues by e-mail and offers links to related Web sites.

Vital Stats:

Access method:	WWW
To access:	http://www.coa.uky.edu/ADReview
E-mail:	jwgeddes@aging.coa.uky.edu

American Health Assistance Foundation

The American Health Assistance Foundation offers news updates about Alzheimer's disease, a list of publications about Alzheimer's that can be ordered from the foundation, information about small grants that are available to help pay for the care of Alzheimer's patients, and details about grants available to researchers. The foundation is a nonprofit organization.

Vital Stats:

Access method:	WWW
To access:	http://www.ahaf.org
E-mail:	sbarnard@ahaf.org

Doctor's Guide to Alzheimer's Disease Information & Resources

This site has dozens of news stories about Alzheimer's disease, a good collection of links to other Alzheimer's-related documents and sites, and information about relevant Usenet newsgroups. It's part of the Doctor's Guide to the Internet (p. 14), which is sponsored by P/S/L NuMedia.

Vital Stats:

Access method:	WWW
To access:	http://www.pslgroup.com/ALZHEIMER.HTM
E-mail:	webmaster@pslgroup.com

ANXIETY

alt.recovery.panic-anxiety.self-help

The alt.recovery.panic-anxiety.self-help newsgroup is aimed at people who are trying to help themselves stop suffering panic and anxiety attacks.

Vital Stats:

Access method:	Usenet newsgroup
To access:	news:alt.recovery.panic-anxiety.self-help

alt.support.anxiety-panic

This very active newsgroup, which averages several dozen posts per day, provides support for people who have anxiety and panic disorders.

Vital Stats:

Access method:	Usenet newsgroup
To access:	news:alt.support.anxiety-panic

the Anxiety-Panic internet resource (tAPir)

This site provides basic information about anxiety disorders such as panic attacks, phobias, shyness, generalized anxiety, obsessive-compulsive behavior, and post-traumatic stress. Much of the material is provided by people with anxiety disorders.

　The site also has book reviews, news about medical studies, stories of people with anxiety disorders, a bulletin board, and links to lots of related Web sites.

Vital Stats:

Access method:	WWW
To access:	http://www.algy.com/anxiety
E-mail:	tapir@algy.com

Doctor's Guide to Anxiety Disorders Information & Resources

This site has more than a dozen news stories about anxiety disorders, a good collection of links to other anxiety-related documents and sites, and information about relevant Usenet newsgroups. It's part of the Doctor's Guide to the Internet (p. 14), which is sponsored by P/S/L NuMedia.

Vital Stats:

Access method: WWW
To access: http://www.pslgroup.com/ANXIETY.HTM
E-mail: webmaster@pslgroup.com

National Anxiety Foundation

This site offers basic information about anxiety disorders such as generalized anxiety disorder, phobia, panic disorder, post-traumatic stress disorder, obsessive compulsive disorder, social phobia, and atypical anxiety. The site, which is operated by the National Anxiety Foundation, also has an annotated list of recommended books and a directory of professionals who specialize in treating anxiety disorders.

Vital Stats:

Access method: WWW
To access: http://www.lexington-on-line.com/naf.html

Panic & Anxiety Disorders

This site offers nicely annotated links to dozens of Internet sites that provide information about panic and anxiety disorders. It's operated by a person who has experienced panic disorder.

The links are arranged by topic. Some of the subjects covered include children and teens, medication, obsessive-compulsive disorder, panic disorder, self help, social phobia, specific phobias, stress management, and therapy. The site also has a bulletin board and a chat room.

Vital Stats:

Access method: WWW
To access: http://panicdisorder.miningco.com
E-mail: panicdisorder.guide@miningco.com

CHILDREN

American Academy of Child & Adolescent Psychiatry

The highlight of this site is a series of several dozen brief fact sheets. It's operated by the American Academy of Child & Adolescent Psychiatry.

The fact sheets address such issues as adopted children, bedwetting, child sexual abuse, the child with a long-term illness, children and divorce, children and family moves, children and TV violence, children online, major psychiatric disorders in children, children's sleep problems, depression in children, learning disabilities, adolescent development, psychiatric medication for children, teenagers with eating disorders, and teen suicide, among others. Some of the fact sheets also are available in Spanish and French.

The site also has abstracts of articles published in the *Journal of the American Academy of Child & Adolescent Psychiatry*, press releases, legislative alerts, and links to related Internet sites.

Vital Stats:

Access method:	WWW
To access:	http://www.aacap.org
E-mail:	mrscott@aacap.org

YANX-DEP

Subscribers to the YANX-DEP mailing list discuss child and adolescent anxiety and depression. The list is primarily aimed at mental health professionals and focuses largely on research and clinical practice.

Vital Stats:

Access method:	E-mail
To access:	Send an e-mail message to listserv@maelstrom.stjohns.edu
Subject line:	
Message:	**subscribe yanx-dep *firstname lastname***
E-mail:	YANX-DEP-request@maelstrom.stjohns.edu

DEPRESSION

alt.support.depression

The audience for this newsgroup is people who have clinical depression. It's a very active group, averaging several hundred messages daily.

Vital Stats:

Access method: Usenet newsgroup
To access: news:alt.support.depression

---

alt.support.depression.manic

People with manic depression are the primary audience for this newsgroup.

Vital Stats:

Access method: Usenet newsgroup
To access: news:alt.support.depression.manic

---

alt.support.depression.medication

Discussions in this newsgroup focus on Prozac and other drugs used to treat depression.

Vital Stats:

Access method: Usenet newsgroup
To access: news:alt.support.depression.medication

alt.support.depression.seasonal

The focus of this newsgroup is seasonal affective disorder (SAD).

Vital Stats:

Access method: Usenet newsgroup
To access: news:alt.support.depression.seasonal

---

alt.support.survivors.prozac

People who have had problems taking Prozac and similar drugs used to treat depression exchange information in this newsgroup.

Vital Stats:

Access method: Usenet newsgroup
To access: news:alt.support.survivors.prozac

DEPRESS

Subscribers to the very active DEPRESS mailing list discuss all aspects of depression, including living with the illness, its impact on relationships, and treatment.

Vital Stats:

Access method: E-mail
To access: Send an e-mail message to listserv@soundprint.org
Subject line:
Message: **subscribe DEPRESS *firstname lastname***
E-mail: chris@soundprint.org

Depression Central

Depression Central presents little original information, but has a fantastic set of links to hundreds of sites that provide information about all types of depressive disorders, including major depression, manic depression, and dysthymia. It's operated by a well-known New York psychiatrist.

The links are divided by subjects such as books and videos about depressive disorders, causes of mood disorders, depression in children and adolescents, electroconvulsive therapy, famous people with mood disorders, postpartum depression, psychotherapy, seasonal affective disorder, Social Security disability for people with mood disorders, support groups, suicide and suicide prevention, treatment-resistant mood disorders, Usenet newsgroups devoted to depression, women and depression, and writings by people with mood disorders, among others.

Vital Stats:

Access method:	WWW
To access:	http://www.psycom.net/depression.central.html
E-mail:	Psydoc@PsyCom.Net

Doctor's Guide to Depression Information & Resources

This site has dozens of news stories about depression and a small collection of links to other depression-related documents and sites. It's part of the Doctor's Guide to the Internet (p. 14), which is sponsored by P/S/L NuMedia.

Vital Stats:

Access method:	WWW
To access:	http://www.pslgroup.com/DEPRESSION.HTM
E-mail:	webmaster@pslgroup.com

National Depressive and Manic-Depressive Association

This site features basic information about depression and manic depression. It's operated by the National Depressive and Manic-Depressive Association, a patient organization.

The site also has articles about suicide and depressive illness, rapid cycling in bipolar illness, and treatment failures, among other subjects. And it offers a catalog of books and brochures that can be ordered from the association, a directory of chapters around the country, and links to related sites.

Vital Stats:

Access method:	WWW
To access:	http://www.ndmda.org
E-mail:	myrtis@aol.com

---

soc.support.depression.crisis

People with depression who are experiencing a crisis in their illness can find support in this newsgroup.

Vital Stats:

Access method:	Usenet newsgroup
To access:	news:soc.support.depression.crisis

---

soc.support.depression.family

Family members of people with depression share support in this newsgroup.

Vital Stats:

Access method:	Usenet newsgroup
To access:	news:soc.support.depression.family

---

soc.support.depression.manic

People with manic depression share information and support in this newsgroup.

Vital Stats:

Access method:	Usenet newsgroup
To access:	news:soc.support.depression.manic

soc.support.depression.misc

Various aspects of treating and living with depression are discussed in this newsgroup.

Vital Stats:

Access method: Usenet newsgroup
To access: news:soc.support.depression.misc

---

soc.support.depression.seasonal

People affected by seasonal affective disorder are the primary audience for this newsgroup.

Vital Stats:

Access method: Usenet newsgroup
To access: news:soc.support.depression.seasonal

---

soc.support.depression.treatment

Various aspects of treating depression are discussed in the newsgroup soc.support.depression.treatment.

Vital Stats:

Access method: Usenet newsgroup
To access: news:soc.support.depression.treatment

DIRECTORIES AND SEARCH ENGINES

Dr. Bob's Mental Health Links

This site provides links to several hundred Internet sites devoted to mental health topics. There are links to comprehensive sites, sites about specific subjects, and sites operated by organizations, college and university psychiatry departments, university student counseling centers, and publications, among others.

Vital Stats:

Access method: WWW
To access: http://uhs.bsd.uchicago.edu/~bhsiung/mental.html
E-mail: dr-bob@uchicago.edu

The Internet Sleuth—Mental Health

This database lets you search more than a dozen Internet sites about mental health using a single interface. You must search each site separately. The database is part of The Internet Sleuth search engine.

Vital Stats:

Access method: WWW
To access: http://www.isleuth.com/ment.html
E-mail: sleuth@isleuth.com

Online Dictionary of Mental Health

This great site provides hundreds of nicely annotated links to Internet sites devoted to mental health topics. The links are arranged alphabetically by subject. The site is operated by the Centre for Psychotherapeutic Studies at the University of Sheffield in England and InterPsych.

Another nice feature lets you search more than 100 sites that provide mental health information. You must search each site individually.

Finally, the site provides the European mirror for PsychArticle Search (p. 45).

Vital Stats:

Access method:	WWW
To access:	http://www.shef.ac.uk/~psysc/psychotherapy
E-mail:	Ian.Pitchford@Scientist.com

EATING DISORDERS

alt.recovery.compulsive-eat

Discussions in alt.recovery.compulsive-eat center on attempts to stop eating compulsively.

Vital Stats:

Access method:	Usenet newsgroup
To access:	news:alt.recovery.compulsive-eat

---

alt.support.eating-disord

Participants in this newsgroup discuss anorexia, bulimia, and other eating disorders. It's very active, averaging several dozen messages daily.

Vital Stats:

Access method:	Usenet newsgroup
To access:	news:alt.support.eating-disord

EAT-DIS

Clinical and research aspects of anorexia, bulimia nervosa, obesity, and other eating disorders are discussed on the EAT-DIS mailing list. The primary audience is mental health professionals.

Vital Stats:

Access method:	E-mail
To access:	Send an e-mail message to listserv@maelstrom.stjohns.edu
Subject line:	
Message:	**subscribe eat-dis *firstname lastname***
E-mail:	EATING-DISORDERS-request@maelstrom.stjohns.edu

OASIS

The OASIS mailing list is a support group for people who are recovering from compulsive eating. Many of the subscribers are members of Overeaters Anonymous.

Vital Stats:

Access method:	E-mail
To access:	Send an e-mail message to listserv@maelstrom.stjohns.edu
Subject line:	
Message:	**subscribe OASIS *firstname lastname***
E-mail:	OASIS-request@maelstrom.stjohns.edu

GENERAL RESOURCES

alt.psychology.help

People seeking help with a wide variety of psychological problems participate in the alt.psychology.help newsgroup.

Vital Stats:

Access method: Usenet newsgroup
To access: news:alt.psychology.help

---

alt.society.mental-health

A wide range of mental health issues are discussed in the newsgroup alt.society.mental-health.

Vital Stats:

Access method: Usenet newsgroup
To access: news:alt.society.mental-health

---

alt.support

The newsgroup alt.support has discussions about general support issues.

Vital Stats:

Access method: Usenet newsgroup
To access: news:alt.support

---

alt.support.stuttering

People who stutter can find information and support in this newsgroup.

Vital Stats:

Access method: Usenet newsgroup
To access: news:alt.support.stuttering

American Psychological Association

This site offers about a dozen brochures concerning various psychology topics. It's operated by the American Psychological Association.

Some of the available titles include *Sexual Harassment: Myths and Realities, Questions and Answers About Memories of Childhood Abuse, Raising Children to Resist Violence, Violence on Television, What Makes Kids Care?, Answers to Questions About Sexual Orientation and Homosexuality, What You Should Know About Women and Depression,* and *Ending Discrimination in Health Insurance: Americans Deserve Insurance Parity for Mental Health Disorders.*

Vital Stats:

Access method:	WWW
To access:	http://www.apa.org
E-mail:	public.affairs@apa.org

APA Online

This site offers more than two dozen pamphlets about psychiatric topics. Some of the subjects covered include coping with AIDS and HIV, Alzheimer's disease, anxiety disorders, choosing a psychiatrist, depression, eating disorders, electroconvulsive therapy, the insanity defense, memories of sexual abuse, mental health of the elderly, phobias, psychiatric hospitalization, psychiatric medications, schizophrenia, substance abuse, and teen suicide.

The site, which is operated by the American Psychiatric Association, also has the full text of the twice-monthly newspaper *Psychiatric News,* information about national mental health events and observances, and links to related sites.

Vital Stats:

Access method:	WWW
To access:	http://www.psych.org
E-mail:	webmaster@psych.org

Internet Mental Health

Internet Mental Health is one of the premier Internet sites for mental health information. This wonderful resource was designed by a Canadian psychiatrist.

The site's highlight is a huge collection of detailed information about fifty-two of the most common mental disorders. For each disorder, the site has the American description, European description, treatment information, online diagnostic programs, annotated bibliographies, stories of recovery, booklets from professional organizations and support groups, newspaper and magazine articles, and links to related sites.

Another great section provides extensive information about sixty-seven common psychiatric drugs. For each drug, the site has information about the pharmacology, indications, contraindications, warnings, precautions, adverse effects, overdose, and dosage, among other details.

Vital Stats:

Access method:	WWW
To access:	http://www.mentalhealth.com
E-mail:	editor@mentalhealth.com

Mental Health Infosource

This site offers a large array of information about mental health topics. It's operated by CME Inc., a company that produces conferences and publications about mental health.

The site has background information about numerous disorders, news items, the full text of articles from the *Psychiatric Times* and *Mental Health Economics,* mental health statistics, an "Ask the Expert" feature, links to dozens of mailing lists and Usenet newsgroups, links to Web sites operated by treatment centers, a calendar of mental health association meetings, a calendar of mental health observances, and links to hundreds of mental health Internet sites.

It also offers contact information for mental health associations, psychotropic drug manufacturers, managed care companies, and state medical boards.

Vital Stats:

Access method:	WWW
To access:	http://www.mhsource.com
E-mail:	webmaster@mhsource.com

Mental Health Net

The highlight of Mental Health Net is a collection of information about various mental disorders. The site is operated by CMHC Systems, a company that develops software for mental health organizations.

For each mental disorder, there are articles about symptoms and treatment, followed by annotated links to dozens of Web sites, individual documents, mailing lists, and newsgroups. The site also has excellent links to sites for nonmental medical problems as well, ranging from brain injury to headaches to skin diseases.

The site also provides the full text of the book *Psychological Self-Help,* news articles, a chat area, more than two dozen discussion forums, links to online support resources, contact information for national and international support organizations, and lots more.

Vital Stats:

Access method: WWW
To access: http://cmhc.com
E-mail: Webmaster@CMHC.com

National Institute of Mental Health

Produced by the National Institute of Mental Health (NIMH), this site offers numerous publications about various types of mental illness. Some of the available titles include *Depression: Effective Treatments Are Available, Plain Talk About Depression, Getting Treatment for Panic Disorder, Understanding Panic Disorder, Alzheimer's Disease, Attention Deficit Hyperactivity Disorder, Eating Disorders, Learning Disabilities, Medications—Mental Health/Mental Illness, Obsessive-Compulsive Disorder, Suicide Facts,* and *You Are Not Alone—Mental Health/Mental Illness.*

The site also has a report titled *Mental Illness in America: The NIMH Agenda;* background information about the NIMH, including a list of telephone contacts; information about NIMH studies that are seeking patients; and a huge calendar of medical conferences.

Vital Stats:

Access method: WWW
To access: http://www.nimh.nih.gov
E-mail: nimhinfo@nih.gov

National Mental Health Association

The highlight of this site is two dozen fact sheets about depression, anxiety disorders, panic disorder, obsessive-compulsive disorder, post-traumatic stress disorder, phobias, schizophrenia, seeking help, hospitalization, stigma, stress, coping with loss, electroconvulsive therapy, children's mental health, and suicide, among other topics. It's operated by the National Mental Health Association.

The site also has information about pending legislation affecting mental health, a glossary of health care reform terms, updates on state health care reform efforts, and links to related Web sites.

Vital Stats:

Access method: WWW
To access: http://www.nmha.org
E-mail: nmhainfo@aol.com

National Mental Health Services Knowledge Exchange Network

This site provides information about prevention, treatment, and rehabilitation services for mental illness. It's operated by the National Center for Mental Health Services, which is part of the U.S. Department of Health and Human Services.

The site has fact sheets about mental illnesses in children, a pamphlet about what to look for in managed mental health care, papers about helping victims of natural disasters, a calendar of mental health conferences and events, statistics about mental health, and information about and links to research centers and clearinghouses on mental health issues.

In addition, it offers a database containing information about more than 1,800 organizations and government agencies that provide mental health services, a database containing names and contact information for people interested in mental health issues, and a huge collection of links to other mental health resources on the Internet.

Vital Stats:

Access methods: WWW, dial-in
To access: http://www.mentalhealth.org
E-mail: ken@mentalhealth.org
Dial-in access: 800-790-2647

P-SOURCE

Subscribers to the P-SOURCE mailing list discuss Internet resources related to psychiatry and mental health.

Vital Stats:

Access method:	E-mail
To access:	Send an e-mail message to listserv@maelstrom.stjohns.edu
Subject line:	
Message:	**subscribe P-SOURCE *firstname lastname***
E-mail:	P-SOURCE-request@maelstrom.stjohns.edu

PSY-MEDIA

Subscribers to the PSY-MEDIA mailing list discuss the portrayal of mental health and mental health issues in the media. It's hosted by the American Psychological Association.

Vital Stats:

Access method:	E-mail
To access:	Send an e-mail message to listserv@lists.apa.org
Subject line:	
Message:	**subscribe PSY-MEDIA *firstname lastname***
E-mail:	psy-media-request@listp.apa.org

---

sci.med.psychobiology

The connections between psychiatry and biology are discussed in this newsgroup.

Vital Stats:

Access method:	Usenet newsgroup
To access:	news:sci.med.psychobiology

sci.psychology Newsgroups

Participants in these two newsgroups discuss various issues related to psychology.

Vital Stats:

Access method: Usenet newsgroups
To access: news:sci.psychology, news:sci.psychology.misc

---

sci.psychology.announce

Announcements related to psychology are posted in this moderated newsgroup.

Vital Stats:

Access method: Usenet newsgroup
To access: news:sci.psychology.announce

---

sci.psychology.psychotherapy

This very active newsgroup, which averages fifty messages daily, discusses a wide range of issues related to psychotherapy.

Vital Stats:

Access method: Usenet newsgroup
To access: news:sci.psychology.psychotherapy

The Student Counseling Virtual Pamphlet Collection

This site provides links to dozens of pamphlets produced by student counseling centers at colleges and universities around the country. The site is operated by the University of Chicago Student Counseling and Resource Service.

The pamphlets are divided by subject. Some of the topics covered include alcohol and substance abuse, anxiety, depression, eating disorders, family issues, relationships, sexual assault, sexual orientation, sleep, stress, study skills, time management, and traumatic events. There also is a nice selection of pamphlets for people who are concerned about friends or loved ones.

Vital Stats:

Access method:	WWW
To access:	http://uhs.uchicago.edu/scrs/vpc/vpc.html
E-mail:	dr-bob@uchicago.edu

Substance Abuse and Mental Health Services Administration

The Substance Abuse and Mental Health Services Administration (SAMHSA) site has statistics about substance abuse and mental illness, information about SAMHSA programs, articles and publications about managed behavioral health care, and a calendar of managed care events.

Vital Stats:

Access method:	WWW
To access:	http://www.samhsa.gov
E-mail:	mbowrin@samhsa.gov

OBSESSIVE-COMPULSIVE DISORDER

alt.support.ocd

People with obsessive-compulsive disorder exchange information and support in this newsgroup.

Vital Stats:

Access method: Usenet newsgroup
To access: news:alt.support.ocd

OCD-L

Subscribers to the OCD-L mailing list discuss various aspects of obsessive-compulsive disorder.

Vital Stats:

Access method: E-mail
To access: Send an e-mail message to listserv@vm.marist.edu
Subject line:
Message: **subscribe OCD-L *firstname lastname***
E-mail: OCD-L-request@vm.marist.edu

PERSONALITY DISORDERS

alt.support.personality

People with personality disorders are the primary audience for this newsgroup.

Vital Stats:

Access method:	Usenet newsgroup
To access:	news:alt.support.personality

BORDERPD

The BORDERPD mailing list is a support group for people with borderline personality disorder, their loved ones, and medical professionals.

Vital Stats:

Access method:	E-mail
To access:	Send an e-mail message to listserv@maelstrom.stjohns.edu
Subject line:	
Message:	**subscribe BORDERPD *firstname lastname***
E-mail:	BORDERPD-request@maelstrom.stjohns.edu

SADM

The SADM mailing list is a support group for people with dissociative identity disorder or multiple personality disorder. It particularly focuses on helping survivors of childhood sexual abuse.

Vital Stats:

Access method:	E-mail
To access:	Send an e-mail message to listserv@maelstrom.stjohns.edu
Subject line:	
Message:	**subscribe SADM *firstname lastname***
E-mail:	SADM-request@maelstrom.stjohns.edu

POST-TRAUMATIC STRESS DISORDER

alt.support.trauma-ptsd

People who have survived trauma and who suffer from post-traumatic stress disorder are the primary audience for this newsgroup.

Vital Stats:

Access method: Usenet newsgroup
To access: news:alt.support.trauma-ptsd

TRAUMATIC-STRESS

This mailing list is devoted to discussions of investigating, assessing, and treating immediate and long-term consequences of traumatic events.

Vital Stats:

Access method: E-mail
To access: Send an e-mail message to listserv@listp.apa.org
Subject line:
Message: **subscribe traumatic-stress *firstname lastname***
E-mail: traumatic-stress-request@listp.apa.org

RECOVERY

alt.abuse.recovery

The newsgroup alt.abuse.recovery is for people recovering from all types of abuse.

Vital Stats:

Access method: Usenet newsgroup
To access: news:alt.abuse.recovery

---

alt.recovery

The alt.recovery newsgroup is aimed at people involved in any type of recovery program.

Vital Stats:

Access method: Usenet newsgroup
To access: news:alt.recovery

---

alt.recovery.addiction.sexual

Recovering from sexual addiction is the subject of the alt.recovery.addiction.sexual newsgroup.

Vital Stats:

Access method: Usenet newsgroup
To access: news:alt.recovery.addiction.sexual

alt.recovery.codependency

The alt.recovery.codependency newsgroup is aimed at people who want to stop participating in mutually destructive relationships.

Vital Stats:

Access method: Usenet newsgroup
To access: news:alt.recovery.codependency

---

alt.sexual.abuse.recovery

Both men and women who have suffered sexual abuse are welcome to participate in the alt.sexual.abuse.recovery newsgroup.

Vital Stats:

Access method: Usenet newsgroup
To access: news:alt.sexual.abuse.recovery

SCHIZOPHRENIA

alt.support.schizophrenia

People with schizophrenia and their loved ones are the primary audiences for this newsgroup.

Vital Stats:

Access method: Usenet newsgroup
To access: news:alt.support.schizophrenia

Doctor's Guide to Schizophrenia Information & Resources

This site has more than a dozen news stories about schizophrenia, a good collection of links to other schizophrenia-related documents and sites, and information about relevant Usenet newsgroups. It's part of the Doctor's Guide to the Internet (p. 14), which is sponsored by P/S/L NuMedia.

Vital Stats:

Access method: WWW
To access: http://www.pslgroup.com/SCHIZOPHR.HTM
E-mail: webmaster@pslgroup.com

SUICIDE

alt.suicide.holiday

Despite its name, the newsgroup alt.suicide.holiday is really a general discussion of suicide. Many people who post messages are having suicidal thoughts.

Vital Stats:

Access method:	Usenet newsgroup
To access:	news:alt.suicide.holiday

---

suicide-support

The suicide-support mailing list is a support group to discuss suicidal feelings, thoughts, intentions, or previous attempts.

Vital Stats:

Access method:	E-mail
To access:	Send an e-mail message to majordomo@research.canon.com.au
Subject line:	
Message:	**subscribe suicide-support**
E-mail:	greyham@research.canon.com.au

---

suicide-survivors

The suicide-survivors mailing list is a support group for people who have had some-one close to them commit suicide.

Vital Stats:

Access method:	E-mail
To access:	Send an e-mail message to majordomo@research.canon.com.au
Subject line:	
Message:	**subscribe suicide survivors**
E-mail:	greyham@research.canon.com.au

NEUROLOGICAL DISORDERS

GENERAL

alt.support.disorders.neurological

People affected by neurological disorders are the primary audience for this newsgroup.

Vital Stats:

Access method: Usenet newsgroup
To access: news:alt.support.disorders.neurological

alt.support.epilepsy

The alt.support.epilepsy newsgroup provides information and support for people with epilepsy.

Vital Stats:

Access method: Usenet newsgroup
To access: news:alt.support.epilepsy

American Academy of Neurology

The highlight of this site is a collection of brief fact sheets about various neurological problems, including Alzheimer's disease, brain tumors, carpal tunnel syndrome, epilepsy, head injuries, Parkinson's disease, and stroke, among others. The site is operated by the American Academy of Neurology, a professional organization.

The site also offers a patient information guide with contact information for organizations devoted to various illnesses and conditions, links to other neurology sites, and lesson plans about the nervous system, the brain, and other subjects.

Vital Stats:

Access method:	WWW
To access:	http://www.aan.com
E-mail:	aan@aan.com

The Internet Sleuth—Neuroscience

This database lets you search nearly a dozen Internet sites about neurology using a single interface. You must search each site separately. The database is part of The Internet Sleuth search engine.

Vital Stats:

Access method:	WWW
To access:	http://www.isleuth.com/medi-neuro.html
E-mail:	sleuth@isleuth.com

National Institute of Neurological Disorders and Stroke

The National Institute of Neurological Disorders and Stroke site offers dozens of pamphlets about disorders of the brain and nervous system. There are pamphlets about attention deficit disorder, autism, carpal tunnel syndrome, headaches, learning disabilities, multiple sclerosis, muscular dystrophy, Parkinson's disease, post-polio syndrome, restless legs, sleep apnea, spinal cord injury, and many other topics.

One of the site's highlights is its extensive collection of documents about stroke prevention, warning signs, risk factors, clinical trials, recovery, and research.

Vital Stats:

Access method:	WWW
To access:	http://www.ninds.nih.gov
E-mail:	NINDSwebmaster@nih.gov

MULTIPLE SCLEROSIS

alt.support.mult-sclerosis

This very active newsgroup is aimed at people with multiple sclerosis (MS).

Vital Stats:

Access method: Usenet newsgroup
To access: news:alt.support.mult-sclerosis

International MS Support Foundation

This site features articles about dozens of topics related to multiple sclerosis, including genetics, fatigue, stress, scooters, medication, mobility, exercise, anxiety, MS lesions, and tests, among others. It's operated by the International MS Support Foundation, a nonprofit organization founded in 1996 by a person with MS.

The site also has information about research and clinical trials, a glossary, descriptions of drugs, a bulletin board, chat rooms, recipes, links to lots of related sites, and much more.

Vital Stats:

Access method: WWW
To access: http://www.msnews.org
E-mail: sumption@aspin.asu.edu

National Multiple Sclerosis Society

This site offers information about treatment of various MS symptoms, research updates, and news about public policy issues. It's operated by the National Multiple Sclerosis Society, a nonprofit organization.

The site also has a glossary, contact information for chapters around the country, contact information for clinics that specialize in treating MS, a list of books about MS, and a list of publications that can be obtained from the society.

The World of Multiple Sclerosis

This site has basic information about multiple sclerosis, news items about research and treatment, and answers to frequently asked questions. It's operated by the International Federation of Multiple Sclerosis Societies, a nonprofit umbrella organization for the thirty-six national MS member societies around the world.

The site also has links to Web sites operated by national MS societies, a glossary, a database of MS research projects around the world, a calendar of MS events in various countries, annotated reviews of books about MS, and lots more.

The entire site is provided in English, and some information is also available in French, German, Italian, Spanish, Arabic, Estonian, Finnish, Greek, Hungarian, Icelandic, Hebrew, Japanese, and Serbo-Croat.

SKIN DISORDERS

AcneNet

AcneNet provides just about everything you might want to know about acne. The site has basic facts about acne, explanations of what causes acne, descriptions of the types of acne lesions, discussions of various treatments, and a glossary. It's operated by Roche Laboratories Inc. in cooperation with the American Academy of Dermatology.

Vital Stats:

Access method: WWW
To access: http://www.derm-infonet.com/acnenet

alt.support.lupus

This newsgroup is aimed at people who have lupus.

Vital Stats:

Access method: Usenet newsgroup
To access: news:alt.support.lupus

alt.support.psoriasis

The skin condition psoriasis is discussed in this newsgroup.

Vital Stats:

Access method: Usenet newsgroup
To access: news:alt.support.psoriasis

---

alt.support.skin-diseases

Various types of skin diseases are discussed in this newsgroup.

Vital Stats:

Access method: Usenet newsgroup
To access: news:alt.support.skin-diseases

---

alt.support.skin-diseases.psoriasis

Various aspects of living with psoriasis are discussed in this newsgroup.

Vital Stats:

Access method: Usenet newsgroup
To access: news:alt.support.skin-diseases.psoriasis

---

alt.support.skin-diseases.vitiligo

Messages in this newsgroup focus on the skin disease vitiligo.

Vital Stats:

Access method: Usenet newsgroup
To access: news:alt.support.skin-diseases.vitiligo

American Academy of Dermatology

The best feature at this site is a collection of three dozen patient education pamphlets about various skin conditions. Some of the topics covered include acne, athlete's foot, moles, poison ivy, scabies, sun protection for children, tanning, and warts. The site is operated by the American Academy of Dermatology, a professional organization.

Another highlight is a special section on skin cancer. It has articles about what skin cancer looks like, detecting melanoma, preventing skin cancer, how to perform a self-examination, and risk factors for melanoma, among other topics.

The site also has contact information for patient organizations on skin disorders and dozens of other medical topics, contact information for academy members around the country, press releases, and links to related Internet sites.

Vital Stats:

Access method:	WWW
To access:	http://www.aad.org

ECZEMA

The ECZEMA mailing list is a support group for people who suffer from eczema. Health care providers and pharmaceutical researchers also are welcome to subscribe.

Vital Stats:

Access method:	E-mail
To access:	Send an e-mail message to listserv@maelstrom.stjohns.edu
Subject line:	
Message:	**subscribe ECZEMA *firstname lastname***
E-mail:	ECZEMA-request@maelstrom.stjohns.edu

National Psoriasis Foundation

This site offers answers to frequently asked questions about psoriasis, links to related Web sites, and statistics on psoriasis. It also has information about types of psoriasis, treatment methods, research, and studies that are seeking volunteers. It's operated by the National Psoriasis Foundation, a nonprofit organization.

Vital Stats:

Access method: WWW
To access: http://www.psoriasis.org
E-mail: getinfo@npfusa.org

Pinch.com

Pinch.com provides archives of postings from four Usenet newsgroups about skin problems: alt.support.skin-diseases, alt.support.skin-diseases.psoriasis, alt.support.skin-diseases.vitiligo, and alt.support.skin-diseases.hidradenitis. The site is operated by a private individual.

Another handy feature is a collection of links to search engines at more than a dozen Internet sites that provide information about skin disorders. The webmaster has provided sample searches for many of the databases.

Vital Stats:

Access method: WWW
To access: http://www.pinch.com/skin
E-mail: ed@pinch.com

SLEEP DISORDERS

alt.support.sleep-disorder

Sleep disorders such as sleep apnea are the focus of this newsgroup.

Vital Stats:

Access method:	Usenet newsgroup
To access:	news:alt.support.sleep-disorder

Doctor's Guide to Insomnia Information & Resources

This site has a few articles about sleep disorders and a small collection of links to other sleep-oriented documents and sites. It's part of the Doctor's Guide to the Internet (p. 14), which is sponsored by P/S/L NuMedia.

Vital Stats:

Access method:	WWW
To access:	http://www.pslgroup.com/INSOMNIA.HTM
E-mail:	webmaster@pslgroup.com

National Sleep Foundation

The highlight of this site is a collection of brochures about sleep problems and disorders. Some of the available titles include *The Nature of Sleep, When You Can't Sleep, Sleep & Aging, Sleep Apnea, Sleep and the Traveler, Melatonin: The Facts, Strategies for Shift Workers, Sleep and Pain,* and *Living with Narcolepsy.* The site is operated by the National Sleep Foundation, a nonprofit organization established in 1990.

The site also has facts about sleep disorders and sleep deprivation, newsletters, press releases, and annotated links to other sleep-related Web sites.

Vital Stats:

Access method:	WWW
To access:	http://www.sleepfoundation.org
E-mail:	natsleep@erols.com

Sleep Home Pages

This jumbled site is primarily aimed at sleep researchers, although some consumers also may find it useful. It's operated by the Brain Information Service at the University of California-Los Angeles (UCLA).

One of the site's highlights is BiblioSleep, a database that contains bibliographic information and abstracts (where available) for all papers about sleep published from 1994 to the present. You can browse the database by author, category, or keyword.

The site also offers numerous discussion forums about sleep research and sleep disorders, an e-mail alert service that provides citations for new publications in the sleep field, a directory of sleep researchers around the world, and annotated links to lots of related sites.

Vital Stats:

Access method:	WWW
To access:	http://bisleep.medsch.ucla.edu
E-mail:	bisleep@ucla.edu

The Sleep Medicine Home Page

The Sleep Medicine Home Page offers no original information, but has a great set of links to Internet documents and Web sites about sleep disorders. It's operated by a private individual.

The links provide information about various sleep disorders, sleep-related newsgroups and mailing lists, professional associations, sleep-related foundations and associated organizations, professional journals, sleep research organizations, medications and neurotransmitters, sleep disorder centers, news items about sleep, and products related to sleep.

Vital Stats:

Access method:	WWW
To access:	http://www.users.cloud9.net/~thorpy
E-mail:	thorpy@aecom.yu.edu

SleepNet

SleepNet attempts to link all of the sleep information located on the Internet, and does a fine job of it. The site's highlight is its annotated links and ratings for more than 100 sleep-related sites. A private individual operates the site.

SleepNet's links lead to information about sleep deprivation, sleep tests, research, dreams, shift work and jet lag, sleep and aging, sleep disorders in infants and children, sleep apnea, insomnia, restless legs, and narcolepsy, among other subjects. There also are links to sites operated by patient support groups, professional organizations, and sleep disorders programs.

Finally, SleepNet provides discussion forums for the public and health care professionals, as well as links to sites that have news items about sleep.

Vital Stats:

Access method:	WWW
To access:	http://www.sleepnet.com
E-mail:	sandman@sleepnet.com

SUBSTANCE ABUSE

Al-Anon/Alateen

This is the official Web site of Al-Anon and Alateen, which are self-help programs for families and friends of alcoholics. It has background information about Al-Anon and Alateen, twenty questions to help users decide whether they need Al-Anon, and contact information for Al-Anon groups around the world.

The site also has the Twelve Steps and Twelve Traditions of Alcoholics Anonymous, personal stories from Al-Anon's monthly magazine *The Forum,* a calendar of events, and a catalog of publications that can be ordered from Al-Anon.

Vital Stats:

Access method:	WWW
To access:	http://www.al-anon-alateen.org

alt.recovery.aa

The very active alt.recovery.aa newsgroup is aimed at people who participate in Alcoholics Anonymous.

Vital Stats:

Access method:	Usenet newsgroup
To access:	news:alt.recovery.aa

alt.recovery.adult-children

The alt.recovery.adult-children newsgroup is aimed at adults who grew up in families where at least one parent was an alcoholic.

Vital Stats:

Access method: Usenet newsgroup
To access: news:alt.recovery.adult-children

alt.recovery.na

The alt.recovery.na newsgroup is targeted at members of Narcotics Anonymous.

Vital Stats:

Access method: Usenet newsgroup
To access: news:alt.recovery.na

Drug-Free Resource Net

This site has detailed descriptions of various drugs, including amphetamines, cocaine, designer drugs, ecstasy, heroin, LSD, marijuana, methamphetamines, mushrooms, PCP, steroids, tobacco, and alcohol, among others. It's operated by the Partnership for a Drug-Free America, a nonprofit coalition of advertising industry professionals.

One especially useful feature is a collection of photographs of illegal drugs and drug paraphernalia. The site also has a database containing street names for drugs and tips for parents about how to talk with their children about drugs.

Vital Stats:

Access method: WWW
To access: http://www.drugfreeamerica.org

Indiana Prevention Resource Center

This site has a dictionary of slang terms for street drugs, numerous articles about drug use prevention, and dozens of photographs of drugs and drug equipment. It's operated by the Department of Allied Health Science at Indiana University.

    The site also has fact sheets about various drugs, a database containing bibliographic information for journal articles about drug abuse and prevention, a large collection of statistics about drug use by children and adults, links to lots of related Web sites, and much more.

Vital Stats:

Access method:	WWW
To access:	http://www.drugs.indiana.edu
E-mail:	webmaster@www.drugs.indiana.edu

The Internet Sleuth—Substance Abuse

This database lets you search several Internet sites about substance abuse using a single interface. You must search each site separately. The database is part of The Internet Sleuth search engine.

Vital Stats:

Access method:	WWW
To access:	http://www.isleuth.com/sub-abuse.html
E-mail:	sleuth@isleuth.com

Mothers Against Drunk Driving

The Mothers Against Drunk Driving (MADD) site has a nice collection of brochures. Some of the available titles include *Someone You Know Drinks & Drives*, *Drunk Driving: An Unacknowledged Form of Child Endangerment*, *Victim Information Pamphlet*, *Don't Call Me Lucky*, *Your Grief: You're Not Going Crazy*, and *Financial Recovery*.

    The site also has extensive statistics about drunk driving, ratings of drunk driving efforts in each state, details about victim assistance services provided by MADD, position statements, a database containing contact information for MADD chapters around the country, a national calendar of substance abuse events, news stories about alcohol use and abuse, and links to lots of related Web sites.

Vital Stats:

Access method: WWW
To access: http://www.madd.org
E-mail: info@madd.org

National Institute on Alcohol Abuse and Alcoholism

The National Institute on Alcohol Abuse and Alcoholism site has a database containing abstracts and bibliographic references to journal articles, books, conference papers, reports, and other works about alcohol abuse and alcoholism. The database contains about 100,000 records dating back to the late 1960s.

The site also has pamphlets about alcoholism, aging and alcohol abuse, drinking and pregnancy, and how to reduce your drinking; a list of free research monographs and other publications that can be ordered online; and the full text of *Alcohol Alerts,* a quarterly publication that has news about research findings. The institute is part of the National Institutes of Health.

Vital Stats:

Access method: WWW
To access: http://www.niaaa.nih.gov
E-mail: webmaster@www.niaaa.nih.gov

National Institute on Drug Abuse

The National Institute on Drug Abuse (NIDA) site offers fact sheets about specific drugs, drug abuse and pregnancy, women and drug abuse, and other topics. It also has a guide for parents about drug use among young people, articles about research, extensive grant information, a catalog of NIDA publications, a calendar of events, and press releases.

In addition, the site has speeches and congressional testimony by NIDA officials, reports titled *Inhalant Abuse: Its Dangers Are Nothing to Sniff at* and *Anabolic Steroids: A Threat to Body and Mind,* links to other Internet sites about drug abuse, and a publication for schools and community groups entitled *Preventing Drug Use Among Children and Adolescents: A Research-Based Guide.*

Vital Stats:

Access method:	WWW
To access:	http://www.nida.nih.gov
E-mail:	Webmaster@lists.nida.nih.gov

Online AA Recovery Resources

This site has background information about Alcoholics Anonymous, various AA publications, telephone numbers for AA groups around the world, a calendar of events, materials about the history of AA, information about online AA meetings, AA-related computer programs, and links to lots of related sites.

The site is in English, although some materials also are available in German, Spanish, Norwegian, Danish, and Portuguese. It's operated by a private individual, not by Alcoholics Anonymous.

Vital Stats:

Access method:	WWW
To access:	http://www.recovery.org/aa
E-mail:	bill@recovery.org

PREVline (Prevention Online)

PREVline offers hundreds of files about alcohol, tobacco, and other drugs from the National Clearinghouse for Alcohol and Drug Information. The site has publications about prevention, resource guides, basic descriptions of street drugs, a publications catalog, and links to recent news articles about alcohol, tobacco, and other drugs.

Vital Stats:

Access methods:	WWW, FTP
To access:	http://www.health.org *or* ftp://ftp.health.org
Login (FTP only):	**anonymous**
Password (FTP only):	your e-mail address
Path (FTP only):	*pub/ncadi*
E-mail:	webmaster@health.org

Tranquility

The Tranquility mailing list is an online meeting of Al-Anon, a group that aims to help families of alcoholics. Weekly discussion subjects are posted to the list, and subscribers are welcome to discuss other issues as well.

Vital Stats:

Access method:	E-mail
To access:	Send an e-mail message to majordomo@world.std.com
Subject line:	
Message:	**subscribe Tranquility**
E-mail:	journey4me@aol.com

PREVENTION AND TREATMENT

AGING ISSUES

Administration on Aging

The Administration on Aging site offers numerous brochures on health topics. Some sample titles include *Taking Care of Your Teeth and Mouth, Hearing and Older People, What to Do About Flu, Aging and Your Eyes, Prostate Problems,* and *High Blood Pressure: A Common but Controllable Disorder.*

The site also has links to Web sites operated by state agencies on aging, directories of area agencies on aging and state long-term care ombudsmen, and lots more.

Vital Stats:

Access method:	WWW
To access:	http://www.aoa.dhhs.gov
E-mail:	esec@ban-gate.aoa.dhhs.gov

LTCARE-L

Subscribers to the LTCARE-L mailing list discuss research findings and public policy issues related to aging, physical and cognitive disability, and long-term care. The list is operated by the U.S. Department of Health and Human Services.

Vital Stats:

Access method:	E-mail
To access:	Send an e-mail message to listserv@list.nih.gov
Subject line:	
Message:	**subscribe LTCARE-L**
E-mail:	LTCARE-L-request@list.nih.gov

ALTERNATIVE MEDICINE

Acupuncture.com

Acupuncture.com offers extensive information for consumers, students, and practitioners about traditional Chinese therapies such as acupuncture, herbology, Qi Gong, Chinese nutrition, and Tui Na and Chinese massage. It's operated by the Yo San University of Traditional Chinese Medicine in Santa Monica, California.

   The site has background articles about the various treatments, abstracts of research articles, treatment testimonials, contact information for practitioners of traditional Chinese medicine around the world, a list of insurance companies that cover acupuncture treatments, information about acupuncture laws in each state, reviews of books and software about Chinese medicine, links to more than 100 other alternative medicine sites on the Internet, and lots more.

Vital Stats:

Access method:	WWW
To access:	http://www.Acupuncture.com
E-mail:	AcuCom@aol.com

Alternative Health News Online

This site provides links to dozens of Internet sites about alternative health. The links provide information about diet and nutrition, mind/body control, alternative medical systems, manual healing, longevity, wellness, healthy living, and other subjects. The site also has news briefs and articles about new clinical findings.

Vital Stats:

Access method: WWW
To access: http://www.altmedicine.com
E-mail: FPGraz@aol.com

The Alternative Medicine Homepage

This site provides no original information of its own but offers links to dozens of other sites that have information about such alternative therapies as folk medicine, herbal medicine, homeopathy, new age healing, chiropractic, acupuncture, and naturopathy, among others. The Alternative Medicine Homepage was created by a reference librarian at the University of Pittsburgh's Falk Library of the Health Sciences.

Vital Stats:

Access method: WWW
To access: http://www.pitt.edu/~cbw/altm.html
E-mail: cbw@med.pitt.edu

Dr. Bower's Complementary and Alternative Medicine Home Page

This site has links to hundreds of Internet sites that offer information about such complementary and alternative treatments as acupuncture, applied kinesiology, aromatherapy, biofeedback, body mind medicine, chiropractic, essence therapy, herbal medicine, homeopathy, music therapy, osteopathy, and reflexology, among many others. The site is operated by an associate professor at the University of Virginia School of Medicine.

Vital Stats:

Access method: WWW
To access: http://galen.med.virginia.edu/~pjb3s/Complementary_
                    Practices.html
E-mail: pbower@virginia.edu

The Internet Sleuth—Alternative Medicine

This database lets you search eight Internet sites about alternative medicine using a single interface. You must search each site separately. The database is part of The Internet Sleuth search engine.

Vital Stats:

Access method: WWW
To access: http://www.isleuth.com/heal-alt.html
E-mail: sleuth@isleuth.com

misc.health.alternative

All aspects of alternative medicine are discussed in the newsgroup misc.health.alternative, which averages 100 messages daily.

Vital Stats:

Access method: Usenet newsgroup
To access: news:misc.health.alternative

Office of Alternative Medicine

The Office of Alternative Medicine (OAM) site provides limited background information about various alternative medical treatments, answers to frequently asked questions about complementary and alternative medicine, and advice about how to search for alternative medicine subjects in the medical literature. The office is part of the National Institutes of Health.

   The site also offers a calendar of complementary and alternative medicine events worldwide, a list of specialty centers that are conducting research in the field, a list of OAM-funded research, a quarterly newsletter, and press releases.

Vital Stats:

Access method: WWW
To access: http://altmed.od.nih.gov
E-mail: webmaster@altmed.od.nih.gov

CHILDREN'S HEALTH

American Academy of Pediatrics

The American Academy of Pediatrics site offers hundreds of documents, ranging from a schedule of recommended childhood immunizations to the full text of all articles from the journal *Pediatrics* starting with the January 1997 issue.

One of the site's highlights is a collection of more than 200 policy statements. They discuss such issues as AIDS in schools, adolescent assault victims, asbestos exposure in schools, assisting disabled children, bicycle helmets, children witnesses, children and television, confidentiality in adolescent health care, distinguishing sudden infant death from child abuse fatalities, drug-exposed infants, health needs of homeless children and families, homosexuality and adolescence, the impact of music lyrics and videos on children, lactose intolerance, media violence, PCBs in breast milk, school transportation safety, sexual assaults and adolescents, shaken baby syndrome, suicide by adolescents and young adults, and teenage drivers, among others.

Another interesting section offers more than a dozen model bills about child health issues. There are bills about all-terrain vehicles, child abuse, child bicycle safety, child health insurance, postdelivery care for mothers and newborns, children and guns, swimming pool safety, and other topics.

The site also has brochures about protecting children from poison, raising children to resist violence, talking to teens about sex, children's television, children and the environment, and other topics; files about air bag safety and reducing the risk of Sudden Infant Death Syndrome; information about legislative developments affecting pediatrics; press releases and congressional testimony; and a catalog of patient and professional publications.

Vital Stats:

Access method:	WWW
To access:	http://www.aap.org
E-mail:	kidsdocs@aap.org

CaringKids

CaringKids is a mailing list for people age eighteen and under who have family members or friends with life threatening or debilitating illnesses. List members are encouraged to exchange information, share their feelings, and establish friendships with other kids in similar circumstances. Adults are not allowed to participate in the list.

Vital Stats:

Access method: E-mail
To access: Send an e-mail message to listserv@maelstrom.stjohns.edu
Subject line:
Message: **subscribe CaringKids *firstname lastname***
E-mail: CaringKids-request@maelstrom.stjohns.edu

CaringParents

The CaringParents mailing list is aimed at adults who are concerned about kids affected by serious illness—either their own illness or the illness of someone they love. Cancer is frequently discussed, although the list is not limited to cancer.

Vital Stats:

Access method: E-mail
To access: Send an e-mail message to listserv@maelstrom.stjohns.edu
Subject line:
Message: **subscribe CaringParents *firstname lastname***
E-mail: CaringParents-Request@maelstrom.stjohns.edu

ChildSecure

Dozens of useful articles about child health and safety are available on this site. It's operated by ChildSecure, a commercial firm that sells baby and child care products.

The health articles cover such topics as colds and flu, pediatric ear infections, immunization schedules, Sudden Infant Death Syndrome, breast feeding, colic and crying, child psychiatry, attention disorder, avoiding E. coli infection, treating burns, preventing birth defects, and feeding babies, among others. Some of the safety issues discussed include fire safety, lead paint, carbon monoxide, crib and bedding safety, toy safety, poisons, playground safety, and bicycle helmet safety.

The site also has news from the American Academy of Pediatrics about child health and safety, details about consumer alerts and product recalls issued by the Consumer Product Safety Commission and the Food and Drug Administration, and reviews of books and videos about child health and safety.

Vital Stats:

Access method:	WWW
To access:	http://www.childsecure.com
E-mail:	comments@childsecure.com

CPPARENT

Subscribers to the CPPARENT mailing list discuss issues related to the parenting of children who have cerebral palsy. Both parents and children are welcome to join the list.

Vital Stats:

Access method:	E-mail
To access:	Send an e-mail message to listserv@maelstrom.stjohns.edu
Subject line:	
Message:	**subscribe CPPARENT *firstname lastname***
E-mail:	CPPARENT-request@maelstrom.stjohns.edu

CSHCN-L

The CSHCN-L mailing list is aimed at people who care for children with special health care needs.

Vital Stats:

Access method:	E-mail
To access:	Send an e-mail message to listserv@lists.ufl.edu
Subject line:	
Message:	**subscribe CSHCN-L *firstname lastname***
E-mail:	CSHCN-L-request@lists.ufl.edu

KidsHealth at the AMA

One of the most useful features at KidsHealth at the AMA is a collection of articles about providing first aid to children. They cover such topics as eye injuries, fever, frostbite, head injuries, heat illness, insect stings, nosebleeds, seizures, tooth injuries, and vomiting. The site is operated by the American Medical Association and the Nemours Foundation.

Another excellent feature is a guide to baby development from birth to age two. It discusses communication, feeding, growth, learning and play, medical care, movement, the senses, and sleep.

The site also has recent articles about pediatric health from Reuters, contact information for state poison control centers nationwide, and articles about fire safety, preventing household accidents, baby product safety, auto safety, germs, childhood infections, childhood immunizations, and related subjects.

Vital Stats:

Access method:	WWW
To access:	http://www.ama-assn.org/KidsHealth
E-mail:	insight@ama-assn.org

KidsHealth.org

The KidsHealth.org site offers hundreds of articles, separated into sections for parents and children. The site is operated by the Nemours Foundation.

The parents section is the strongest part of the site. It offers more than 100 articles about attention disorder, death, divorce, night terrors, sleep, stress, teenage suicide, temper tantrums, childhood infections, laboratory tests, asthma, broken bones, common orthopedic conditions, ear infections, tonsils and tonsillectomies, pediatric dentistry, gastrointestinal problems, managing pain, bedwetting, healthy food choices, sugar and behavior, exercise, ergonomics, and other topics. It also has reviews of selected kids' toys and games.

The kids section has articles about such topics as death, divorce, eating disorders, menstruation, puberty, healthy eating, sports and nutrition, how the body works, acne, the brain, AIDS, and deafness, among others.

Vital Stats:

Access method:	WWW
To access:	http://KidsHealth.org/index2.html
E-mail:	webmaster@KidsHealth.org

misc.kids.health

All aspects of children's health are discussed in this newsgroup.

Vital Stats:

Access method:	Usenet newsgroup
To access:	news:misc.kids.health

National Institute of Child Health and Human Development

This site has patient publications about Cushing's Syndrome, endometriosis, McCune-Albright Syndrome, precocious puberty, vasectomy safety, pituitary tumors in children, Sudden Infant Death Syndrome, gestational diabetes, uterine fibroids, vaginitis, and other topics. It also has press releases and background information about the National Institute of Child Health and Human Development, which is part of the National Institutes of Health.

Vital Stats:

Access method:	WWW
To access:	http://www.nih.gov:80/nichd

The National Organization on Fetal Alcohol Syndrome

This site has basic information about fetal alcohol syndrome, tips for parents and caregivers of fetal alcohol syndrome children, details about The National Organization on Fetal Alcohol Syndrome (NOFAS) and its programs, and a list of newsletters, books, reports, and support groups about fetal alcohol syndrome. NOFAS is a non-profit organization.

Vital Stats:

Access method:	WWW
To access:	http://www.nofas.org
E-mail:	nofas@erols.com

National Sudden Infant Death Syndrome Resource Center

This site has background publications about Sudden Infant Death Syndrome (SIDS), information about state SIDS programs around the country, a bibliography of materials about infant positioning and SIDS, and a publication titled *After Sudden Infant Death Syndrome: Facing Anniversaries, Holidays, and Special Events.* The center is operated by the Maternal and Child Health Bureau in the U.S. Department of Health and Human Services.

Vital Stats:

Access method:	WWW
To access:	http://www.circsol.com/SIDS
E-mail:	info@circsol.com

Pediatric/Adolescent Gastroesophageal Reflux Association

This site provides basic information about gastroesophageal reflux in children, along with links to other sites about gastroesophageal reflux. It's operated by the Pediatric/Adolescent Gastroesophageal Reflux Association, a nonprofit volunteer group.

Vital Stats:

Access method:	WWW
To access:	http://www.reflux.org
E-mail:	GERGROUP@aol.com

PEDIATRIC-PAIN

All aspects of pediatric pain management are discussed on the PEDIATRIC-PAIN mailing list. The list is primarily aimed at clinicians and researchers, although anyone is welcome to join.

Vital Stats:

Access method:	E-mail
To access:	Send an e-mail message to MAILSERV@ac.dal.ca
Subject line:	
Message:	**subscribe PEDIATRIC-PAIN**
E-mail:	owner-pediatric-pain@ac.dal.ca

Pediatric Points of Interest

Pediatric Points of Interest provides no original information of its own, but has links to more than 3,500 Web sites and mailing lists that provide information about children's health. There are links to organizations, hospitals, parenting resources, resources for professionals, patient education materials, journals and newsletters, and other types of information. The site was created by Dr. Christoph U. Lehmann, and is sponsored by the pediatrics departments at Johns Hopkins University and the Marshall University School of Medicine.

Vital Stats:

Access method:	WWW
To access:	http://www.med.jhu.edu/peds/neonatology
Mirror site (Europe):	http://medweb.uni-muenster.de/mirror/poi/poi.html
E-mail:	clehmann@welchlink.welch.jhu.edu

PEDINFO

PEDINFO offers links to hundreds of Web sites, mailing lists, and Usenet newsgroups of interest to pediatricians. Each link has a brief annotation.

The sites provide information about adolescent medicine, allergies, child abuse, dentistry, disabilities, drug abuse, growth, immunizations, injury prevention, nursing, nutrition, pain management, preventive care, psychiatry, safety, sports medicine, surgery, and many other topics. PEDINFO is provided by the University of Alabama at Birmingham.

Vital Stats:

Access method:	WWW
To access:	http://www.uab.edu/pedinfo
European mirror:	http://www.nice.it/pedinfo
E-mail:	spooner@uab.edu

SickKids

SickKids is a mailing list designed for people age eighteen and under who are ill. On the list, members can talk about their feelings and frustrations, ask questions, share poems and stories, tell jokes, and otherwise support each other. Adults are not allowed to participate.

Vital Stats:

Access method:	E-mail
To access:	Send an e-mail message to listserv@maelstrom.stjohns.edu
Subject line:	
Message:	**subscribe SickKids *firstname lastname***
E-mail:	SickKids-Request@maelstrom.stjohns.edu

SIDS Network

The SIDS Network site offers more than 1,000 files about Sudden Infant Death Syndrome (SIDS) and related disorders. The network is a nonprofit organization.

The files provide answers to questions frequently asked by parents and siblings, information about how to help those who are grieving, dozens of personal stories written by people affected by the death of an infant from SIDS, and a list of books, videos, and other resources about SIDS, pregnancy loss, stillbirth, or neonatal death.

Other files provide legislative news, contact information for SIDS organizations and support groups around the country, and dozens of articles about sleep-related issues, sleep apnea and monitors, SIDS research, and related issues.

Vital Stats:

Access method:	WWW
To access:	http://sids-network.org
E-mail:	sidsnet@sids-network.org

DENTAL HEALTH

ADA Online

ADA Online, which is operated by the American Dental Association, has information for consumers about tooth whitening, bad breath, finding a dentist, dental insurance benefits, preventing baby bottle tooth decay, cleaning teeth and gums, root canal treatment, diet and dental health, gum disease, fluoridation, infection control, tobacco, and related topics.

It also offers abstracts of articles published in *The Journal of the American Dental Association,* news releases, a calendar of dental conferences, and links to other dental sites on the Internet.

Vital Stats:

Access method:	WWW
To access:	http://www.ada.org
E-mail:	publicinfo@ada.org

Dental Related Internet Resources

This site offers hundreds of links to Internet sites that provide information about all aspects of dentistry, including fluoride, dental phobia and anxiety, sports dentistry, pet care, orthodontics, and oral surgery, among other subjects. It provides no original information of its own.

Vital Stats:

Access method:	WWW
To access:	http://www.dental-resources.com
E-mail:	webmaster@dental-resources.com

The Internet Sleuth—Dentistry

This database lets you search nearly a dozen Internet sites about dentistry using a single interface. You must search each site separately. The database is part of The Internet Sleuth search engine.

Vital Stats:

Access method: WWW
To access: http://www.isleuth.com/dent.html
E-mail: sleuth@isleuth.com

National Institute of Dental Research

The National Institute of Dental Research site has publications titled *Snack Smart for Healthy Teeth, A Healthy Mouth for Your Baby, Diabetes and Periodontal Disease,* and *Seal Out Dental Decay.* It also offers information about research being conducted at the institute, a calendar of events, press releases, and links to other dental-related Internet sites. The institute is part of the National Institutes of Health.

Vital Stats:

Access method: WWW
To access: http://www.nidr.nih.gov
E-mail: nidrinfo@od31.nidr.nih.gov

National Oral Health Information Clearinghouse

The clearinghouse provides the Oral Health Database, which has titles, abstracts, and availability information for publications and health education materials. The clearinghouse is operated by the National Institute of Dental Research, which is part of the National Institutes of Health.

Vital Stats:

Access method: WWW
To access: http://www.aerie.com/nihdb/nohic/ohtest.html
E-mail: nidr@aerie.com

DRUGS (PRESCRIPTION)

CenterWatch Clinical Trials Listing Service

This fantastic site offers information about more than 5,200 clinical trials of drugs that are actively recruiting patients. It's operated by CenterWatch, which publishes newsletters and books about clinical trials.

The trials are divided into twenty disease categories, and under each category the trials are further divided by state and country. For each listing, the site provides background information about the trial and the facility where it's being performed.

The site also offers:

- Listings of drugs approved by the U.S. Food and Drug Administration (FDA) since 1995. The listings are divided by year, and then by therapeutic area.

- Profiles of more than 150 clinical research centers, divided by therapeutic area and geographic region.

- Background information about how clinical research is conducted.

- An e-mail service that will notify you automatically about new trials in a particular therapeutic area or about drugs newly approved by the FDA in a particular area.

Vital Stats:

Access method: WWW
To access: http://www.centerwatch.com
E-mail: cntrwatch@aol.com

The Internet Sleuth—Pharmacology

This database lets you search more than a half-dozen Internet sites about prescription drugs using a single interface. You must search each site separately. The database is part of The Internet Sleuth search engine.

Vital Stats:

Access method:	WWW
To access:	http://www.isleuth.com/pharm.html
E-mail:	sleuth@isleuth.com

Medication Info Search

Fact sheets at this site provide basic information about dozens of common prescription medications. The sheets discuss uses, how to take the medication, side effects, precautions, drug interactions, missed doses, and storage. The site is provided by the Cheshire Medical Center, a hospital in New Hampshire.

Vital Stats:

Access method:	WWW
To access:	http://www.cheshire-med.com/services/pharm/ med-form.cgi
E-mail:	Pharmacy@Cheshire-med.com

Needy Meds

Needy Meds provides details about programs operated by pharmaceutical manufacturers to help people who can't afford to buy prescription drugs. You can browse the information by manufacturer or drug name.

Vital Stats:

Access method:	WWW
To access:	http://www.needymeds.com
E-mail:	LibOverly@pobox.com

Pharmaceutical Connections

This site provides links to Internet sites operated by several dozen drug companies, ranging from Abbott Labs to Whitehall Robins. Each link has a few words describing what's available at the site.

Vital Stats:

Access method:	WWW
To access:	http://www.docsweb.com/pharm.htm
E-mail:	doctors@docsweb.com

PharmInfoNet

One of the highlights of PharmInfoNet is a database containing articles about prescription drugs. You can search the database or browse it by tradename or generic name. PharmInfoNet is operated by VirSci Corporation.

Another interesting feature allows users to submit questions about specific drugs. The questions are answered by a panel of experts. The site also has a database of press releases about new pharmaceutical and biotechnology products and a huge glossary of drug and medical terms.

Vital Stats:

Access method:	WWW
To access:	http://pharminfo.com
E-mail:	johnmack@virsci.com

RxList

RxList has lengthy articles about nearly 300 prescription drugs. The articles cover everything from the cost of the drug to possible side effects to results from clinical trials. RxList licenses the articles from Mosby, a major medical publisher. RxList is operated by a pharmacist.

One feature is especially helpful if you have an unknown tablet or capsule. You can type the code imprinted on the pill into a database, which will tell you what drug it is.

Another interesting feature lists the top 200 drugs in the United States by prescription volume. Each listing includes the brand name, generic name, and manufacturer.

Vital Stats:

Access method:	WWW
To access:	http://www.rxlist.com
E-mail:	info@rxlist.com

RxMed

RxMed, which is aimed at family physicians, offers patient information sheets about hundreds of illnesses. Each sheet provides information about symptoms, risk factors, prevention, diagnosis and treatment, and possible complications.

The site also provides lengthy articles about hundreds of prescription drugs. Each article provides details about clinical trials, indications, warnings, side effects, and drug interactions, among other issues.

Vital Stats:

Access method:	WWW
To access:	http://www.rxmed.com

FITNESS AND EXERCISE

Fit-L

Subscribers to the Fit-L mailing list discuss a wide range of subjects related to fitness, exercise, diet, and wellness. Some of the topics covered include various exercise programs, exercise equipment, metabolism, wellness programs, personal trainers, and vegetarianism.

Vital Stats:

Access method:	E-mail
To access:	Send an e-mail message to listserv@maelstrom.stjohns.edu
Subject line:	
Message:	**subscribe Fit-L *firstname lastname***
E-mail:	FIT-L-request@maelstrom.stjohns.edu

FitnessLink

FitnessLink offers dozens of articles about stress management, eating for fitness, vitamins and minerals, sports nutrition, choosing the right place to work out, working out at home, aerobic exercise, determining your fitness level, weight training, weight loss, making exercise a habit, and fitness for kids, among other subjects.

One interesting feature lets you submit questions to a panel of fitness experts. The questions are answered online. Another nice feature lets you chat with other fitness enthusiasts.

The site also has weekly fitness tips, news stories about fitness and health, recipes, links to health and fitness newsgroups and mailing lists, contact information for dozens of health and fitness magazines, links to dozens of related Web sites, lots of resources for fitness professionals, and much more.

Vital Stats:

Access method:	WWW
To access:	http://www.fitnesslink.com
E-mail:	info@fitnesslink.com

misc.fitness Newsgroups

Messages in these five newsgroups cover various aspects of physical fitness.

Vital Stats:

Access method:	Usenet newsgroups
To access:	news:misc.fitness, news:misc.fitness.aerobic, news:misc.fitness.misc, news:misc.fitness.walking, news:misc.fitness.weights

soc.senior.health+fitness

Posts to this newsgroup cover all aspects of health and fitness for seniors. Some of the topics discussed include physical and mental health, nutrition, health care facilities for seniors, aerobics, exercise equipment, and senior sports leagues.

Vital Stats:

Access method:	Usenet newsgroup
To access:	news:soc.senior.health+fitness

Start-Now-L

Subscribers to the Start-Now-L mailing list post their daily exercise workouts (or lack thereof) and exchange exercise information.

Vital Stats:

Access method:	E-mail
To access:	Send an e-mail message to majordomo@lists.teleport.com
Subject line:	
Message:	**subscribe start-now-l**
E-mail:	tonyap@teleport.com

Walklist

Members of the Walklist discuss all aspects of recreational walking for exercise and fitness.

Vital Stats:

Access method:	E-mail
To access:	Send an e-mail message to majordomo@lists.teleport.com
Subject line:	
Message:	**subscribe walklist**

Weights-2

Subscribers to the Weights-2 mailing list discuss all aspects of weightlifting.

Vital Stats:

Access method:	E-mail
To access:	Send an e-mail message to majordomo@nbaf.com
Subject line:	
Message:	**subscribe weights-2**

MEN'S HEALTH

alt.support.impotence

People dealing with impotence issues are the audience for this newsgroup.

Vital Stats:

Access method: Usenet newsgroup
To access: news:alt.support.impotence

alt.support.prostate.prostatitis

Men with any type of prostate disorder, including prostate cancer, are the focus of this newsgroup.

Vital Stats:

Access method: Usenet newsgroup
To access: news:alt.support.prostate.prostatitis

Doctor's Guide to Enlarged Prostate (BPH) Information & Resources

This site has more than a dozen news stories about benign prostatic hyperplasia (BPH)—or enlarged prostates—a good collection of links to other prostate-related documents and sites, and information about relevant Usenet newsgroups. It's part of the Doctor's Guide to the Internet (p. 14), which is sponsored by P/S/L NuMedia.

Vital Stats:

Access method:	WWW
To access:	http://www.pslgroup.com/ENLARGPROST.HTM
E-mail:	webmaster@pslgroup.com

Doctor's Guide to Erectile Dysfunction Information & Resources

This site has more than two dozen news stories about impotence and a good collection of links to other impotence-related documents and sites. It's part of the Doctor's Guide to the Internet (p. 14), which is sponsored by P/S/L NuMedia.

Vital Stats:

Access method:	WWW
To access:	http://www.pslgroup.com/ERECTILE.HTM
E-mail:	webmaster@pslgroup.com

Not for Men Only

This site has useful articles about dozens of male health issues. Some of the topics covered include screening for male health problems, cancer, exercise, nutrition, weight loss, kidney stones, prostate problems, impotence, vasectomy, medical symptoms, sexually transmitted diseases, self care, and sexual performance, among many others. The site is operated by the Male Health Center in Dallas, Texas.

Vital Stats:

Access method:	WWW
To access:	http://www.malehealthcenter.com

Prostatitis Home Page

This site offers a hodgepodge of information about prostatitis, much of it provided by patients. It has details about causes and treatment methods, a list of prostatitis clinics, an archive of postings to the sci.med.prostate.prostatitis Usenet newsgroup, papers from various scientific and medical publications, and links to related Web sites. The site is operated by the Prostatitis Foundation.

Vital Stats:

Access method:	WWW
To access:	http://www.prostate.org
E-mail:	ken@ideasmith.com

---

sci.med.prostate.prostatitis, PROSTATITIS

Readers of the sci.med.prostate.prostatitis newsgroup, which is mirrored on the PROSTATITIS mailing list, discuss symptoms, diagnosis, treatment, complications, and the personal impact of prostatitis.

Vital Stats:

Access methods:	Usenet newsgroup, E-mail
To access (Usenet):	news:sci.med.prostate.prostatitis
To access (mailing list):	Send an e-mail message to listserv@maelstrom.stjohns.edu
Subject line:	
Message:	**subscribe prostatitis *firstname lastname***
E-mail:	prostatitis-request@maelstrom.stjohns.edu

NUTRITION AND DIET

alt.health.fasting

Discussions in the alt.health.fasting newsgroup center on the impact of fasting on health.

Vital Stats:

Access method:	Usenet newsgroup
To access:	news:alt.health.fasting

alt.support.diet

This newsgroup provides information and support for people who are trying to lose weight through dieting.

Vital Stats:

Access method:	Usenet newsgroup
To access:	news:alt.support.diet

alt.support.diet.rx

Discussions in this newsgroup focus on taking prescription and over-the-counter drugs to help with weight loss.

Vital Stats:

Access method: Usenet newsgroup
To access: news:alt.support.diet.rx

American Dietetic Association

This site's most useful feature is a collection of dozens of fact sheets about various nutrition topics. Some of the subjects covered include fats and oils, breakfast, calcium, legumes, aspartame, olestra, sodium, feeding infants and toddlers, healthy eating for children, food allergies, reducing cancer risk, lactose intolerance, migraine headaches and food, nutrition for people living with HIV/AIDS, snacks for picky eaters, and vitamin and mineral supplements. The site is operated by the American Dietetic Association (ADA), a professional organization.

The site also has an extensive list of recommended nutrition books, a database of registered dietitians, and ADA position papers on child nutrition, dieting, food technology and safety, and health care reform, among other subjects.

Vital Stats:

Access method: WWW
To access: http://www.eatright.org
E-mail: webmaster@eatright.org

Center for Food Safety & Applied Nutrition

The Center for Food Safety & Applied Nutrition site has everything from background information about the fat substitute olestra to a book titled *Foodborne Pathogenic Microorganisms and Natural Toxins*—otherwise known as the "Bad Bug Book." The center is part of the Food and Drug Administration (FDA).

The site has information about food labels, health fraud, safe food handling, mercury in fish, eating disorders, food allergies, osteoporosis and other bone diseases, biotechnology, food additives, and pesticides and chemical contaminants, among many other subjects. Of particular note is a special section of the site devoted to women's health.

It also has an explanation of which federal agencies regulate food safety, details about how to report problems to the FDA, lesson plans about food safety, press releases, and links to dozens of other Internet sites that provide food and nutrition information.

Vital Stats:

Access method: WWW
To access: http://vm.cfsan.fda.gov/list.html
E-mail: lrd@cfsan.fda.gov

Center for Science in the Public Interest

This site provides everything from a chart showing the caffeine content of various foods and drugs to suggestions for improving food served in schools. It's operated by the Center for Science in the Public Interest (CSPI), a nonprofit advocacy organization.

One of the site's highlights is a collection of reports about dozens of nutrition topics. Some of the available titles include *Chemical Cuisine: CSPI's Guide to Food Additives, Scrambled Eggs: How a Broken Food Safety System Let Contaminated Eggs Become a National Food Poisoning Epidemic, Diner's Guide to Health and Nutrition Claims on Restaurant Menus,* and *Playing Chicken: The Human Cost of Inadequate Regulation of the Poultry Industry.* Classic CSPI reports on movie theater popcorn and Chinese, Mexican, and Italian foods also are available.

The site also offers selected articles from the *Nutrition Action Healthletter,* articles about alcohol advertising from CSPI's Alcohol Policies Project, articles about olestra, testimony before Congress, press releases, links to other health and nutrition Internet sites, and news about public advocacy efforts on food safety, organic foods, and other topics.

Vital Stats:

Access method: WWW
To access: http://www.cspinet.org
E-mail: amanuel@cspinet.org

CyberDiet

CyberDiet offers several interesting interactive programs, including a calculator that determines how many calories you burn by participating in various activities and a program that assesses your daily calorie and nutrient requirements. The site is operated by a registered dietitian.

CyberDiet also has a database of nutritional values for foods from various fast food chains, a seven-day diet and weight loss plan, a daily food planner, recipes, tips for modifying recipes to make them healthier, and lots more.

Vital Stats:

Access method:	WWW
To access:	http://www.cyberdiet.com
E-mail:	eatright@cyberdiet.com

Food Finder

Food Finder's database provides nutrient values for more than 1,000 fast-food items. The site is operated by Olen Publishing, and the data are derived from a handbook published by the consumer division of the Minnesota Attorney General's office.

The database is particularly helpful because you can search it by a number of variables. For example, if you want to know the nutrient value of all food sold by McDonald's, you can search by restaurant name. If you want to find all fast-food items that contain less than ten grams of fat, you can search by maximum fat amount. You also can search by type of food item and by limits on the number of calories, percentage of calories from fat, cholesterol, and sodium.

Vital Stats:

Access method:	WWW
To access:	http://www.olen.com/food
E-mail:	feedback@olen.com

Kids Food CyberClub

The Kids Food CyberClub is aimed at students in third through fifth grades. It has interactive quizzes, games, recipes contributed by children, a list of books about kids and food, and facts about various foods.

The site also offers a teacher's guide with lesson plans and suggestions for activities that children and parents can do together to learn about food and nutrition. The site is operated by the Connecticut Association for Human Services, an education and advocacy organization, with funding from Kaiser Permanente.

Vital Stats:

Access method:	WWW
To access:	http://www.kidsfood.org
E-mail:	webmaster@kidsfood.org

NutriBase

This site's highlight is a database that lists nutrients for more than 19,300 food items. The data come from the U.S. Department of Agriculture, although the site is operated by CyberSoft, a company that produces nutrition books and software packages.

The site also offers a weight-loss calculator, a calorie requirements calculator, charts of desirable weight and body fat, a directory of more than 1,300 food and supplement makers, toll-free telephone numbers for hundreds of food companies, a glossary of food and cooking terms, and a list of suggested food substitutions.

Vital Stats:

Access method:	WWW
To access:	http://www.nutribase.com
E-mail:	edp@nutribase.com

Nutrition Analysis Tool

The Nutrition Analysis Tool is a Web-based program that analyzes the nutrients in the foods you eat. The program can analyze your diet for water, protein, carbohydrates, phosphorus, sodium, vitamin A, riboflavin, vitamin C, monounsaturated fat, cholesterol, calories, fat, total dietary fiber, calcium, iron, potassium, thiamin, niacin, saturated fat, and polyunsaturated fat.

If you think you're deficient in a particular nutrient, the program also will provide suggestions about foods you should eat to balance your diet. The program was created by the Department of Food Science and Human Nutrition at the University of Illinois—Urbana/Champaign.

Vital Stats:

Access method:	WWW
To access:	http://spectre.ag.uiuc.edu/~food-lab/nat

rec.food.veg Newsgroups

These two newsgroups are aimed at vegetarians.

Vital Stats:

Access method:	Usenet newsgroup
To access:	news:rec.food.veg, news:rec.food.veg.cooking

---

sci.med.nutrition

This very active newsgroup about nutrition averages more than fifty messages daily.

Vital Stats:

Access method:	Usenet newsgroup
To access:	news:sci.med.nutrition

Tufts University Nutrition Navigator

This site provides links to more than 150 nutrition-related Internet sites. Each site has been reviewed and rated by nutritionists at the Tufts University School of Nutrition Science and Policy.

The site listings are provided in eight categories you can browse: educators, general nutrition, journalists, kids, health professionals, parents, special dietary needs, and women. There's some overlap among the categories. You also can search the entire site if you prefer.

Vital Stats:

Access method:	WWW
To access:	http://navigator.tufts.edu
E-mail:	jsmith1@emerald.tufts.edu

SPORTS MEDICINE

American Podiatric Medical Association

This site has a set of brochures about sports-related foot care. The brochures discuss topics such as aerobics, children and sports, cycling, running, tennis, and winter sports, among others. The site is operated by the American Podiatric Medical Association.

The site also has a series of general brochures about foot health issues. Some of the topics covered include aging, arthritis, athlete's foot, children's feet, diabetes, foot and ankle injuries, footwear, heel pain, nail problems, walking, and warts.

Vital Stats:

Access method: WWW
To access: http://www.apma.org
E-mail: askapma@apma.org

NISMAT

This site provides articles about therapeutic exercise programs, orthopedic exams, common heart abnormalities, cardiovascular screening of athletes, muscle physiology, oxygen consumption, cumulative trauma disorders in musicians, hamstring pulls, knee injuries in female athletes, protecting your back, shoulder range of motion exercises, tennis elbow, and immediate field care of musculoskeletal injuries, among other topics. The site is operated by the Nicholas Institute of Sports Medicine and Athletic Trauma (NISMAT) at Lenox Hill Hospital.

The site also has lectures given to orthopedic residents and fellows on such subjects as high-fat diets, exercise physiology, rotator cuff tears, and muscle injuries;

training tips for various sports, including skiing and running; and links to related Internet sites.

Vital Stats:

Access method: WWW
To access: http://www.nismat.org
E-mail: webmaster@nismat.org

The Physician and Sportsmedicine Online

This site offers articles from *The Physician and Sportsmedicine,* a monthly print journal. Some sample article titles include "Exercise for Mild Coronary Artery Disease," "Wrist Pain from Overuse," "Persistent Pain After Ankle Sprain," "Osteoporosis in Active Women," and "Don't Miss Gastrointestinal Disorders in Athletes." The site is operated by the McGraw-Hill Companies.

The site also has a directory of sports medicine clinics, contact information for dozens of sports medicine groups, medical news articles from the Olympics, and links to related Web sites.

Vital Stats:

Access method: WWW
To access: http://www.physsportsmed.com
E-mail: shawthor@mcgraw-hill.com

TRANSPLANTATION

Bone Marrow Transplant Resource Netmarks

This site provides no original information, but it has dozens of links to Internet documents and sites about blood and bone marrow transplantation. It's operated by the University of Oklahoma Health Sciences Center.

Vital Stats:

Access method: WWW
To access: http://www.uokhsc.edu/sections/hemaonco/bmtmark.htm
E-mail: hem-onc@uokhsc.edu

CenterSpan

CenterSpan provides links to dozens of Web sites, Usenet newsgroups, and mailing lists that offer information about transplantation. The site is a joint effort of the American Society of Transplant Physicians and the American Society of Transplant Surgeons.

Vital Stats:

Access method: WWW
To access: http://www.centerspan.org/desk/netres.htm
E-mail: webmaster@slackinc.com

SECONDWIND

The SECONDWIND mailing list allows lung transplant recipients, transplant candidates, and their families and friends to discuss respiratory diseases.

Vital Stats:

Access method: E-mail
To access: Send an e-mail message to listserv@home.ease.lsoft.com
Subject line:
Message: **subscribe SECONDWIND *firstname lastname***
E-mail: SECONDWIND-request@home.ease.lsoft.com

Surviving Transplantation

This site provides the full text of the book *Surviving Transplantation: A Personal Guide for Organ Transplant Patients, Their Families, Friends and Caregivers.* The book was written by Dr. John Craven and Susan Farrow, an occupational therapist.

The book has nine chapters: Getting Started, Living with Illness, Waiting for Transplantation, Recovering from Transplantation, Understanding Stress, Dealing with Stress, Working with Others, Knowing When to Ask for Help, and Transplantation and Personal Growth. The book also has a lengthy list of recommended books about transplantation.

Vital Stats:

Access method: WWW
To access: http://www.stjosephs.london.on.ca/SJHC/programs/
                   mental/survive
E-mail: jcraven@julian.uwo.ca

TransWeb

Both through original documents and links to other sites, TransWeb offers a wealth of information about organ transplantation. TransWeb is a nonprofit educational project that's largely operated by volunteers.

Among its highlights, TransWeb provides dozens of accounts of transplant patient experiences, answers to hundreds of questions submitted by users, and articles about transplant medications. It also has a calendar of events, news about athletic events for transplant recipients, answers to questions about organ and tissue donation, links to more than 100 Web sites about transplant topics, and much more.

Vital Stats:

Access method:	WWW
To access:	http://www.transweb.org
E-mail:	transweb@umich.edu

TRAVEL MEDICINE

CDC Travel Information

If you're planning a trip to a foreign country, the CDC Travel Information site is a must-see before you go. It has news about current disease outbreaks around the world, summaries from inspections of international cruise ships, and health recommendations for regions around the world. The site is operated by the federal Centers for Disease Control and Prevention (CDC).

One of the site's highlights is a book titled *Health Information for International Travel,* which has CDC recommendations for every country in the world, vaccination requirements for each country, and a large section of health hints for travelers.

The site also has schedules of recommended childhood immunization and booster shots, as well as articles about traveler's diarrhea, cholera, dengue fever, hepatitis A vaccine, precautions for HIV-infected travelers, malaria, rabies, and typhoid fever, among other topics.

Vital Stats:

Access method: WWW
To access: http://www.cdc.gov/travel
E-mail: ncid@cdc.gov

Medical College of Wisconsin International Travelers Clinic

This site has articles about what to pack in a travel medicine kit, traveling while pregnant, altitude sickness, motion sickness, and various diseases and immunizations. It also offers links to more than two dozen other Internet sites about travel health. The site is operated by the International Travelers Clinic at the Medical College of Wisconsin.

Vital Stats:

Access method:	WWW
To access:	http://www.intmed.mcw.edu/travel.html
E-mail:	barnas@mcw.edu

Travel Health Online

Travel Health Online offers profiles of health conditions for every country in the world. The site is operated by Shoreland Inc., which produces publications and software for health professionals who treat international travelers.

The site also has a directory of travel medicine clinics around the world, copies of many U.S. State Department publications about traveling abroad, and articles about preventive medications and vaccines, travel precautions, and various travel illnesses.

Vital Stats:

Access method:	WWW
To access:	http://www.tripprep.com
E-mail:	webmaster@shoreland.com

WOMEN'S HEALTH

Abortion Clinics OnLine

This site provides a directory of abortion clinics around the United States, and also has a few listings for clinics in Australia, Austria, Belgium, Canada, England, and Spain. Listings are available for private physician's offices, state-licensed abortion clinics, surgical centers, and hospital abortion services. Contact information is provided for each clinic, and there are links to Web sites operated by many clinics.

The site also provides articles about various aspects of abortion rights, links to dozens of articles about different birth control methods, and links to dozens of other Web sites about abortion and women's health.

Vital Stats:

Access method:	WWW
To access:	http://www.gynpages.com
E-mail:	feedback@gynpages.com

alt.infertility Newsgroups

The alt.infertility newsgroups are devoted to various aspects of the causes and treatment of infertility.

Vital Stats:

Access method:	Usenet newsgroups
To access:	news:alt.infertility, news:alt.infertility.alternatives, news:alt.infertility.pregnancy, news:alt.infertility.primary, news:alt.infertility.secondary, news:alt.infertility.surrogacy

alt.support.abortion

The newsgroup alt.support.abortion is aimed at women who have had or are considering having abortions, as well as their partners.

Vital Stats:

Access method: Usenet newsgroup
To access: news:alt.support.abortion

---

alt.support.breast-implant Newsgroups

The alt.support.breast-implant newsgroups are aimed at women who have breast implants. The basic newsgroup averages about a dozen messages a day, while the moderated group averages two messages daily.

Vital Stats:

Access method: Usenet newsgroups
To access: news:alt.support.breast-implant, news:alt.support.breast-implant.moderated

---

alt.support.breastfeeding

Women who are seeking information about breastfeeding are the primary audience for the newsgroup alt.support.breastfeeding.

Vital Stats:

Access method: Usenet newsgroup
To access: news:alt.support.breastfeeding

---

alt.support.endometriosis

This newsgroup is aimed at women who have endometriosis.

Vital Stats:

Access method: Usenet newsgroup
To access: news:alt.support.endometriosis

alt.support.menopause

Women going through menopause are the primary audience for this very active newsgroup, which averages several dozen messages daily.

Vital Stats:

Access method:	Usenet newsgroup
To access:	news:alt.support.menopause

BabyZone

The BabyZone offers little original information, but it has a nice selection of links to articles and Internet sites about infertility, adoption, preparing for pregnancy, pregnancy testing, prenatal testing, diet and exercise during pregnancy, the stages of pregnancy, maternity health, preparing for labor and delivery, childbirth classes, natural childbirth, baby care, and parenting, among other issues. Each listing is rated for quality and briefly annotated.

The site also has message boards about pregnancy, adoption, family planning and infertility, caring for babies, and single parenting.

Vital Stats:

Access method:	WWW
To access:	http://siteguider.com

Doctor's Guide to Menopause Information & Resources

This site has dozens of news articles about menopause and links to other menopause-oriented documents and sites. It's part of the Doctor's Guide to the Internet (p. 14), which is sponsored by P/S/L NuMedia.

Vital Stats:

Access method:	WWW
To access:	http://www.pslgroup.com/MENOPAUSE.HTM
E-mail:	webmaster@pslgroup.com

grief-choice

This mailing list provides support for women who have had an abortion. No one else can join, and the list owner's approval is required to subscribe. The list is sponsored by the GriefNet Web site (p. 271).

Vital Stats:

Access method:	E-mail
To access:	Send an e-mail message to majordomo@mailser.ic.net
Subject line:	
Message:	**subscribe grief-choice *e-mail address***
E-mail:	stephen@griefnet.org

Health Resource Directory

The Health Resource Directory provides links to dozens of documents and Internet sites about women's health issues. The links are divided by subject: breast cancer, endometriosis, hormone replacement therapy, hysterectomy, infertility, institutions, mammography, menopause, menstruation, obstetrics and gynecology, online women's magazines, organizations, osteoporosis, ovarian cancer, pregnancy, premenstrual syndrome, reproductive health, sexuality, and tubal ligation.

Vital Stats:

Access method:	WWW
To access:	http://www.stayhealthy.com/hrdfiles/hrd00009.html
E-mail:	win@stayhealthy.com

The Internet Sleuth—Women's Health

This database lets you search a half-dozen Internet sites about women's health using a single interface. You must search each site separately. The database is part of The Internet Sleuth search engine.

Vital Stats:

Access method:	WWW
To access:	http://www.isleuth.com/heal-wome.html
E-mail:	sleuth@isleuth.com

JAMA Contraception Information Center

This site offers articles about various birth control methods from the Planned Parenthood Federation of America and answers to frequently asked questions about contraception from Family Health International. It's produced by the *Journal of the American Medical Association*.

The site also has news stories about contraception from Reuters Health Information, articles from *JAMA* and other medical journals, clinical guidelines, contact information for support groups, and links to related Internet sites.

Vital Stats:

Access method:	WWW
To access:	http://www.ama-assn.org/special/contra
E-mail:	Contraception@ama-assn.org

---

misc.health.infertility

People dealing with fertility problems exchange information and support in this newsgroup.

Vital Stats:

Access method:	Usenet newsgroup
To access:	news:misc.health.infertility

---

misc.kids.breastfeeding

This active newsgroup averages several dozen messages daily about breastfeeding.

Vital Stats:

Access method:	Usenet newsgroup
To access:	news:misc.kids.breastfeeding

misc.kids.pregnancy

All aspects of pregnancy, ranging from planning pregnancies to childbirth, are discussed in this newsgroup. It averages more than 100 messages daily.

Vital Stats:

Access method:	Usenet newsgroup
To access:	news:misc.kids.pregnancy

Online Birth Center

Through original material and links to other sites, the Online Birth Center offers hundreds of articles. The articles cover such topics as midwifery, pregnancy, birthing, breastfeeding, infertility, childhood diseases, nutrition and pregnancy, high-risk situations and complications, alternative health resources, books, videotapes, and mailing lists and newsgroups, among others. The site is operated by a private individual.

Vital Stats:

Access method:	WWW
To access:	http://www.efn.org/~djz/birth/birthindex.html
E-mail:	djz@efn.org

---

sci.med.obgyn

Various aspects of obstetrics and gynecology are discussed in this newsgroup.

Vital Stats:

Access method:	Usenet newsgroup
To access:	news:sci.med.obgyn

---

soc.support.pregnancy.loss

People affected by a miscarriage share support and information in this newsgroup.

Vital Stats:

Access method:	Usenet newsgroup
To access:	news:soc.support.pregnancy.loss

Take Wellness to Heart

Take Wellness to Heart provides information for women about heart disease and stroke. The site, which is operated by the American Heart Association, has information about reducing your risk, post menopause hormone therapy, nutrition, physical activity, preventing a second heart attack or stroke, cholesterol screening, stroke support groups, and many other subjects.

It also offers questions to ask your doctor, a scientific statement from the American Heart Association about cardiovascular disease in women, lists of the warning signs and risk factors of heart disease and stroke, and the *Heart and Stroke A-Z Guide.*

Vital Stats:

Access method: WWW
To access: http://women.americanheart.org
E-mail: dstokes@amhrt.org

talk.abortion

Brace yourself if you read this newsgroup, which averages a whopping 250 messages daily on all facets of the abortion issue.

Vital Stats:

Access method: Usenet newsgroup
To access: news:talk.abortion

HEALTH CARE ISSUES

DEATH AND DYING

adult-parents

The adult-parents mailing list is aimed at adults who are dealing with the loss, chronic illness, or terminal illness of a parent. It's sponsored by the GriefNet Web site (p. 271).

Vital Stats:

Access method:	E-mail
To access:	Send an e-mail message to majordomo@mailserv.ic.net
Subject line:	
Message:	**subscribe adult-parents *e-mail address***
E-mail:	stephen@griefnet.org

adult-sibs

The adult-sibs mailing list is a support group for adults and older adolescents who have had a sibling die, whether recently or long ago. It's sponsored by the GriefNet Web site (p. 271).

Vital Stats:

Access method:	E-mail
To access:	Send an e-mail message to majordomo@mailserv.ic.net
Subject line:	
Message:	**subscribe adult-sibs *e-mail address***
E-mail:	stephen@griefnet.org

alt.support.grief

Participants in the alt.support.grief newsgroup provide comfort to each other.

Vital Stats:

Access method: Usenet newsgroup
To access: news:alt.support.grief

---

alt.support.grief.pet-loss

People grieving over the death of a pet are the primary audience for this newsgroup.

Vital Stats:

Access method: Usenet newsgroup
To access: news:alt.support.grief.pet-loss

FACING-AHEAD

The FACING-AHEAD mailing list is aimed at helping people face the death of a loved one.

Vital Stats:

Access method: E-mail
To access: Send an e-mail message to listserv@listserv.acor.org
Subject line:
Message: **subscribe FACING-AHEAD *firstname lastname***
E-mail: FACING-AHEAD-request@listserv.acor.org

---

grief-aids

Anyone dealing with HIV or AIDS—patients, loved ones, caregivers, and others—can subscribe to this mailing list. It's affiliated with the GriefNet Web site (p. 271).

Vital Stats:

Access method:	E-mail
To access:	Send an e-mail message to majordomo@mailserv.ic.net
Subject line:	
Message:	**subscribe grief-aids *e-mail address***
E-mail:	ataplow@bigfoot.com

grief-chat

Any topic related to death, dying, bereavement, or other major loss can be discussed on the grief-chat mailing list. It's affiliated with the GriefNet Web site (p. 271).

Vital Stats:

Access method:	E-mail
To access:	Send an e-mail message to majordomo@mailserv.ic.net
Subject line:	
Message:	**subscribe grief-chat *e-mail address***
E-mail:	stephen@griefnet.org

grief-coping

The grief-coping mailing list is a support group for anyone coping with a life-threatening illness—people who are ill, their loved ones, and caregivers. It's sponsored by the GriefNet Web site (p. 271).

Vital Stats:

Access method:	E-mail
To access:	Send an e-mail message to majordomo@mailserv.ic.net
Subject line:	
Message:	**subscribe grief-coping *e-mail address***
E-mail:	stephen@griefnet.org

grief-grands

The grief-grands mailing list is for grandparents who have had a grandchild die from any cause. It's affiliated with the GriefNet Web site (p. 271).

Vital Stats:

Access method:	E-mail
To access:	Send an e-mail message to majordomo@mailserv.ic.net
Subject line:	
Message:	**subscribe grief-grands *e-mail address***
E-mail:	stephen@griefnet.org

grief-men

The grief-men mailing list is aimed at men whose spouse or partner has died. It's affiliated with the GriefNet Web site (p. 271).

Vital Stats:

Access method:	E-mail
To access:	Send an e-mail message to majordomo@mailserv.ic.net
Subject line:	
Message:	**subscribe grief-men *e-mail address***
E-mail:	stephen@griefnet.org

grief-pets

People who have lost a pet or whose pet faces imminent death are the primary audience for this mailing list. It's sponsored by the GriefNet Web site (p. 271).

Vital Stats:

Access method:	E-mail
To access:	Send an e-mail message to majordomo@mailserv.ic.net
Subject line:	
Message:	**subscribe grief-pets *e-mail address***
E-mail:	stephen@griefnet.org

grief-violence

This mailing list is a support group for people who have lost a loved one due to violence. It's sponsored by the GriefNet Web site (below).

Vital Stats:

Access method: E-mail
To access: Send an e-mail message to majordomo@mailserv.ic.net
Subject line:
Message: **subscribe grief-violence *e-mail address***
E-mail: stephen@griefnet.org

grief-widowed *and* griefwidowed-movingon

These two mailing lists are aimed at anyone who has lost a partner or a spouse. They're affiliated with the GriefNet Web site (below). The lists are slightly different:

- grief-widowed is a general support group for people who have lost a partner or a spouse.
- griefwidowed-movingon is for those who have lost a partner or a spouse and have moved beyond the first stages of dealing with their loss.

Vital Stats:

Access method: E-mail
To access: Send an e-mail message to majordomo@mailserv.ic.net
Subject line:
Message: **subscribe *listname e-mail address***
E-mail: stephen@griefnet.org

GriefNet

GriefNet offers a small collection of resources about dying and bereavement. It's operated by Rivendell Resources, a nonprofit organization.

The site has articles about various aspects of grief and loss, information about mailing lists operated by GriefNet, descriptions of books about grief, and links to other Web sites that provide similar information.

Vital Stats:

Access method: WWW
To access: http://griefnet.org
European mirror: http://www.griefnet.demon.co.uk
E-mail: rivendel@ic.net

Grieving Parents Lists

The GriefNet Web site (p. 271) operates nine mailing lists that provide support for parents who have had a child die, whether recently or long ago. The general list is grieving-parents, which is for parents who had a child die at any age and from any cause. The other eight lists are spin-offs:

- griefparents-accidents is for parents of a child who died from any accidental cause.
- griefparents-adultchild is for parents whose child was an adult when death occurred.
- griefparents-neonate is for parents who have suffered a miscarriage, a stillbirth, or the death of a child soon after birth.
- griefparents-onlychild is for parents whose only child died.
- griefparents-suicide is for parents whose child committed suicide.
- grief-sids is for parents whose child died from Sudden Infant Death Syndrome (SIDS).
- griefparents-newbirth is for parents who are dealing with a pregnancy and birth of a child after having an earlier child die.
- griefparents-substances is for parents of a child whose death was related to substance abuse.

Vital Stats:

Access method: E-mail
To access: Send an e-mail message to majordomo@mailserv.ic.net
Subject line:
Message: **subscribe *listname e-mail address***
E-mail: stephen@griefnet.org

hospice

The hospice mailing list is aimed at hospice volunteers. On the list, they discuss helping patients, dealing with feelings that arise from hospice work, and related issues.

Vital Stats:

Access method:	E-mail
To access:	Send an e-mail message to listserv@whitman.edu
Subject line:	
Message:	**subscribe hospice *firstname lastname***

---

kids-to-kids

This mailing list is a support group for children who are coping with any major loss. It's affiliated with the GriefNet Web site (p. 271).

Vital Stats:

Access method:	E-mail
To access:	Send an e-mail message to majordomo@mailserv.ic.net
Subject line:	
Message:	**subscribe kids-to-kids *e-mail address***
E-mail:	stephen@griefnet.org

National Hospice Organization

This site, which is operated by a trade association for hospices, offers basic information about hospice care and statistics about hospice use in the United States. It also has a database you can search to find a local hospice, contact information for state hospice associations, a position paper on physician-assisted suicide, and links to lots of related Internet sites.

Vital Stats:

Access method:	WWW
To access:	http://www.nho.org
E-mail:	drsnho@cais.com

talk.euthanasia

Euthanasia and other end-of-life issues are discussed in this newsgroup.

Vital Stats:

Access method:	Usenet newsgroup
To access:	news:talk.euthanasia

Webster's Death, Dying & Grief Guide

This site provides hundreds of links to Web sites, Usenet newsgroups, and mailing lists devoted to death, dying, and grief. It's operated by a nurse.

The linked sites provide information about such topics as caregiving, depression, online memorials, hospice care, pet or animal loss, survivors of death, funerals, wills, death in the arts and literature, cemeteries, eulogies, and many other topics.

The Webster site also has an annotated list of books about death, dying, and grief.

Vital Stats:

Access method:	WWW
To access:	http://www.katsden.com/death/index.html
E-mail:	webster@katsden.com

ENVIRONMENTAL HEALTH

Agency for Toxic Substances and Disease Registry

If you're looking for information about hazardous substances and public health, the Agency for Toxic Substances and Disease Registry (ATSDR) site is the place to check. The agency is part of the Department of Health and Human Services.

The site's highlight is the HazDat database, which provides data about releases of hazardous substances from about 2,000 Superfund sites or spills and the effects of the substances on human health. The database provides information about site characteristics, contaminants found, maximum contaminant concentration levels, impact on population, community concerns, public health threat categorization, and physical hazards at the site, among other subjects.

There are several ways to search the database. Perhaps the easiest is to use the national map and click on the state you want. Doing so will produce a list of all contaminated sites in that state, and lead to further details about individual locations.

The site also has fact sheets about individual toxic chemicals, a guide to communicating health risk information to the public, congressional testimony by ATSDR staff, DOS software for researchers who are examining disease clusters, information about what levels of specific toxic substances pose a health risk, a list of the top twenty hazardous substances, a paper titled *Impact of Lead-Contaminated Soil on Public Health*, links to other Internet sites that provide information about toxic substances and health, and lots more.

Vital Stats:

Access method:	WWW
To access:	http://atsdr1.atsdr.cdc.gov:8080
E-mail:	lmp1@cdc.gov

arsenic

Members of the arsenic mailing list discuss the environmental and occupational health effects of arsenic exposure.

Vital Stats:

Access method:	E-mail
To access:	Send an e-mail message to listserv@uci.edu
Subject line:	
Message:	**subscribe ARSENIC *firstname lastname***
E-mail:	menzel@uci.edu

HealthE

Subscribers to the HealthE mailing list exchange information about potential environmental threats to physical, emotional, and psychological health and well-being.

Vital Stats:

Access method:	E-mail
To access:	Send an e-mail message to listserv@home.ease.lsoft.com
Subject line:	
Message:	**subscribe HealthE *firstname lastname***
E-mail:	HEALTHE-request@home.ease.lsoft.com

Human Radiation Experiments Information Management System (HREX)

This site provides searchable databases containing more than 250,000 pages of historical documents about human radiation experiments conducted during the cold war. The declassified documents originated with the Central Intelligence Agency and the departments of Defense, Energy, Health and Human Services, and Veterans Affairs. HREX is operated by the Energy Department.

Vital Stats:

Access method:	WWW
To access:	http://hrex.dis.anl.gov
E-mail:	hrex@dis.anl.gov

National Institute of Environmental Health Sciences

This site has a small collection of publications about environmental health. Some of the available titles include *Questions and Answers about Electric and Magnetic Fields Associated with the Use of Electric Power*, *Lead: The #1 Environmental Hazard to Many Children*, *Medicine and the Layman: Environment and Disease*, *Lead and Your Health*, and *With Respect to Life: Protecting Human Health and the Environment Through Laboratory Animal Research*. The institute is part of the National Institutes of Health.

Vital Stats:

Access method:	WWW
To access:	http://www.niehs.nih.gov
E-mail:	rozier@niehs.nih.gov

National Pesticide Telecommunications Network

This site has more than a dozen articles about toxicology issues such as bioaccumulation, carcinogenesis, toxic effects on skin, movement of pesticides in the environment, and pesticide regulation. It's a joint project of Oregon State University and the U.S. Environmental Protection Agency (EPA).

The site also offers contact information and links to Web sites operated by pesticide companies, contact information for state and regional poison control centers around the country, links to pesticide databases at other Internet sites, links to EPA documents about pesticides, and links to Web sites operated by state pesticide regulatory agencies.

Vital Stats:

Access method:	WWW
To access:	http://ace.ace.orst.edu/info/nptn
E-mail:	nptn@ace.orst.edu

National Safety Council

One of the best sections of this site is the Environmental Health Center, which has fact sheets about air pollution, alternatives to household chemicals, asbestos, biological contaminants, carbon monoxide, flood recovery, formaldehyde, hazardous and toxic chemicals, indoor air quality, lead poisoning, ozone, pesticides, radiation, radon, and sick building syndrome, among other subjects. The site is operated by the National Safety Council.

Two extensive handbooks are excellent resources for reporters (and anyone else interested in the topics). They are *Reporting on Climate Change: Understanding the Science* and *Covering the Coasts: A Reporter's Guide to Coastal and Marine Resources.*

Another highlight is a set of background papers about dozens of chemicals. The papers provide descriptions, chemical properties, health effects, economics, and regulations. Some of the chemicals described include acetone, arsenic, asbestos, benzene, cadmium, chlorine, cyanide, DDT, hydrochloric acid, lead, mercury, phosphoric acid, toluene, and vinyl chloride.

Vital Stats:

Access method:	WWW
To access:	http://www.nsc.org
E-mail:	webmaster@nsc.org

National Toxicology Program

The highlight of this site is a report listing all chemicals that are suspected or known to be carcinogens. The site also has extensive technical information about chemicals tested by the National Toxicology Program, *Federal Register* notices, a calendar of events, press releases, and abstracts of long-term carcinogenesis studies, short-term toxicity studies, immunotoxicity studies, reproductive toxicity studies, and teratology studies.

Vital Stats:

Access method:	WWW
To access:	http://ntp-server.niehs.nih.gov
E-mail:	Rowley@niehs.nih.gov

Office of Human Radiation Experiments

The Office of Human Radiation Experiments site offers extensive information about human radiation experiments conducted during the cold war. The office is part of the Energy Department.

The site has the full text of recently declassified documents, oral histories with researchers involved in human radiation experiments, historical photographs, an

Energy Department report that summarizes more than 400 human radiation experiments, descriptions of record sets about human radiation experiments located at various federal facilities, and links to other Internet sites that have information about the subject.

Vital Stats:

Access method:	WWW
To access:	http://www.ohre.doe.gov
E-mail:	ohre-support@dis.anl.gov

ETHICS AND FRAUD

BIOMED-L

Subscribers to the BIOMED-L mailing list discuss biomedical ethics. Some of the subjects discussed include the right to die, drug legalization, euthanasia, hospices, fetal cell transplant, patient autonomy, respirator withdrawal, and overtreatment of infants.

Vital Stats:

Access method:	E-mail
To access:	Send an e-mail message to listserv@listserv.nodak.edu
Subject line:	
Message:	**subscribe BIOMED-L *firstname lastname***
E-mail:	BIOMED-L-request@listserv.nodak.edu

Biomedical & Health Care Ethics Resources on WWW

This site provides links to dozens of health care ethics institutions and organizations, publications, and on-line forums for discussing bioethics. It's operated by the Centre for Applied Ethics at the University of British Columbia.

Vital Stats:

Access method:	WWW
To access:	http://www.ethics.ubc.ca/resources/biomed
E-mail:	chrismac@ethics.ubc.ca

The Center for BioEthics

The highlight of this site is its collection of materials about physician-assisted suicide, including the U.S. Supreme Court's 1997 decision on the subject, amicus briefs in the case, the text of various federal and state laws, and links to numerous related sites. The site is operated by the Center for BioEthics at the University of Pennsylvania.

Another nice feature is a collection of links to Web sites and Usenet newsgroups about such issues as abortion, AIDS, bioethics, cloning, genetics, insurance, law, and plagues, among other topics. The site also has articles about genetics issues, articles by center faculty on various bioethics topics, and a list of dozens of books about bioethics.

Vital Stats:

Access method:	WWW
To access:	http://www.med.upenn.edu/~bioethic
E-mail:	mcgee@mail.med.upenn.edu

Healthfraud

Subscribers to the Healthfraud mailing list discuss health frauds and quackery. It's a very active list, averaging forty posts per day. The list is cosponsored by the Georgia Council Against Health Fraud and Quackwatch, which also has a Web site (p. 283).

Vital Stats:

Access method:	E-mail
To access:	Send an e-mail message to healthfraud-subscribe@ssr.com
Subject line:	
Message:	
E-mail:	sbinfo@quackwatch.com

MacLean Center for Clinical Medical Ethics

The MacLean Center provides hundreds of links to Internet sites devoted to such topics as genetics, death and dying, brain death, alternative medicine, health care policy and reform, home care, suffering and mental health, and animal rights. The center is part of the University of Chicago.

Vital Stats:

Access method:	WWW
To access:	http://ccme-mac4.bsd.uchicago.edu/CCME.html
E-mail:	kerielam@midway.uchicago.edu

National Bioethics Advisory Commission Homepage

The highlight of this National Bioethics Advisory Commission (NBAC) site is a 125-page report the NBAC issued in June 1997 about human cloning. The NBAC, which was created by executive order in October 1995, makes recommendations to federal agencies on bioethical issues involving research with humans.

The site also has transcripts of meetings, press releases, a schedule of upcoming meetings, the NBAC charter, and a list of NBAC members.

Vital Stats:

Access method:	WWW
To access:	http://www.bioethics.gov

National Human Genome Research Institute

The National Human Genome Research Institute site has discussions of the ethical issues involved in human genetics research, news about genetic discoveries, background information about the Human Genome Project, grant information, fact sheets, press releases, and links to other Internet sites that offer genetic and genomic resources. The institute is part of the National Institutes of Health.

Vital Stats:

Access method:	WWW
To access:	http://www.nhgri.nih.gov
E-mail:	webmaster@nhgri.nih.gov

Quackwatch

Quackwatch is a wonderful source for information about health fraud and quackery. It offers dozens of articles about how to spot health quackery, common ploys used to defraud the public, signs of a "quacky" Web site, questionable products and therapies, questionable advertisements, individuals and organizations with dubious backgrounds, how to fight quackery, AIDS-related quackery and fraud, and many related topics.

Quackwatch is operated by Stephen Barrett, M.D., a retired psychiatrist who has written numerous books about health fraud. Quackwatch also cosponsors the Healthfraud mailing list (p. 281).

Vital Stats:

Access method:	WWW
To access:	http://www.quackwatch.com
E-mail:	sbinfo@quackwatch.com

UB Center for Clinical Ethics and Humanities in Health Care

This site has a superb collection of links to other Internet sites that are devoted to various bioethics issues. Some of the topics covered include physician-assisted suicide, hospital and palliative care, advance directives, medical record privacy, and genetics.

The site also provides links to many bioethics journal articles and documents. It's operated by the Center for Clinical Ethics and Humanities in Health Care at the University of Buffalo.

Vital Stats:

Access method:	WWW
To access:	http://wings.buffalo.edu/faculty/research/bioethics
E-mail:	jfreer@acsu.buffalo.edu

HEALTH CARE POLICY

HEALTHPOL

Subscribers to the HEALTHPOL mailing list discuss health care policy issues affecting the United States. The primary audience is health care professionals, although anyone can subscribe.

Vital Stats:

Access method:	E-mail
To access:	Send an e-mail message to listserv@home.ease.lsoft.com
Subject line:	
Message:	**subscribe HEALTHPOL _firstname lastname_**
E-mail:	moz@mich.com

HEALTHRE

Health care reform is discussed on the HEALTHRE mailing list.

Vital Stats:

Access method:	E-mail
To access:	Send an e-mail message to listserv@lsv.uky.edu
Subject line:	
Message:	**subscribe HEALTHRE _firstname lastname_**
E-mail:	HEALTHRE-request@lsv.uky.edu

LIST.HEALTHPLAN

Subscribers to LIST.HEALTHPLAN receive White House announcements about health care reform by e-mail. The list does not permit any discussion about the announcements. The list is operated by a private volunteer with assistance from the Institute for Global Communications. Although subscriptions are free, the moderator requests contributions to help cover his costs.

Vital Stats:

Access method:	E-mail
To access:	Send an e-mail message to SFreedkin@igc.apc.org
Subject line:	**subscribe LIST.HEALTHPLAN *your Internet address***
Message:	**add: *your Internet address (firstname lastname)***
E-mail (questions):	SFreedkin@igc.apc.org

Marijuana Policy Project

This site has dozens of articles about efforts to legalize the medicinal use of marijuana. The articles cover such topics as marijuana arrests, U.S. Supreme Court decisions, legislative actions, and moves by the Clinton administration. The site is operated by the Marijuana Policy Project (MPP), an advocacy organization.

The project also publishes the MPPupdates e-mail newsletter (below).

Vital Stats:

Access method:	WWW
To access:	http://www.mpp.org
E-mail:	mpp@mpp.org

MPPupdates

MPPupdates is a mailing list that provides periodic news updates and information about legislative efforts to legalize the medicinal use of marijuana. The list is operated by the Marijuana Policy Project (MPP), an advocacy organization that also operates a Web site (above).

Vital Stats:

Access method:	E-mail
To access:	Send an e-mail message to majordomo@igc.org
Subject line:	
Message:	**subscribe MPPupdates**
E-mail:	mpp@mpp.org

National Coalition on Health Care

The highlights of this site are reports about the rising number of uninsured workers, health care quality, and health care spending. It's operated by the National Coalition on Health Care, a nonpartisan coalition supported by foundations that seeks to secure health insurance for all and improve the quality of care.

The site also has the results of a poll about how Americans perceive the health care system and fact sheets on health care costs, health care coverage, health care for children, care for the elderly, and public health.

Vital Stats:

Access method:	WWW
To access:	http://www.nchc.org
E-mail:	info@nchc.org

National Rural Health Association

This site has a good collection of issue papers about health issues affecting rural America. The papers discuss such topics as HIV/AIDS in rural America, emergency medical services in rural and frontier areas, rural health clinics, the role of telemedicine in rural health care, and managed care in rural areas, among other topics. The site is operated by the National Rural Health Association, a nonprofit organization.

Other highlights include news from the association's governmental affairs office in Washington, information about rural health provisions in national legislation, a list of federal bills and regulations related to rural health, congressional testimony, links to Web sites operated by federal agencies involved in rural health care, and links to other Web sites about rural health.

Vital Stats:

Access method: WWW
To access: http://nrharural.org
E-mail: mail@nrharural.org

The OTA Legacy

The OTA Legacy offers reports about health care policy prepared by the congressional Office of Technology Assessment (OTA), which existed from 1972 until 1995. The site is operated by the Woodrow Wilson School of Public and International Affairs at Princeton University.

Some of the available titles include *Institutional Protocols for Decisions About Life-Sustaining Treatments*, *Adverse Reactions to HIV Vaccines: Medical, Ethical, and Legal Issues*, *The Effectiveness of AIDS Prevention Efforts*, *Losing a Million Minds: Confronting the Tragedy of Alzheimer's Disease and Other Dementias*, *Costs and Effectiveness of Prostate Cancer Screening in Elderly Men*, *Does Health Insurance Make a Difference?*, *Health Care in Rural America*, and *Hospital Financing in Seven Countries*.

Vital Stats:

Access method: WWW
To access: http://www.wws.princeton.edu:80/~ota
E-mail: ota@edith.princeton.edu

---

sci.med.cannabis

The medical use of marijuana is discussed in this newsgroup.

Vital Stats:

Access method: Usenet newsgroup
To access: news:sci.med.cannabis

talk.politics.medicine

Participants in this newsgroup discuss various ethical and political issues related to medicine.

Vital Stats:

Access method: Usenet newsgroup
To access: news:talk.politics.medicine

HEALTH INSURANCE

California Coalition for Ethical Mental Health Care

Various materials about managed mental health care are provided at this site. It's operated by the California Coalition for Ethical Mental Health Care, a consumer group that seeks to preserve the quality, integrity, and confidentiality of mental health care.

The site has a brochure titled *Myths of Managed Mental Health Care,* a position paper titled *Confidentiality of Patient Records and Managed Care: Legal and Ethical Issues,* proposed state legislation, legislative testimony, legislative updates, a newsletter, a huge bibliography of books and articles, and dozens of great links to related sites.

A warning: when you connect to this site, it starts playing part of the William Tell Overture. Why? Who knows—but it's kind of cool.

Vital Stats:

Access method:	WWW
To access:	http://pw2.netcom.com/~donmar/CCEMHC.html
E-mail:	RuthCliff@aol.com

Health Care Financing Administration

The Health Care Financing Administration (HCFA) site specializes in information about Medicare and Medicaid. It has numerous consumer publications, including *The Medicare Handbook, Guide to Health Insurance for People with Medicare, What Everyone Should Know About Skilled Nursing Facilities Under Medicare, Advanced*

Directives, Medicare Hospice Benefits, Guide to Choosing a Nursing Home, and
Medicare Managed Care.

The site also has a directory of local contacts for Medicare information, a list of
state and federal Medicaid contacts, a fact sheet about managed care in Medicare and
Medicaid, tips for avoiding Medicare fraud, extensive statistics on Medicare and
Medicaid, fact sheets about HCFA programs, speeches and congressional testimony
by HCFA officials, and an HCFA employee telephone directory.

Vital Stats:

Access method:	WWW
To access:	http://www.hcfa.gov
E-mail:	WebMaster@hcfa.gov

Managed Care

This site contains the full text of the magazine *Managed Care,* which is aimed at
physicians and HMO executives. The articles cover such topics as reimbursement
and compensation, contracting, forming networks and alliances, dealing with
Medicare and Medicaid, accreditation, and working with doctors and hospitals. The
site, which also offers daily news items about managed care, is operated by Stezzi
Communications.

Vital Stats:

Access method:	WWW
To access:	http://www.managedcaremag.com
E-mail:	webmaster@managedcaremag.com

MBHC

Subscribers to the MBHC (Managed Behavioral Health Care) mailing list discuss
various aspects of managed behavioral health care, including the impact of health
care reform in the United States and comparisons with other behavioral health care
systems around the world.

Vital Stats:

Access method:	E-mail
To access:	Send an e-mail message to listserv@maelstrom.stjohns.edu
Subject line:	
Message:	**subscribe mbhc *firstname lastname***
E-mail:	MBHC-OWNER@maelstrom.stjohns.edu

Medicare and You

Medicare and You offers the full text of numerous pamphlets about Medicare published by the federal Health Care Financing Administration. Some of the titles available include *Your Medicare Handbook, How to Help Stop Medicare from Being Ripped Off, Guide to Choosing a Nursing Home, Medicare Hospice Benefits, Advance Directives, Medicare and Home Health Care, Medicare Managed Care,* and *What Everyone Should Know About Skilled Nursing Facilities Under Medicare.* The site is operated by the Health Care Service Corporation, the Medicare contractor for the states of Illinois and Michigan.

The site also has answers to dozens of frequently asked questions about Medicare, fact sheets about various aspects of Medicare coverage, details about recent Medicare changes, and information about the role of Medicare as a secondary payer.

Vital Stats:

Access method:	WWW
To access:	http://www.medicareinfo.com

LEGAL ISSUES

Health Law

This site has news briefs from the *New York Law Journal,* columns about health law issues, and links to federal health statutes and state health codes. It's part of the Law Journal EXTRA! site, which is operated by The New York Law Publishing Co.

Vital Stats:

Access method:	WWW
To access:	http://www.ljx.com/practice/health/index.html
E-mail:	feedback@ljextra.com

The Health Law Resource

This site offers a superb collection of links to specific documents and Internet sites about health care law. The links are divided by topic: telemedicine, bioethics, privacy, Medicare and Medicaid, fraud and abuse, and mergers. The site is operated by a Pennsylvania attorney.

Vital Stats:

Access method:	WWW
To access:	http://www.netreach.net/~wmanning
E-mail:	wmanning@netreach.net

OCCUPATIONAL HEALTH AND SAFETY

MCS-IMMUNE-NEURO

This mailing list is devoted to discussions of chemical injuries and sensitivities. The list owner is director of electronic communications for the Chemical Injury Information Network, a nonprofit organization.

Vital Stats:

Access method: E-mail
To access: Send an e-mail message to listserv@maelstrom.stjohns.edu
Subject line:
Message: **subscribe MCS-IMMUNE-NEURO *firstname lastname***
E-mail: MCS-IMMUNE-NEURO-request@maelstrom.stjohns.edu

misc.health.injuries.rsi Newsgroups

Participants in these two newsgroups discuss repetitive strain injuries.

Vital Stats:

Access method: Usenet newsgroups
To access: news:misc.health.injuries.rsi.misc,
                       news:misc.health.injuries.rsi.moderated

misc.health.therapy.occupational

Various aspects of occupational therapy are discussed in this newsgroup.

Vital Stats:

Access method:	Usenet newsgroup
To access:	news:misc.health.therapy.occupational

Occ-Env-Med-L

Subscribers to the Occ-Env-Med-L mailing list exchange messages about occupational and environmental medicine. The primary audience for the list is clinicians, public health experts, and safety and hygiene professionals.

Vital Stats:

Access method:	E-mail
To access:	Send an e-mail message to majordomo@list.mc.duke.edu
Subject line:	
Message:	**subscribe occ-env-med-l**
E-mail:	green011@mc.duke.edu

Occupational Safety and Health Administration Home Page

The Occupational Safety and Health Administration (OSHA) Home Page has a wide range of information about protecting employees in the workplace. It offers dozens of safety-related fact sheets and numerous publications, including *Handbook for Small Business, Consultation Services for the Employer, Employee Workplace Rights, Employer Rights & Responsibilities, Federal Employer Rights and Responsibilities Following an OSHA Inspection,* and *Guidelines for Workplace Violence Prevention Programs for Night Retail Establishments.* Another large collection of OSHA materials is available from the OSHA Computerized Information System (p. 295).

The home page also has an OSHA report titled *The New OSHA—Reinventing Worker Safety and Health,* a directory of OSHA offices around the country, press releases, speeches and congressional testimony by OSHA officials, and the full text of the Occupational Safety and Health Act of 1970.

In addition, it has lists of free publications available from OSHA, a list of states that conduct their own occupational safety and health inspections under plans approved by OSHA, a searchable database called "Most Frequently Violated Standards" that lets you determine the most frequently violated OSHA standards for a particular SIC code, and links to other Internet sites that offer safety and health information.

Vital Stats:

Access method:	WWW
To access:	http://www.osha.gov
E-mail:	webmaster@www.osha.gov

OSHA Computerized Information System (OCIS)

The OSHA Computerized Information System (OCIS) has a huge collection of technical documents related to worker health and safety. The site complements the Occupational Safety and Health Administration (OSHA) Home Page (p. 294).

OCIS offers the full text of OSHA regulations and interpretations of the regulations, OSHA notices published in the *Federal Register,* OSHA directives, and the full text of OSHA's *Field Inspection Reference Manual.*

The site also has a searchable database of OSHA fact sheets, the full text of Corporate Wide Settlement Agreements (CWSA) between OSHA and corporations, extensive information about ergonomics, numerous publications about worker safety and health in nursing homes, data about the most frequently violated OSHA standards in construction, congressional testimony and speeches by OSHA officials, press releases, and lots more.

Vital Stats:

Access method:	WWW
To access:	http://www.osha-slc.gov
E-mail:	webmaster@osha-slc.gov

PCHEALTH

Subscribers to the PCHEALTH mailing list discuss health problems caused by computer use. Eyestrain, headaches, and carpal tunnel syndrome are just some of the subjects discussed. The list is moderated.

Vital Stats:

Access method:	E-mail
To access:	Send an e-mail message to listserv@listserv.aol.com
Subject line:	
Message:	**subscribe PCHEALTH *firstname lastname***
E-mail:	PCHEALTH-request@listserv.aol.com

RSI-EAST

Subscribers to the RSI-EAST mailing list discuss repetitive strain injuries. The primary audience is people who live on the East Coast of the United States. RSI-EAST complements the SOREHAND mailing list (p. 297), which is aimed at people on the West Coast.

Vital Stats:

Access method:	E-mail
To access:	Send an e-mail message to listserv@maelstrom.stjohns.edu
Subject line:	
Message:	**subscribe RSI-EAST *firstname lastname***
E-mail:	RSI-EAST-request@maelstrom.stjohns.edu

---

sci.med.occupational

Occupational therapy and repetitive stress injuries are discussed in this newsgroup.

Vital Stats:

Access method:	Usenet newsgroup
To access:	news:sci.med.occupational

SOREHAND

Carpal tunnel syndrome, tendonitis, and related hand and wrist injuries are the main focus of the SOREHAND mailing list. It's primarily aimed at people who live on the West Coast of the United States. SOREHAND complements the RSI-EAST mailing list (p. 296), which is aimed at people on the East Coast.

Vital Stats:

Access method: E-mail
To access: Send an e-mail message to listserv@itssrv1.ucsf.edu
Subject line:
Message: **subscribe SOREHAND *firstname lastname***
E-mail: SOREHAND-request@itssrv1.ucsf.edu

Typing Injury FAQ

Lots of information about avoiding and dealing with repetitive strain injuries (RSI) is available at this site. It's operated by the Cumulative Trauma Disorder Resource Network, a group of people and organizations interested in repetitive strain injury.

The site offers original articles on everything from alternative keyboards to healing from RSI, a huge listing of products to help computer users and others avoid RSI, and lots of links to other Web sites, mailing lists, and newsgroups about RSI.

Vital Stats:

Access method: WWW
To access: http://www.tifaq.com
E-mail: wcbmaster@tifaq.com

SMOKING

Action on Smoking and Health

This site has breaking news about smoking, previously secret tobacco company documents, and extensive information about the proposed tobacco deal, including the full text of the agreement. It's operated by Action on Smoking and Health, an advocacy organization.

The site also has court decisions in various tobacco suits, the full text of Food and Drug Administration rules regulating smoking, links to other Web sites about smoking, press releases, and articles about nicotine addiction, health hazards from smoking, quitting smoking, workplace smoking, tobacco advertising, tobacco taxes, and other topics.

All of the site's documents are available in English, and some are also provided in French, German, and Spanish.

Vital Stats:
Access method: WWW
To access: http://ash.org

alt.recovery.nicotine

People who are attempting to recover from nicotine addictions are the primary audience for the newsgroup alt.recovery.nicotine.

Vital Stats:

Access method:	Usenet newsgroup
To access:	news:alt.recovery.nicotine

---

alt.smokers

Flame wars are common in the newsgroup alt.smokers, where passionate pro- and antismoking forces do battle.

Vital Stats:

Access method:	Usenet newsgroup
To access:	news:alt.smokers

---

alt.support.non-smokers Newsgroups

These two newsgroups focus on the dangers of second-hand smoke.

Vital Stats:

Access method:	Usenet newsgroups
To access:	news:alt.support.non-smokers, news:alt.support.non-smokers.moderated

---

alt.support.stop-smoking

If you're trying to stop smoking, this newsgroup is a good place to find support from others who are trying to do likewise. The group is extremely active—frequently more than 100 messages are posted in a single day.

Vital Stats:

Access method:	Usenet newsgroup
To access:	news:alt.support.stop-smoking

American Lung Association

This site has dozens of articles about smoking and tobacco control, asthma, asthma and children, lung health in minority communities, lung disease and related diseases, and environmental health. The site is operated by the American Lung Association (ALA), a nonprofit organization.

The site also has fact sheets about various lung diseases, information about how to subscribe to free weekly newsletters about asthma and lung disease, legislative updates, medical news, a database that lists ALA offices around the country, and press releases.

Vital Stats:

Access method:	WWW
To access:	http://www.lungusa.org

Campaign for Tobacco-Free Kids

This site has the full text of the proposed settlement between the tobacco industry and state attorneys general, statements from various organizations responding to the proposed settlement, and a comparison of various initiatives to control tobacco. The site is operated by the National Center for Tobacco-Free Kids, an advocacy organization.

One of the site's highlights is a collection of fact sheets about tobacco marketing and children, tobacco use among youth, tobacco use and ethnicity, and the proposed Food and Drug Administration tobacco rule, among other subjects.

The site also offers summaries of major tobacco legislation introduced in state legislatures, a calendar of anti-tobacco events around the country, press releases, and an excellent collection of annotated links to tobacco-related sites for adults and kids.

Vital Stats:

Access method:	WWW
To access:	http://www.tobaccofreekids.org
E-mail:	info@tobaccofreekids.org

CDC's Tobacco Information and Prevention Source (TIPS)

This site has articles about nicotine dependence, the prevalence of smoking, advertising, smoking cessation, economics, health consequences, international issues, legal and policy issues, secondhand smoke, smokeless tobacco, tobacco production, and youth, among other subjects. It's operated by the federal Centers for Disease Control and Prevention.

One of the highlights is a database containing bibliographic information and abstracts of journal articles, books, reports, government documents, legal documents, editorials, and other items about smoking and health. The database lists more than 56,000 items. A separate list has citations for tobacco-related articles published within the last four weeks.

The site also has guides to quitting smoking, a guide for employers on creating a smoke-free workplace, a timeline of significant developments related to smoking and health between 1964 and 1996, descriptions of actions taken by the federal government to regulate tobacco, the executive summary of a 1994 report by the Surgeon General titled *Preventing Tobacco Use Among Young People,* and quizzes, posters, and facts for children and teens.

Vital Stats:

Access method:	WWW
To access:	http://www.cdc.gov/tobacco
E-mail:	cdcinfo@cdc.gov

EXSMKR-L

Former smokers provide support and information to each other on the EXSMKR-L mailing list.

Vital Stats:

Access method:	E-mail
To access:	Send an e-mail message to listserv@lists.psu.edu
Subject line:	
Message:	**subscribe EXSMKR-L *firstname lastname***
E-mail:	EXSMKR-L-request@lists.psu.edu

NicNet

NicNet provides little original information, but has an excellent set of links to dozens of Internet sites about smoking and tobacco. The links provide information about smoking prevention, smoking cessation, policy, kids, environmental tobacco smoke, cigar smoking, tobacco news, and tobacco research, among other subjects. NicNet is operated by the Arizona Program for Nicotine and Tobacco Research at the University of Arizona.

Vital Stats:

Access method:	WWW
To access:	http://tobacco.arizona.edu
E-mail:	jshober@ccit.arizona.edu

The State Tobacco Information Center

The State Tobacco Information Center offers a huge collection of documents arising from suits by state attorneys general around the country against tobacco companies. The site is operated by the Tobacco Control Resource Center at Northeastern University.

The documents available include tobacco industry papers, documents filed by state attorneys general, motions, judicial orders, opinions, and agreements, among others. The site also has links to the latest news articles about tobacco lawsuits and links to related Web sites.

Vital Stats:

Access method:	WWW
To access:	http://www.stic.neu.edu
E-mail:	tobacco@bigfoot.com

The Tobacco Resolution

Thousands of pages of previously secret tobacco industry documents are available on this site. The documents were made available as part of a lawsuit filed by the Minnesota attorney general against the tobacco companies, which operate the site.

The documents include scientific and marketing research reports, memoranda, executive correspondence, handwritten notes, and other materials. The documents are grouped by company.

The site also has testimony by tobacco industry officials before congressional committees, press releases from tobacco companies, the text of state settlement agreements, and the proposed national agreement reached by the U.S. tobacco industry, state attorneys general, and other parties in June 1997.

Vital Stats:

Access method:	WWW
To access:	http://www.tobaccoresolution.com

TOBACTALK

Subscribers to the TOBACTALK mailing list discuss various tobacco and smoking issues.

Vital Stats:

Access method:	E-mail
To access:	Send an e-mail message to listserv@listserv.arizona.edu
Subject line:	
Message:	**subscribe TOBACTALK *firstname lastname***
E-mail:	TOBACTALK-request@listserv.arizona.edu

GLOSSARY

ASCII   A plain text format that includes no coding.

Baud   A rate that indicates how fast a modem can transfer information. The higher the number, the faster the transfer.

Capture feature   A feature in most communications software programs that allows you to "capture" in a text file the information that's scrolling on your screen from an Internet site. After logging off the site, you can review the file using your word processing program.

Communications software   A software program that allows your computer to "talk" with other computers.

Compressed file   A file that has been made smaller than its original size. Files are compressed so they download more quickly and take up less space. To use them, you must decompress them back to their original size after downloading them. Usually, this requires using a decompression program. However, some files are "self-executing," meaning you don't need a special program to decompress them. These files have an EXE extension on their names. For example, a self-executing file might be called **BBSGUIDE.EXE.** Self-executing files cannot be used on most Macintosh computers.

Decompressed file   *See* Compressed file.

Directory   An Internet site that has a comprehensive set of links to other Internet sites about one or more topics.

Download   To copy a file from a remote computer to your computer.

E-mail   Electronic messages written using a computer and sent to another person's computer. E-mail is basically private, although it can be intercepted as it travels across the Internet.

Emulate   A setting in your communications software that makes your computer act like it's another type of computer. When using the Internet, it's common to make your computer emulate a VT100 terminal.

Extension   A three-letter code at the end of a file name that usually indicates what program was used to create the file. The extension is separated from the rest of the file name by a period. For example, on a file called **BBSGUIDE.W51**, the extension W51 indicates that the file was created using WordPerfect 5.1. Sometimes, the file extension indicates which program was used to compress the file. For example, a file called **BBSGUIDE.ZIP** was compressed using the PKZIP compression program.

FAQ   A list of frequently asked questions, along with answers.

File   A document, graphic image, sound, or computer program. You can download copies of files from Internet sites to your computer.

File transfer protocol (FTP)   An Internet protocol used to transfer copies of files from one computer to another. Most publicly accessible FTP sites allow you to access them using "anonymous FTP." To use anonymous FTP, type **anonymous** when asked for a login and type your e-mail address when asked for a password. This procedure allows you to access and download selected files on the computer without being a registered user of the machine.

Freeware   A software program that you can use free of charge. Some Internet sites have freeware programs that you can download.

FTP   *See* File transfer protocol.

Garbage   Nonsensical characters that appear on your computer screen when you connect to an Internet site. They're commonly caused by noise on the telephone line or incorrect settings in your communications software.

Gateway   An Internet connection that allows you to move from one computer system to another. Many health-related Internet sites have gateways to related Internet sites.

GIF   *See* Graphics interchange format.

Gopher   An Internet program that organizes files into hierarchical menus.

Graphics interchange format (GIF)   A popular format for compressing and storing graphic files such as photographs. You need a viewer program to decompress and open the files.

Home page   A site on the World Wide Web, which is part of the Internet.

Internet   A vast international network of computer networks.

Listserv   *See* Mailing list.

Login   A word or words you must type to access some Internet sites after connecting to them.

Mail server   A computer that responds to e-mail requests for files. If you send a properly formatted e-mail message to a mail server, it will send back the file you requested.

Mailing list   Regular postings of topical e-mail messages to which you can subscribe. Some mailing lists allow discussion, and any message sent to the list goes to every subscriber. Others are one-way only, and are used to distribute press releases or other documents.

Meta directory   An Internet site that has links to directories about particular topics. The directories provide links to specific sites about the topic.

Mirror site   A duplicate version of a World Wide Web site located on a second computer. Mirrors are created for popular sites to lessen the load on them.

Modem   A piece of hardware that transforms data into electronic signals that computers can exchange over ordinary telephone lines.

Newsgroup   *See* Usenet newsgroups.

Password   A code used to access some Internet sites. At most publicly accessible FTP sites, **anonymous** is the password.

Path   The route you follow at an Internet site to reach a piece of information. The path can take you through layers of directories before you reach the file you want.

PDF file   A file in Portable Document Format. These files can only be read using Adobe Acrobat Reader software, which is available for free at http://www.adobe.com/acrobat.

Prompt   A message from the Internet site asking what you want to do next. Some prompts present a list of options from which you can choose.

Protocol   The "rules" two computers must follow to exchange messages or files. On the Internet, two of the more common protocols are file transfer protocol (FTP) and Telnet.

Server   A computer on the Internet that has files that are available to other computers. Any time you access an Internet site, you're connecting to a server.

Shareware   A computer program you can try for free. If you decide to keep it, you must send the shareware fee to the program's author. Some health-related Internet sites have shareware programs that you can download.

Telnet   An Internet protocol that allows you to connect to another computer and use it as if it were sitting on your desk. For example, you can use Telnet to access electronic card catalogs at some medical libraries.

Uniform resource locator   An Internet address for a site or file.

Upload   To copy a file from your computer to another computer.

URL   *See* Uniform resource locator.

Usenet newsgroups   Thousands of discussion groups where users can exchange messages about specific topics.

User   A person who uses the Internet.

Wildcard   A capability that allows you to search for a file using only a partial file name. You can type part of the file name and a wildcard symbol such as *, and the computer will search for all files containing the partial name.

World Wide Web (WWW)   A hypertext-based interface to the Internet. Hypertext files have links to other, related files or Internet sites embedded within them. To access the related file or site, you click on the link.

WWW   *See* World Wide Web.

Zipped   *See* Compressed file.

INDEX

infections and complications, 67, 70, 72
International Association of Physicians in AIDS Care, 70
Internet Sleuth—AIDS, 70
JAMA HIV/AIDS Information Center, 71
mental health issues, 67
minority issues, 70
misc.health.aids, 71
National AIDS Information Clearinghouse, 29
National AIDS Treatment Advocacy Project, 71
National Commission on AIDS, 72
National Institute of Allergy and Infectious Diseases (NIAID), 72
and nursing, 72
nutrition and diet, 67, 70, 246
organizations, 67, 68, 69, 71
patents, 72–73
patient support, 69, 70, 71
pediatrics, 70, 228
physician guidelines, 71
political issues, 66
prevention, 63, 64, 67, 68, 287
protease inhibitors, 70, 71
publications, 68, 70
quackery, 283
in rural areas, 286
in schools, 225
sci.med.aids, 64, 72
and travel, 256
treatment, 34, 63, 67, 68, 70
USPTO Patent Databases, 72–73
vaccines, 70, 72, 287
and women's health, 70
www.aidsnyc.org, 73
Alcohol and alcohol abuse, 26, 29, 34, 52, 192, 247
and aging, 215
Al-Anon, 212, 217
Alateen, 212
Alcohol Alerts, 215
Alcohol and Alcoholism, 41
Alcoholics Anonymous, 212, 216
alt.recovery.aa, 212
alt.recovery.adult-children, 213
and bone disorders, 87
drunk driving, 214–215
fetal alcohol syndrome, 141, 229
National Institute on Alcohol Abuse and Alcoholism, 215
Online AA Recovery Resources, 216
pregnancy and drinking, 215
Allergies, 14, 53, 55, 58, 74–77
ALLERGY, 74
Allergy Basics Center, 74–75
alt.med.allergy, 75
alt.support.food-allergies, 75

American Academy of Allergy, Asthma & Immunology, 75–76
CEL-KIDS, 76
CELIAC, 76
in children, 74, 76, 231
Doctor's Guide to Allergies, 77
food allergies, 74, 75, 246
hay fever, 74
latex and rubber allergies, 74, 77
nasal allergies, 29
National Institute of Allergy and Infectious Diseases (NIAID), 72
skin allergies, 74
Skin & Allergy News, 33
ALS (amyotrophic lateral sclerosis), 85–86
alt.abuse.recovery, 197
alt.health, 25
alt.health.cfids-action, 119
alt.health.fasting, 245
alt.infertility, 258
alt.med, 25
alt.med.allergy, 75
alt.med.cfs, 119
alt.med.cfs.open, 120
alt.psychology.help, 186
alt.recovery, 197
alt.recovery.aa, 212
alt.recovery.addiction.sexual, 197
alt.recovery.adult-children, 197
alt.recovery.codependency, 198
alt.recovery.compulsive-eat, 184
alt.recovery.na, 213
alt.recovery.nicotine, 298–299
alt.recovery.panic-anxiety.self-help, 174
alt.sexual.abuse.recovery, 198
alt.smokers, 299
alt.society.mental-health, 186
alt.suicide.holiday, 200
alt.support, 186
alt.support.abortion, 259
alt.support.anxiety-panic, 174
alt.support.arthritis, 78
alt.support.asthma, 81
alt.support.ataxia, 84
alt.support.attn-deficit, 137–138
alt.support.breast-implant, 259
alt.support.breastfeeding, 259
alt.support.cancer, 98
alt.support.cancer.prostate, 115
alt.support.cancer.testicular, 118
alt.support.cerebral-palsy, 89
alt.support.chronic-pain, 123
alt.support.crohns-colitis, 133
alt.support.depression, 177
alt.support.depression.manic, 177
alt.support.depression.medication, 177

American Diabetes Association, 126
American Dietetic Association, 246
American Foundation for the Blind, 139
American Health Assistance Foundation, 173
American Heart Association, 44, 157–158
American Heart Journal, 33
American Institute for Cancer Research Online, 98–99
American Journal of Epidemiology, 46
American Journal of Preventive Medicine, 41
American Lung Association, 300
American Medical Association (AMA), 22–23, 25, 40, 228
American Podiatric Medical Association, 251
American Psychiatric Association, 44, 187
American Psychological Association, 187
American Society of Cataract & Refractive Surgery, 149
American Society of Clinical Oncology, 99
American Speech-Language-Hearing Association, 147
Americans with Disabilities Act (ADA), 139, 141–145
Amputations, 141
Amyotrophic lateral sclerosis, 85–86
Anabolic steroids, 215
Anatomy, 56
Anemia, aplastic, 108
Animal research, 277, 281
Anorexia, 184. *See also* Eating disorders
Antibiotic resistance, 43
Anti-Cancer Drug Design, 41
Anxiety and panic disorders, 14, 27, 35, 38, 174–175, 189–190, 192. *See also* Mental Health
    alt.recovery.panic-anxiety.self-help, 174
    alt.support.anxiety-panic, 174
    Anxiety-Panic internet resource, the (tAPir), 174
    in children, 175, 176
    Doctor's Guide to Anxiety Disorders, 175
    National Anxiety Foundation, 175
    Panic & Anxiety Disorders, 175
    phobias, 174, 175, 187, 190, 233
APA Online (American Psychiatric Association), 187
Aplastic anemia, 108
Archives of Dermatology, 40
Archives of Family Medicine, 40
Archives of General Psychiatry, 40, 46
Archives of Internal Medicine, 40, 46
Archives of Neurology, 40
Archives of Ophthalmology, 40, 46
Archives of Otolaryngology-Head & Neck Surgery, 40
Archives of Pediatrics & Adolescent Medicine, 40
Archives of Psychiatry, 41
Archives of Surgery, 40
Archives of Women's Health, 41
Archives Specialty Journals, 40

Aromatherapy, 223
Arsenic, 276, 278
Arthritis, 25, 33, 51, 53, 55, 78–80, 141, 144
    alt.support.arthritis, 78
    American College of Rheumatology, 78
    Arthritis & Rheumatism, 78
    Arthritis Care and Research, 78
    Arthritis Foundation, 79
    in children, 79
    Doctor's Guide to Arthritis, 79
    and exercise, 80
    misc.health.arthritis, 79
    National Institute of Arthritis and Musculoskeletal and Skin Diseases, 80
    rheumatology, 17, 78
Asbestos, 225, 277, 278
ASCO Online (American Society of Clinical Oncology), 99
Asthma, 25, 27, 29, 38, 44, 72, 74, 81–82
    alt.support.asthma, 81
    American Academy of Allergy, Asthma & Immunology, 75–76
    in children, 39, 228, 300
    Doctor's Guide to Asthma, 81
    drugs, 82
    JAMA Asthma Information Center, 82
    organizations, 82
    prevention, 82
Ataxia, 84
Athlete's foot, 207
Attention deficit disorder, 137–138, 202
Attention deficit hyperactivity disorder, 27, 189
Attention disorder, 226, 228
Autism, 202

BabyZone, 260
Back pain, 24, 38, 39, 78
    in children, 39
    chiropractic, 223
Balance disorders, 27
Barrett, Stephen, 283
BCN-FLASH, 92
Bedwetting, 176, 228
Behavioral risk factors, 34, 35, 49, 51
Behavioral sciences, 34
Benign prostatic hyperplasia (BPH). *See* Prostate disorders
beyond-hearing, 147
BiblioSleep, 210
Biliary disorders, 58
Biochemical markers, of bone metabolism, 87
Bioethics. *See* Ethics and fraud
Biofeedback, 223
BIOMED-L, 280
Biomedical & Health Care Ethics Resources on WWW, 280

Biomedical ethics. *See* Ethics and fraud
Biomedical sciences, 13, 50
BioSites, 13
Biotechnology, 45, 246
Bipolar illness, 180
Birth control, 27, 33, 55, 258, 261–262
Birth defects, 26, 226
Birth rate, 60
bit.listserv.medlib-l, 48
Blindness. *See* Eye care
Blood disorders, 53, 58, 83, 135. *See also* Leukemia
and myeloma
    alt.support.hemophilia, 83
    alt.support.scleroderma, 83
    National Heart, Lung, and Blood Institute, 161
Blood pressure, 14, 25, 27, 55, 221
Blood supply, 30
Blood vessel disease. *See* Heart and cardiovascular
system
BMT-TALK, 105
The Body: A Multimedia AIDS and HIV
Information Resource, 67
Body mind medicine, 223
Bone and muscle disorders, 51, 53, 58, 84–88, 246.
See also Osteoporosis
    and alcohol abuse, 87
    alt.support.ataxia, 84
    alt.support.dystonia, 84
    alt.support.jaw-disorders, 85
    alt.support.marfan, 85
    alt.support.spina-bifida, 85
    biochemical markers of bone metabolism, 87
    bone density and mass, 87
    bone loss and depression, 87
    broken bones, in children, 228
    Doctor's Guide to ALS (Lou Gehrig's Disease),
    85–86
    estrogen and bone loss, 87
    female athletes and bone health, 87
    hip replacement, 80
    muscle tone, 84
    National Institute of Arthritis and
    Musculoskeletal and Skin Diseases, 80
    orthopedic conditions in children, 228
    orthopedic surgery, 86
    Osteoporosis and Related Bone Diseases National
    Resource Center, 87–88
    sci.med.diseases.als, 86
    sci.med.orthopedics, 86
    tendonitis, 297
    X-Linked Myotubular Myopathy, 140
Bone marrow transplants, 93, 100, 105, 107, 253
    Bone Marrow Transplant Resource Netmarks,
    253
Borderline personality disorder, 195
BORDERPD, 195

Boston Children's Hospital, 38
BPH (benign prostatic hyperplasia). *See* Prostate
disorders
Brain, 46
Brain diseases and injuries, 39, 53, 89–91, 141, 189
    alt.support.cerebral-palsy, 89
    American Brain Tumor Association, 89
    brain death, 281
    brain tumors, 89, 90, 202
    BRAINTMR, 90
    cerebral palsy, 89, 227
    DISCUSS-TBI, 90
    National Parkinson Foundation, 90
    PARKINSN, 91
    Parkinson's disease, 90, 91, 202
    TBI-FAM, 91
    TBI-SPRT, 91
    traumatic brain injuries, 90, 91
Breast cancer, 14, 35–36, 38, 44, 55, 92–96
    advocacy, 93, 95, 96
    BCN-FLASH, 92
    bone marrow transplants, 93, 100, 105, 107, 253
    BREAST-CANCER, 92–93
    Breast Cancer Information Clearinghouse, 93
    breast reconstruction, 93
    clinical trials, 95, 96
    Community Breast Health Project, 93–94
    detection and diagnosis, 35, 49, 92, 93, 95, 99
    and diet, 93
    Doctor's Guide to Breast Cancer, 94
    frequently asked questions, 96
    genetic testing, 95, 99
    insurance and legal issues, 93, 95
    mammography, 24, 60, 95, 261
    in men, 94
    and minorities, 37
    National Action Plan on Breast Cancer, 95
    National Alliance of Breast Cancer Organizations,
    95
    National Breast Cancer Coalition, 96
    patient rights, 93
    prevention, 92, 93
    publications, 93, 95, 96
    risk factors, 93, 95
    self-examinations, 96
    support groups, 95, 96
    survivorship, 93, 96
    Tamoxifen (drug), 93
    treatment, 92, 93, 99
    tumor-related prognostic factors, 99
    warning signs, 38
    Y-ME National Breast Cancer Organization, 96
    and young women, 95
Breast implants, 259
Breastfeeding, 226, 231, 259, 262, 263
British Medical Journal, 40–41, 46

CDC's Tobacco Information and Prevention Source (TIPS), 301
CEL-KIDS, 76
Celiac disease, 76
Center for BioEthics, The, 281
Center for Food Safety & Applied Nutrition, 246–247
Center for Science in the Public Interest, 247
Centers for Disease Control and Prevention (CDC), 26, 43, 51, 67–68, 126–127, 256, 301
CenterSpan, 253
CenterWatch Clinical Trials Listing Service, 235
Central nervous system, 39
Cerebral palsy, 89, 227
Cervical cancer, 49, 55
CFIDS. *See* Chronic fatigue syndrome
CFS. *See* Chronic fatigue syndrome
Chemical injuries and sensitivities, 121, 293
Chemicals, 34, 278
Chicken pox, 29
Child abuse and neglect, 39, 187, 225, 231
Childbearing. *See* Pregnancy and childbirth
children with DIABETES, 127
Children's health, 31, 34, 52, 225–233. *See also*
  Adolescent health; Pediatrics; Pregnancy and
  childbirth; Sudden Infant Death Syndrome
  (SIDS)
    AIDS, 70, 228
    allergies, 74, 76, 231
    American Academy of Child & Adolescent
      Psychiatry, 176
    arthritis, 79
    asthma, 39, 228, 300
    back pain, 39
    bedwetting, 176, 228
    birth defects, 26, 141, 226, 229
    broken bones, 228
    cancer, 104
    CaringKids, 226
    CaringParents, 226
    celiac disease, 76
    cerebral palsy, 89, 227
    childhood diseases, 29, 263
    ChildSecure, 226–227
    chronic fatigue syndrome, 120, 121
    colds and flu, 226
    colic, 226
    CPPARENT, 227
    CSHCN-L, 227
    and death, 228, 273
    dentistry, 228, 231
    diabetes, 126, 127, 131
    disabilities, 140, 141, 145, 225, 231
    and divorce, 176, 228
    drug abuse, 213, 214, 215, 231
    ear infections, 14, 29, 226, 228

eating disorders, 176, 228
ergonomics, 228
and family moves, 176
first aid, 228
fitness and exercise, 228, 239
gastroesophageal reflux, 230
gastrointestinal problems, 228
growth, 231
hearing impairment, 35, 228
immunizations, 43, 225, 226, 231, 256
KidsHealth at the AMA, 228
KidsHealth.org, 228
lab tests, 228
learning disabilities, 138, 141, 176, 189, 202
legislation affecting, 225
mental health, 175, 176, 179, 190, 231
misc.kids.health, 229
National Institute of Child Health and Human
  Development, 229
nutrition, 228, 231, 246, 248–249, 250
orthopedic conditions, 228
pain management, 228, 230, 231
parenting, 41, 55, 260
preventive care, 231
safety issues, 226–227, 228, 231
serious illnesses, 176, 226, 232
shaken baby syndrome, 225
SickKids, 232
sleep disorders, 176, 211, 228
sports and sports medicine, 231, 251
stress, 228
sugar and behavior, 228
suicide, 272
sun protection, 207
surgery, 231
television violence, 176, 187, 225
temper tantrums, 228
tonsils, 228
Chinese medicine, 222
Chiropractic, 223
Cholera, 256
Cholesterol, 14, 158, 264
Chronic fatigue and immune dysfunction syndrome
  (CFIDS). *See* Chronic fatigue syndrome (CFS)
Chronic fatigue syndrome (CFS), 26, 27, 38, 72,
  119–122, 144
    alt.health.cfids-action, 119
    alt.med.cfs, 119
    alt.med.cfs.open, 120
    CFIDS Association of America, 120
    CFIDS-L, 119
    CFS-L, 119
    CFS-NEWS, 120–121
    CFS-OPEN, 120
    CFS-Y, 121
    in children, 120, 121

National Oral Health Information Clearinghouse, 234

oral disorders, 58

oral health, 52, 53

oral surgery, 233

orthodontics, 233

periodontal disease, 233, 234

Depression, 14, 24–25, 27, 29, 33, 38, 43, 177–181, 187. *See also* Mental Health

and aging, 35

alt.support.depression, 177

alt.support.depression.manic, 177

alt.support.depression.medication, 177

alt.support.depression.seasonal, 178

alt.support.survivors.prozac, 178

bipolar illness, 180

and bone loss, 87

in children and adolescents, 176, 179

clinical depression, 177

crisis support, 180

DEPRESS, 178

Depression Central, 179

Doctor's Guide to Depression, 179

drugs, 177, 178

dysthymia, 179

electroconvulsive therapy, 179, 187, 190

family support, 180

manic depression, 177, 179–180

National Depressive and Manic-Depressive Association, 179–180

postpartum depression, 179

Prozac, 177, 178

psychotherapy, 179, 192

publications, 179, 180

and relationships, 178

seasonal affective disorder (SAD), 178, 179, 181

soc.support.depression.crisis, 180

soc.support.depression.family, 180

soc.support.depression.manic, 180

soc.support.depression.misc, 181

soc.support.depression.seasonal, 181

soc.support.depression.treatment, 181

and Social Security disability, 179

and suicide, 179, 180

support groups, 179

treatment, 178, 180, 181, 189

treatment-resistance disorders, 179

and women, 179, 187

Dermatology, 39, 40, 46. *See also* Skin disorders

American Academy of Dermatology, 44, 207

Archives of Dermatology, 40

Diabetes, 17, 25, 38, 41, 51–53, 125–132, 135, 144

adults_cwd, 125

advocacy, 129

alt.support.diabetes, 125

alt.support.diabetes.kids, 126

American Diabetes Association, 126

CDC Diabetes Home Page, 126–127

characteristics of, 127, 129

in children and teens, 126, 127, 131, 132

complications, 126, 127–128

detection, 126, 127, 129

Diabetes, 126

Diabetes Care, 46

Diabetes Forecast, 126

Diabetes in America, 127–128

Diabetes Information Center, 128

Diabetes Mall, 128

Diabetes Monitor, 129

diabetic mailing list, 129

dictionary, 127

Doctor's Guide to Diabetes, 130

drugs, 128, 129

and family planning, 129

gestational, 229

and health insurance, 128

insulin and hypoglycemia, 127

insulin pumps, 129

Internet Sleuth—Diabetes, 130

Juvenile Diabetes Foundation International, 130

legislation, 126, 127, 130

living with, 126

misc.health.diabetes, 131

mortality data, by state, 126

National Diabetes Information Clearinghouse, 131

National Institute of Diabetes and Digestive and Kidney Diseases (NIDDK), 135

nutrition and fitness, 126, 129

On-line Diabetes Resources, 132

patient rights, 126

and periodontal disease, 234

prevalence and incidence, 126, 127

publications, 126, 130, 131

and quackery, 129

research, 126, 127, 128

risk factors, 127

state programs, 126

sugarfree food, 129

supplies for, 126, 128

treatment, 126, 128

Diagnostic tests and procedures, 28, 31, 52, 55

for children, 228

for diabetes, 126

radiology tests, 28

Dialysis, 35

Diarrhea, 256

Dictionaries, 33, 34

for diabetes, 127

OneLook Dictionaries, 59

Online Dictionary of Mental Health, 182–183

for prostate cancer, 116

National Toxicology Program, 278
Office of Human Radiation Experiments, 278–279
Epidemiology, 46
Epilepsy, 14, 201, 202
Ergonomics, 228
Esophageal cancers, 109
Essence therapy, 223
Estrogen, and bone loss, 87
Ethics and fraud, 52, 246, 280–283, 287, 288, 292. *See also* Quackery
  and AIDS/HIV, 71
  bioethics, 29, 280, 281, 283, 292
  BIOETHICSLINE, 54
  Biomedical & Health Care Ethics Resources on WWW, 280
  biomedical ethics, 280
  BIOMED-L, 280
  California Coalition for Ethical Mental Health Care, 289
  Center for Bioethics, The, 281
  Healthfraud, 281
  MacLean Center for Clinical Medical Ethics, 281–282
  National Bioethics Advisory Commission Homepage, 282
  National Human Genome Research Institute, 282
  UB Center for Clinical Ethics and Humanities in Health Care, 283
Ethnic medicine, 18
Euthanasia, 41, 54, 274, 280
Exercise. *See* Fitness and exercise
EXSMKR-L, 301
Eye care, 35, 53, 149–151
  and aging, 221
  alt.support.glaucoma, 149
  American Foundation for the Blind, 139
  American Society of Cataract & Refractive Surgery, 149
  Archives of Ophthalmology, 40, 46
  blindness, 139, 144
  cataracts, 24, 149
  EyeNet, 150
  Glaucoma Research Foundation, 150
  National Eye Institute, 150–151
  ophthalmologic disorders, 58
  ophthalmology, 17, 40, 46
  Prevent Blindness America, 151
  sci.med.vision, 151
  visual disabilities, 137

FACING-AHEAD, 268
Falls, prevention of, 87
Family and Medical Leave Act, 93, 144
Family Guide Encyclopedia of Medical Care, 55
Family Guide to Prescription Drugs, 55
Family Guide to Women's Health, 55

Family medical records, 53
Family medicine, 17, 38, 40
Family Village, 140–141
Farrow, Susan, 254
Fasting, 245
Fat, in foods, 27
FDA Consumer, 30
FDA Enforcement Report, 30
Federal government
  agencies, 57
  health information centers and clearinghouses, 36, 37
  offices, 58–59
  publications, 16, 24, 27–28, 33
Female reproductive system, 29, 55. *See also* Women's health
Fetal alcohol syndrome, 141, 229
Fetal cell transplant, 280
Fiber, in diet, 38
Fibroids, 55, 229
Fibromyalgia, 78, 121, 122
Fibrous dysplasia, 87
Firearm-related deaths, 60
First aid, 21, 31–32, 52, 228
Fitness and exercise, 21, 25–29, 31–33, 35, 41, 239–241. *See also* Sports medicine
  and aging, 240
  and arthritis, 78
  for children, 228, 239
  and diabetes, 126, 129
  Fit-L, 239
  FitnessLink, 239–240
  and men, 243
  misc.fitness, 240
  and postmenopausal women, 87
  during pregnancy, 260
  soc.senior.health+fitness, 240
  Start-Now-L, 240–241
  walking, 38, 240, 241
  weightlifting, 239, 240, 241
  Weights-2, 241
Flu, 72, 221, 226
Folk medicine, 223
Food, 27, 30, 31, 34, 38, 55. *See also* Nutrition and diet
  additives, 246, 247
  allergies. *See* Allergies
  safety and foodborne illness, 27, 38, 246–247
Food and Drug Administration (FDA), 30, 64
Food Finder, 248
Food stamps, 144
Foodborne Pathogenic Microorganisms and Natural Toxins, 246
Foot care, 207, 251
Fraud. *See* Ethics and fraud
Funding Guide, 36
Fungal research, 72

InfoNet, 30
Information, quality of, 4–6
Inhalant abuse, 215
Inpatient surgeries, 23
Insect stings and bites, 58, 74
Insomnia, 14, 38, 209, 211. *See also* Sleep disorders
Insurance. *See* Health insurance
Intensive care units, 23
Internal medicine, 40, 46
International AIDS Patent Database, 72–73
International Association of Physicians in AIDS Care, 70
International MS Support Foundation, 203
International Myeloma Foundation, 106
Internet FDA, 30
Internet Grateful Med, 56–58
Internet Mental Health, 188
Internet Resources for Special Children, 141
Internet Sleuth, The, 18
   AIDS, 70
   alternative medicine, 224
   cancer, 97–98
   cardiology, 160
   dentistry, 234
   diabetes, 130
   health, 31
   heart disease, 161
   journals, 42
   mental health, 182
   neuroscience, 202
   news, 42
   pharmacology, 236
   substance abuse, 214
   women's health, 261
Intestinal diversions, 135

JAMA (Journal of the American Medical Association), 5, 41, 42, 46, 71
JAMA Asthma Information Center, 82
JAMA Contraception Information Center, 262
JAMA HIV/AIDS Information Center, 71
JAMA Migraine Information Center, 155
JAMA Sexually Transmitted Disease Information Center, 166
JAN on the Web, 141–142
Jaw disorders, 85
Johns Hopkins Medical Institutions, 30, 44
Journal of Clinical Oncology, 46, 102
Journal of Neuroscience, The, 41
Journal of Psychopharmacology, The, 41
Journal of the American Academy of Child & Adolescent Psychiatry, 176
Journal of the American Medical Association (JAMA), 5, 41, 42, 46, 71
Journal of the National Cancer Institute, 46

Journals, 18, 33–34, 40–47, 50
   abstracts, 16, 33–34, 40–42, 44–46, 54–55
   Alzheimer's Disease Review, 173
   Archives Specialty Journals, 40
   British Medical Journal, 40–41, 46
   CA: A Cancer Journal for Clinicians, 99
   Combined Health Information Database, 51–52
   Docnet MediS Search, 41
   Dr. Felix's Free MEDLINE Page, 53–54
   HealthSTAR database, 55, 57
   Internet Sleuth—Journals, 42
   Journal of Clinical Oncology, 46, 102
   Journal of the American Medical Association (JAMA), 5, 41, 42, 46, 71
   New England Journal of Medicine, 41, 44, 45, 46
   OLDMEDLINE, 57
   Physician and Sportsmedicine, The, 252
   PsychArticle Search, 45
   psychiatry journals, 33, 40, 41, 45, 46, 176, 187, 188
   psychology journals, 45, 189
   PubMed, 59
   social science journals, 45
   TOC-L, 44, 45–46
   WebMedLit, 46
Juvenile Diabetes Foundation International, 130

Keller, Helen, 139
Kidney diseases, 44, 52, 53, 55, 135, 167–169. *See also* Urinary disorders
   AAKP Renal Flash, 167
   alt.support.kidney-failure, 167
   American Association of Kidney Patients, 167, 168
   dialysis, 35
   kidney cancer, 110
   KIDNEY-ONC, 110
   kidney stones, 243
   National Institute of Diabetes and Digestive and Kidney Diseases (NIDDK), 135
   National Kidney and Urologic Diseases Information Clearinghouse, 167, 168
   National Kidney Foundation, 168–169
   Nephron Information Center, 169
kids_cwd, 131
Kids Food CyberClub, 248–249
kids-to-kids, 273
KidsHealth at the AMA, 228
KidsHealth.org, 228
Kinesiology, 223

L-M-SARCOMA, 110
Labor and delivery, 55. *See also* Pregnancy and childbirth
Laboratory tests. *See* Diagnostic tests and procedures

PubMed, 59
SDILINE, 57
Medscape, 33–34
MEL (Michigan Electronic Library), 19
MEL-L, 111
Melanoma, 35, 111, 207. *See also* Skin cancer
Melatonin, 33, 210
Menopause, 14, 28, 38, 55, 260, 261
Men's health, 52, 55, 242–244. *See also* Prostate
cancer; Prostate disorders
    alt.support.impotence, 242
    breast cancer in men, 94
    cancer, 94, 243
    Doctor's Guide to Erectile Dysfunction, 243
    impotence, 35, 242, 243
    Not for Men Only, 243
    nutrition and diet, 243
    osteoporosis, 87
    reproductive health, 21, 26, 29, 243
    vasectomy, 33, 229, 243
Menstruation, 228, 261
Mental health, 21, 26, 31, 53, 170–200. *See also*
  Alzheimer's disease; Anxiety and panic disorders;
  Depression; Eating disorders; Psychiatry;
  Psychology; Recovery; Suicide
    and aging, 187
    and AIDS/HIV, 66
    alt.psychology.help, 186
    alt.society.mental-health, 186
    alt.support, 186
    alt.support.stuttering, 186
    American Academy of Child & Adolescent
      Psychiatry, 176
    American Psychiatric Association, 44, 187
    American Psychological Association, 187
    APA Online, 187
    bibliographies, 188
    calendars of events, 188, 190
    California Coalition for Ethical Mental Health
      Care, 289
    and children, 176, 190
    diagnostics, 188, 189
    directories and search engines, 182–183
    Dr. Bob's Mental Health Links, 182
    electroconvulsive therapy, 179, 187, 190
    emotional health, 29, 53, 192
    health insurance, 187, 190, 193
    hospitalizations, 190
    Internet Mental Health, 188
    Internet Sleuth—Mental Health, 182
    legislation, 190
    media portrayal of, 191
    Mental Health Economics, 188
    Mental Health Infosource, 188
    Mental Health Net, 189
    mood disorders, 55

National Institute of Mental Health, 189
National Mental Health Association, 190
National Mental Health Services Knowledge
  Exchange Network, 190
natural disaster victims, 190
obsessive-compulsive disorder, 174, 175, 189, 190,
  194
Online Dictionary of Mental Health, 182–183
organizations, 182, 188, 190
personality disorders, 195
post-traumatic stress disorder, 174, 175, 190, 196
prevention, 190
P-SOURCE, 191
PSY-MEDIA, 191
psychiatric drugs, 188
publications, 182, 188
rehabilitation, 190. *See also* Disabilities and
  rehabilitation
research, 190
schizophrenia, 14, 187, 190, 199
sci.med.psychobiology, 191
sci.psychology, 192
sci.psychology-announce, 192
sci.psychology.psychotherapy, 192
sexual assault, 55, 192
sexual orientation, 187, 192, 225
statistics, 188, 190
Student Counseling Virtual Pamphlet Collection,
  192–193
Substance Abuse and Mental Health Services
  Administration, 193
support groups, 186, 188
treatment, 188, 189, 190
YANX-DEP, 176
Mental retardation, 141. *See also* Disabilities and
  rehabilitation; Mental health
Merck & Co., 58
Merck Manual of Diagnosis and Therapy, The, 58
*Merck Manual of Medical Information—Home
  Edition, The,* 58
MeSH (Medical Subject Headings), 14
Meta directories, 15, 18
Metabolic disorders, 58. *See also* Diabetes;
  Endocrinology and endocrine disorders
Michigan Electronic Library (MEL), 19
Microbiology, 28
Midwifery, 263
Migraine headaches. *See* Headaches
Minority health, 17, 141, 143, 300
    AIDS and HIV, 70
    Office Of Minority Health Resource Center,
      36–37
    osteoporosis and African American women, 98
Miscarriage, 55, 263
misc.fitness, 240
misc.handicap, 142

National Multiple Sclerosis Society, 203–204

National Oral Health Information Clearinghouse, 234

National Organization for Rare Disorders, 29

National Organization on Fetal Alcohol Syndrome, 229

National Parkinson Foundation, 90

National Pesticide Telecommunications Network, 277

National Psoriasis Foundation, 207–208

National Rehabilitation Information Center, 143

National Rural Health Association, 286–287

National Safety Council, 277–278

National Sleep Foundation, 210

National Sudden Infant Death Syndrome Resource Center, 230

National Toxicology Program, 278

Natural disaster victims, 190

Natural healing, 31

Naturopathy, 223

NCCS, 102

Neck and head surgery, 40

NEDLIB-L, 48

Needy Meds, 236

Nephron Information Center, The, 169

Neurological disorders, 53, 58, 201–204. *See also* Alzheimer's disease; Multiple sclerosis; Stroke
  alt.support.disorders.neurological, 201
  American Academy of Neurology, 202
  Archives of Neurology, 40
  epilepsy, 14, 201, 202
  Internet Sleuth—Neuroscience, 202
  Journal of Neuroscience, The, 41
  National Institute of Neurological Disorders and Stroke, 202
  neurology, 17, 32, 40, 46
  neurosurgery, 32
  paralysis, 141
  Parkinson's disease, 90, 91, 202

New England Journal of Medicine, 41, 44, 45, 46

New York Law Journal, 292

News sources, 14, 18, 21, 24–25, 32–34, 38, 40–47
  CNN Health, 41
  Internet Sleuth—News, 42
  Medical Tribune Online, 43
  MMWR, 43
  Newswise, 44
  nlmfiles, 50
  PR Newswire Health/Biotech, 45
  Reuters, 21, 25, 38, 46–47
  www.reutershealth.com, 46–47
  Your Health Daily, 47

NicNet, 302

Nicotine addiction. *See* Smoking

NIDDK WWW Server, 135

NIH Clinical Research Studies, 35

NISMAT, 251–252

NLM Locator, 50

nlmfiles, 50

Nose disorders, 38. *See* Ear, nose, and throat conditions

Not for Men Only, 243

Nursing, 56, 59, 72

Nursing homes, 27, 290, 291

Nutrition and diet, 17, 21, 25–28, 31–35, 52, 55, 135, 144, 245–250
  and AIDS and HIV, 66, 70, 246
  alt.health.fasting, 245
  alt.support.diet, 245
  alt.support.diet.rx, 246
  American Dietetic Association, 246
  and breast cancer, 93
  and cancer, 98, 103, 246
  Center for Food Safety & Applied Nutrition, 246–247
  Center for Science in the Public Interest, 247
  for children, 228, 231, 246, 248–249, 250
  CyberDiet, 248
  and diabetes, 126
  fats, 27
  fiber, 38
  food additives, 246, 247
  Food Finder, 248
  food safety and foodborne illness, 27, 38, 39, 246–247
  food sites, 27, 30, 31, 34, 38, 55
  Kids Food Cyber Club, 248–249
  for men, 243
  NutriBase, 249
  nutrient values, 248, 249
  Nutrition Analysis Tool, 249
  Nutrition and Your Health: Dietary Guidelines for Americans, 36
  olestra, 246, 247
  and Parkinson's disease, 90
  during pregnancy, 34, 260, 263
  rec.food.veg, 250
  sci.med.nutrition, 250
  sports nutrition, 239
  Tufts University Nutrition Navigator, 250
  vegetarianism, 27, 239, 250
  vitamin and mineral supplements, 33, 49, 239, 246
  for women, 247, 250, 264

Nutritional disorders, 58. *See also* Eating disorders

OASIS, 185

Obesity, 14, 41, 43, 135, 184. *See also* Weight control

Obsessive-compulsive disorder, 174, 175, 189, 190, 194
  alt.support.ocd, 194
  OCD-L, 194

PED-ONC, 104
Pediatrics, 225
PEDINFO, 231
Periodontal disease, 233, 234. *See also* Dental health
Personal health, 28, 25
Personality disorders, 195
    alt.support.personality, 195
    borderline personality disorder, 195
    BORDERPD, 195
    multiple personality disorder, 195
    SADM, 195
Pesticides, 34, 246, 277
Pet loss, 268, 270, 274
Pharmaceutical companies, press releases from, 45
Pharmaceutical Connections, 237
Pharmacology. *See also* Prescription drugs
    clinical pharmacology, 58
    clinical psychopharmacology, 39
    Internet Sleuth—Pharmacology, 236
    PharmInfoNet, 237
Physical agents, disorders due to, 58
Physical fitness. *See* Fitness and exercise
Physical medicine and rehabilitation, 17. *See also*
  Disabilities and rehabilitation
Physician and Sportsmedicine Online, The, 252
Physician-assisted suicide, 281, 283
Physician Select (AMA), 22
Physicians. *See* Doctors
Pinch.com, 208
Pituitary tumors, 229
Plagues, 281
Plastic surgery, 55
PMS (premenstrual syndrome), 55, 261
Podiatry, 251
Poison control centers, 33, 53, 228
Poison ivy, 207
Poisoning, lead, 26, 275, 277, 278
Poisoning and bites, 58, 74
Polio, 163, 202
Postpartum depression, 179
Post-traumatic stress disorder, 174, 175, 190, 196
    alt.support.trauma-ptsd, 196
    TRAUMATIC-STRESS, 196
PR Newswire Health/Biotech, 45
Preclinical sciences, 56, 59
Precocious puberty, 229
Pregnancy and childbirth, 29, 31, 34, 41, 52, 55, 260, 261, 263
    alternative health resources, 263
    baby development, 228
    BabyZone, 260
    birth control, 26, 33, 55, 258, 261–262
    birth defects, 26, 226
    birthing, 263
    breastfeeding, 226, 231, 259, 262, 263
    childbearing, 34

    childbirth classes, 260
    complications, 33, 263
    and drinking, 215
    exercise, 260
    female reproductive system, 29
    fetal alcohol syndrome, 141, 229
    gestational diabetes, 229
    high-risk pregnancy, 263
    infant mortality rate, 60
    infertility, 28, 33, 55, 258, 260–263
    labor and delivery, 55
    midwifery, 263
    misc.kids.pregnancy, 263
    natural childbirth, 260
    nutrition, 34, 260, 263
    obstetrics and gynecology, 58, 261, 263
    Online Birth Center, 263
    postpartum depression, 179
    pregnancy loss, 38, 55, 232, 263, 272
    prenatal testing, 55, 260
    smoking and pregnancy, 52
    soc.support.pregnancy.loss, 263
    stages of, 260
    testing for pregnancy, 260
    travel and, 256
PREMEDLINE, 57
Premenstrual syndrome (PMS), 55, 261
Prenatal issues. *See* Pregnancy and childbirth
Prescription drugs, 14, 24, 26, 29, 30–31, 33, 56, 235–238. *See also* Clinical trials; Pharmacology
    for AIDS and HIV, 54, 56, 66, 69, 70, 71
    for Alzheimer's disease, 171, 172
    for asthma, 82
    CenterWatch Clinical Trials Listing Service, 235
    commonly prescribed, 53
    for depression, 177, 178
    for diabetes, 128, 129
    Family Guide to Prescription Drugs, 55
    Internet Sleuth—Pharmacology, 236
    Medication Info Search, 236
    for mental health, 189
    Needy Meds, 236
    Pharmaceutical Connections, 237
    PharmInfoNet, 237
    proper use of, 53
    Prozac, 177, 178
    psychiatric drugs, 188
    RxList, 237–238
    RxMed, 238
    Tamoxifen, 93
    Thalidomide, 49
    toxicological effects of, 34
Presidential Advisory Committee on Gulf War Veteran's Illnesses, 152–153
Press releases, 30, 44, 45, 65, 95
Prevent Blindness America, 151

OneLook Dictionaries, 59
PubMed, 59
Social Statistics Briefing Room, 60
Reflexology, 223
Reflux, 134, 230, 242
Refractive surgery, 149
Rehabilitation. *See* Disabilities and rehabilitation;
Recovery
Rehabilitation Act of 1973, 144
Relationships, 29, 192
Repetitive strain injuries (RSI), 293, 296, 297
Reproductive system, 21, 26, 29, 55. *See also*
Pregnancy and childbirth
Research, 35, 43, 57. *See also* Clinical trials
Agency for Health Care Policy and Research, 24
aging, 221
AIDS and HIV, 65–66, 68
Alzheimer's disease, 171, 172, 173
animal research, 277, 281
brain tumors, 90
cancer, 98–99, 100
chronic fatigue syndrome (CFS), 120
dental research, 233
diabetes, 126, 127, 128
disabilities and rehabilitation, 141, 145
facilities and institutions for, 57
fungal, 72
information on, 20
mental health, 190
National Advisory Council for Health Care
Policy, Research, and Evaluation, 24
National Human Genome Research Institute, 282
NIH Clinical Research Studies, 35
press releases, 44
rare diseases, 37
women and, 34
Respiratory diseases, 53. *See also* Lung disorders
Restless legs, 202, 211
Reuters, 21, 25, 38, 46–47
Rheumatology. *See* Arthritis
Rural health care, 17, 18, 286–287
RxList, 237–238
RxMed, 238

SAD. *See* Seasonal affective disorder
SADM, 195
Safety issues, 17, 21, 26, 43, 49, 52. *See also*
Occupational health and safety
for children, 226–227, 228, 231
National Safety Council, 277–278
Sarcomas, 104, 110
Scabies, 207
Schizophrenia, 14, 187, 190, 199
School health, 51
sci.med, 37

sci.med.aids, 64, 72
sci.med.cannabis, 287
sci.med.cardiology, 161
sci.med.diseases.als, 86
sci.med.diseases.cancer, 104
sci.med.diseases-hepatitis, 164
sci.med.diseases.lyme, 165
sci.med.diseases.osteoporosis, 88
sci.med.nutrition, 250
sci.med.obgyn, 263
sci.med.occupational, 296
sci.med.orthopedics, 86
sci.med.prostate.cancer, 116
sci.med.prostate.prostatitis, 244
sci.med.psychobiology, 191
sci.med.vision, 151
sci.psychology, 192
sci.psychology.announce, 192
sci.psychology.psychotherapy, 192
Scleroderma, 83
SDILINE, 57
Search engines. *See* Directories and search engines
Search NIH Web-Space, 20
Seasonal affective disorder (SAD), 178, 179, 181
SECONDWIND, 254
Senior citizens. *See* Aging
Sex, 29, 38, 243
safe sex, 64, 66
Sexual abuse, 176, 187, 195, 198
Sexual addiction, 197
Sexual assault, 55, 192
Sexuality, 21, 29, 31, 34, 55, 138
Sexually transmitted diseases, 26, 55, 64, 72, 166,
243
herpes, 29, 166
JAMA Sexually Transmitted Disease Information
Center, 166
Shaken baby syndrome, 225
Shingles, 29
Shoulder pain, 38
Shyness, 174
Sick building syndrome, 278
SickKids, 232
SIDS. *See* Sudden Infant Death Syndrome
Sinusitis, 146
Six Senses Review, 18
Skin cancer, 28, 207. *See also* Melanoma
Skin care, 38
Skin disorders, 33, 51, 53, 189, 205–208. *See also*
Dermatology
acne, 205, 207, 228
allergies, 74. *See also* Allergies
alt.support.skin-diseases, 206
American Academy of Dermatology, 207
athlete's foot, 207
bites and stings, 58, 74

burns, 226
canker sores, 26
dermatologic disorders, 58
ECZEMA, 207
lupus, 80, 205
moles, 207
National Institute of Arthritis and
 Musculoskeletal and Skin Diseases, 80
Pinch.com, 208
poison ivy, 207
psoriasis, 80, 206, 207–208
Skin & Allergy News, 33
vitiligo, 206, 208
warts, 207
Sleep disorders, 29, 38, 41, 192, 209–211
and aging, 210, 211
alt.support.sleep-disorder, 209
BiblioSleep, 210
in children, 176, 211, 228
Doctor's Guide to Insomnia, 209
insomnia, 14, 38, 209, 211
narcolepsy, 211
National Sleep Foundation, 210
pain management and sleep, 210
sleep apnea, 29, 38, 202, 209, 210, 211
sleep deprivation, 210, 211
Sleep Home Pages, 210
Sleep Medicine Home Page, 211
SleepNet, 211
Smoking, 52, 298–303. *See also* Lung disorders
Action on Smoking and Health, 298
alt.recovery.nicotine, 298–299
alt.smokers, 299
alt.support.non-smokers, 299
alt.support.stop-smoking, 299
American Lung Association, 300
Campaign for Tobacco-Free Kids,
 300
cancer and tobacco companies, 98
CDC's Tobacco Information and Prevention
 Source (TIPS), 301
in children and adolescents, 300, 302
EXSMKR-L, 301
NicNet, 302
and pregnancy, 52
second-hand smoke, 299, 301, 302
State Tobacco Information Center, 302
tobacco, 30, 216, 233, 300, 302–303
Tobacco Resolution, The, 302–303
TOBACTALK, 303
soc.senior.health+fitness, 240
soc.support.depression.crisis, 180
soc.support.depression.family, 180
soc.support.depression.manic, 180
soc.support.depression.misc, 181
soc.support.depression.seasonal, 181

soc.support.depression.treatment, 181
soc.support.pregnancy.loss, 263
Social phobia, 175
Social science journals, 45
Social Statistics Briefing Room, 60
SOREHAND, 297
Spamming, 4
Special Olympics International, 144–145
Speech disorders, 90, 147, 186
Spina bifida, 85
Spinal cord injury, 137, 141, 202. *See also* Disabilities
 and rehabilitation
Sports medicine, 251–252
American Podiatric Medical Association,
 251
for children, 231
NISMAT, 251–252
Physician and Sportsmedicine Online, The, 252
Sports nutrition, 239
Start-Now-L, 240–241
State Tobacco Information Center, 302
Steroids, anabolic, 215
Stillbirth, 232
Stings and bites, 58, 74
Stomach cancer, 112
Stomach disorders. *See* Digestive diseases
STOMACH-ONC, 112
Stress management, 26, 33, 38, 55, 144, 175, 192,
 228, 239
Stroke, 14, 24, 28, 41, 202, 264
Doctor's Guide to Stroke, 158–159
National Institute of Neurological Disorders and
 Stroke, 202
Stroke, 41
STROKE-L, 162
and women, 264
Student Counseling Virtual Pamphlet Collection,
 The, 192–193
Stuttering, 186
Substance abuse, 17, 52, 187, 192, 212–217. *See also*
Alcohol and alcohol abuse
 Al-Anon/Alateen, 212
 alt.recovery.aa, 212
 alt.recovery.adult-children, 213
 alt.recovery.na, 213
 death of a child, 272
 Drug-Free Resource Net, 213
 Indiana Prevention Resource Center, 214
 inhalant abuse, 215
 Internet Sleuth—Substance Abuse, 214
 Mothers Against Drunk Driving, 214–215
 National Institute on Alcohol Abuse and
  Alcoholism, 215
 National Institute on Drug Abuse, 215–216
 Online AA Recovery Resources, 216
 PREVline (Prevention Online), 216

Substance Abuse and Mental Health Services
   Administration, 193
   Tranquility, 217
Sudden Infant Death Syndrome (SIDS), 225, 226,
   229, 230, 232–233, 272
   National Sudden Infant Death Syndrome
      Resource Center, 230
   SIDS Network, 232
Suffixes, on addresses, 4
Sugar, and behavior, 228
Suicide, 189, 190, 200. *See also* Depression
   and depression, 179, 180
   physician-assisted, 281, 283
   prevention, 179
   support groups, 200
   teen suicide, 176, 187, 225, 228, 272
Sun protection, 207
Support groups, 32, 33, 57
Surgery, 23, 24, 28, 40
   Archives of Surgery, 40
   cataract and refractive, 149
   and children, 231
   head and neck, 40
   inpatient, 23
   neurosurgery, 32
   oral, 233
   orthopedic, 86
   outpatient, 23
   plastic surgery, 55
Surviving Transplantation, 254
Swallowing problems, 90
Symptoms, 52

Take Wellness to Heart, 264
talk.abortion, 264
talk.euthanasia, 274
talk.politics.medicine, 288
Tamoxifen (drug), 93
Tanning, 207
tAPir (the Anxiety-Panic internet resource), 174
Taste disorders, 38
TBI-FAM, 91
TBI-SPRT, 91
TC-NET, 118
Technology Assessment, Office of (OTA), 287
Teen suicide, 176, 187, 225, 228
teens_cwd, 132
Teeth. *See* Dental health
Telemedicine, 35, 49, 292
Television violence, 176, 187, 225
Temper tantrums, 228
Temple University, 44
Tendonitis, 297
Terminal illness, coping with, 144
Testicular cancer, 118
   alt.support.cancer.testicular, 118

TC-NET, 118
   Testicular Cancer Resource Center, 118
Thalidomide, 49
Thrive, 38
Throat conditions. *See* Ear, nose, and throat
   conditions
Thyroid cancer, 113
Tile.Net, 20
Tinnitus, 35, 146–147
TIPS (CDC's Tobacco Information and Prevention
   Source), 301
Tobacco. *See* Smoking
Tobacco Resolution, The, 302–303
TOBACTALK, 303
TOC-L, 44, 45–46
Tonsils, 228
Total hip replacement, 80
Toxic substances, 246, 275, 277–278. *See also*
   Environmental health
TOXLINE, 34
Trace Research & Development Center, 145
Tranquility, 217
Transplantation, 17, 38, 72, 253–255
   Bone Marrow Transplant Resource Netmarks,
      253
   bone marrow transplants, 93, 100, 105, 107, 253
   CenterSpan, 253
   fetal cell transplant, 280
   lung transplants, 254
   SECONDWIND, 254
   Surviving Transplantation, 254
   TransWeb, 254–255
Trauma, 196
Traumatic brain injuries, 90, 91
TRAUMATIC-STRESS, 196
Travel medicine, 25, 26, 256–257
   and AIDS/HIV, 256
   altitude sickness, 256
   CDC Travel Information, 256
   Health Information for International Travel, 256
   Medical College of Wisconsin International
      Travelers Clinic, 256–257
   and pregnancy, 256
   Travel Health Online, 257
   travel-related diseases, 39
   vaccinations, 33, 256, 257
Tubal ligation, 261
Tufts University Nutrition Navigator, 250
Typhoid fever, 256
Typing Injury FAQ, 297

UB Center for Clinical Ethics and Humanities in
   Health Care, 283
Ulcers, 14, 29
United Ostomy Association, 135–136
University of California-Los Angeles, 44